UNCOMMON
LOVE

UNCOMMON
LOVE

A Love that Finds You

A 365 DAY
DAILY DEVOTIONAL

Paula Sellars

UNCOMMON LOVE
A Love that Finds You

© Copyright 2019 – Paula Sellars

ISBN: 978-1-798880-91-3

For Worldwide Distribution, Printed in the U.S.A.

DEDICATION

First, to my Father God....Whose love never quits. (Psalm 136) His encouragement to me to write helped me to pick up the pen. I had no idea what He was about to do as He told me what to put down on paper. I wrote some things that were still not real to me yet, but were a glimpse of what was to come—while at the same time the truth about Him wanting to be my Father went deeper into my heart. No one impacts us like our fathers and mothers, so you can only imagine how much more we will be impacted when we know how much our Father God personally loves each one of us.

To my dear husband Ron....I cannot thank God enough for you. He gave me a very kind, supportive husband from whom I get pictures of what God's love is really like. Thank you, Ron, for always believing in me.

To my children...Who the Father kept using as an example when speaking to me about His love. He would remind me how I felt about my own children to help me get in touch with His parental love for me.

ACKNOWLEDGEMENTS

Ron…Thank you again to my dear husband Ron, who is my biggest fan, who picked me up when I had my moments. You always blessed me with just the right words to say.

Dave Hess…I want to thank you for being an expression of Father's love to me in your kindness and believing in me.

Karen Webb…Heartfelt thanks to you, dear lady, for your guidance, and continual support. What a great blessing you have been to me.

Stephen Hill…sometimes we will never know how much we impact others, and this is the case with you, Stephen. You took the time to stop and be present with me in my life with this book from across the world. Thank you for letting me feel Father's love through you. There were many special moments where I would sit overwhelmed, a very good overwhelmed, by what Father was doing with this book, and one of those moments was with you when you were present and heard my heart.

A special thank you to two very special young ladies Phillppa Cawdell and Jassrin Jacob for the fun time we had taking pictures at INS for this book.

To my dear friends, you know who you are, who have been waiting patiently for this book. Thank you for all your encouragement and cheering me onward.

ENDORSEMENTS

"There is always something very different about someone who knows the Father because they walk with Him in everyday life and have proven his faithfulness, his mercy and his tangible comfort to someone who knows only the doctrine of God being our Father. The one who knows him experientially, has the assurance that whatever life circumstances and tribulations come to them they will have an inner knowing, confidence and underlying peace. In this book *Uncommon Love*, we clearly see that Paula Sellars has walked through many trials and much personal pain out of which come these beautiful daily readings. I am sure that no matter where you are on the path to becoming a son or daughter of our Heavenly Father you will find that each entry will be the perfect one for you to meditate on to bring life, hope and encouragement for that day!"

Denise Jordan,
Co-Founder Fatherheart Ministries
Author. *Forgotten Feminine*

"Paula Sellars has produced a treasure trove, mined out of deep personal experience. *Uncommon Love* speaks of the journey of someone walking in reality, not trying to hide her struggles and weaknesses but bringing herself every day before a heavenly Father who loves her without any conditions. This book is full of shining jewels of hearing the Father speak to His beloved. As you read this it will give you confidence to relate to God in an intimate way, without performance, without expectations and without shame. I heartily recommend it!"

Stephen Hill,
Author of *Primal Hope:
Finding Confidence Beyond Religion*
and *John: A Prophetic Revelation*

"Imagine waking up in the morning or going to bed at night having your mind and emotions bathed in the beauty of God's love. I believe this is what will happen to you as you read Paula's wonderful devotional, *Uncommon Love*. You will find your heart melted as you encounter and experience the passionate and tender affections of your heavenly Father revealed in her writing. And, you'll be carried along in conversations with the One who not only loves you but likes you and can't get enough of you! I'm honored to be able to recommend this book to you."

S. J. Hill,
Author of *What's God Really Like,
Enjoying God, and A Love for the Ages*

"God is love, but few experience it when we need it the most. Paula Sellars' book, *Uncommon Love*, will break every tradition of how God thinks of you. On your worst day you will hear Him singing shouts of victory as He declares you a champion and heals your battle scars."

Bill Yount
Author of *The Power of Real*

TABLE OF CONTENTS

PREFACE

Like so many, the nurturing and healthy attachments that a child needs to thrive were not there. My world was full of surviving an abusive and chaotic childhood, with parents that were very broken. My dad being an alcoholic, was full of rage. My mom, although she was able at times to let us know she cared, just could not be present. I have heard that children are good observers but poor interpreters. My dad barely said a word to me, but I do remember him saying many times, "If you are good to me, I will be good to you." I tried so hard to be good and when I couldn't get his love, I interpreted this as there must be something wrong with me.

Throughout my teen years I was in and out of three reform schools for running away from home. There was nobody around that really seemed to care except for a very kind Catholic nun at St. Joseph's Reform School. She would sit and just talk to me when I got in trouble and it was never about my behavior. Then, suddenly she was gone. They sent her to a different assignment.

The next road I went down was years of drugs and party-ing. One day, I came to the conclusion that I was addicted to heroin, and I thought to myself that I would just die a drug addict. At this point, miraculously, I started hearing people talk about the "Jesus people" coming to town; surprisingly I remember feeling a flicker of hope inside. My friends dragged me to a Catholic charismatic meeting and there Jesus turned my life upside down. I was instantly delivered from heroin. It was truly a miracle. A lady named Frieda started to talk to me about Jesus' love coming to her in her pain. Suddenly, I fell to the floor sobbing for what seemed like hours.

For thirty years after this experience, Jesus was my friend and still is, but I didn't connect to anything He said about His Father. I would tell myself to just accept that fact that I would never have a father. In July 2001, we stopped at a Jack Frost conference on our way to my son's wedding and there I had an encounter with the Father as soon as I walked in the door. It was as if the Father was waiting at the door for me, waiting to tell me that He was not mad at me. That is what He said to me through this kind grandfather figure who we ran into as soon as we walked in the door. This very kind man prayed for me while I wept on his shoulder and I was suddenly surrounded with the presence of the Father's love. My life once again was radically changed.

God is so wise and kind, never trying to force His way into my life as Father because of my "father" pain, until He knew I was ready. How exciting in that moment to find out the Father loved me and it has been equally exciting to find out how much He wants to talk to me. The God who created heaven and earth is my Father and wants to talk to me!

While I was listening to Him, learning to hear his voice to write this book, He spoke to some of my deepest fears and insecurities. I didn't realize how much of my "father" pain controlled my life, and how this distorted my picture of Father God. I loved hanging out with Jesus, he did not stir up my Father pain.

I had a prophetic word years ago, way before I met Father, that He was going to re-parent me, but I never gave much thought to it. I am convinced, more than ever, after writing this book that Father God wants us to know Him as our Father, and loves to talk to his kids. He is always trying to reach us and many times we miss it because we are not aware that we have a Father like Him that loves us the way He does. Stephen Hill from *Fatherheart Ministries* says, "We think we have to go after Him and try and find Him, but He is the one coming after us trying to reach us."

FOREWORD

When I first opened my heart to Jesus, I did it with eternity in mind. The phrase I remember responding to, was something like: "Repent of your sin, ask Jesus into your heart, and you will go to heaven when you die." I still believe this to be true. I believe that I need to turn from sin and selfishness. I believe that I need to ask Jesus to forgive me and free me from sin. And I also believe that when I die, as a believer in Jesus, I will forever be with Him in His Heavenly Kingdom.

Yet, I limited my relationship with Jesus to something that I would only come to enjoy in the afterlife. While focusing solely on my "retirement home" after death, I completely missed the joy of living in my Father's House here and now.

Over time, I discovered that Jesus came to show us what *His Father* is like. He said, "If you've seen Me, you've seen and experienced who My Father is." He said, "No one comes to the Father but through Me." He didn't simply say, "No one comes *to Heaven* but through Me." He said, "I've come to bring you to *My Father*, so that you may know and experience His love—just like I do."

I will always remember the day I surrendered to Jesus' love for me. I remember the peace that came from knowing that nothing—not even death—would ever separate me from Him. Not now. Not in eternity.

But I also remember the day I realized that He came to bring me into a relationship with His Father. To let me experience the same kind of love that the Father has for His Son, Jesus.

Being loved by His Father—who is also *my* Father—has absolutely changed my life. I've learned to live loved. I've learned to really love others as a much-loved son.

The book you are about to read, written by my friend Paula, will touch your heart in a very personal, powerful way. Paula's painful past has been overwhelmed by the revelation of the Father's love for her. The following pages are not filled with vague theories or flowery ideas. She welcomes us into her world, to experience the journey of a daughter learning to let her Father love her.

My prayer is that you too will plunge into His heart for you. May His love become your great joy and settled reality!

Dave Hess,
Senior Pastor
Christ Community Church
Camp Hill, PA

INTRODUCTION

I heard the Father speak to my heart and say...

"I saw you, I watched you, waiting for the day I knew your heart would be open to see Me as your Father. I waited and planned with great anticipation for that moment when you realized that I am the Father you always longed for. Now, My child, take My hand as I open up a whole new world of My love and show you the kind of Father I will be to you."

The Father wants to come to us in our everyday struggles, to care for us, to take our hand and guide us with His counsel, no matter what kind of junk is in our hearts. (Psalm 73:21) Why was Jesus urging us to go see the Father? (Matthew 6:6) What did He know about Him that He wanted us to know? He could have said, "Go see *My* Father" or "Go see *the* Father" but He said, "Go see *your* Father and close the door." Jesus Himself is saying it, right here, that God is our Father. Jesus knew the Father wanted to be alone with us to give us His time and full attention. He was very secure in His relationship with His Father and wanted us to know what He knew—knowing how blessed we would feel and how much it would help us to know Him like He did. So, He encouraged us to go see *our* Father, who was also His Father. Jesus knew His place as God's Son; He was not jealous of us, so when we learn what He knew, we will not be jealous or feel inferior around others that Father God loves. This idea was a struggle for me since I grew up with my father, and many adults in my family, having favorites. In the secret place, we will find out many things about our Papa God that will secure our world. Did you ever think about what it would be like to go see your Father God and close the door? Just picture this, you and your Father, who is "The Almighty God," sitting together and all He wants is to spend time with you alone. We can believe Jesus loves us because He is a friend of sinners, but when you think about your Father God—whatever your experience was growing up with your own father—this will affect your view of Him. We have no idea just how much He loves us; how much He longs to father us. You can hear His heart in Jeremiah 3:19, when He says, "I just wanted you to call Me Father." Pray for the Father to reveal Himself to you in the following pages. Jesus said to Peter in Matthew 16:17 that man did not reveal to him who Jesus was, but the Father in heaven did. Just as man could not reveal Jesus to Peter, man cannot reveal the Father to you. (Matthew 11:27) The exciting news is that we can know and experience Him as a Father with the help of His Holy Sprit and He wants this for us. He knows how much we need a Father, even if we did have a good earthly father. Even the best father ever in our eyes does not compare to His incredible love for us. My prayer for you is that the Holy Spirit will bring fresh and continual revelation of how the Father feels about you as you turn the pages. I have been on a quest to know the Father since I had an encounter with Him in 2001. Before that, I hung out with my friend and Lord, Jesus, not knowing that I could have a relationship with the Father too! One day Matthew 6:6 came alive and He started speaking to me about Jesus telling us to go see our Father. This was like a burning bush experience. Suddenly, two eagles showed up in a tree across the creek in front of our house, and many know that eagles represent the prophetic. They sat there for almost five months, coming and going every day to the same branch and as soon as I asked Father about the eagles, was He trying to tell me something, He told me to write this book and that He would tell me what to say. I didn't have to wait very long, He was right there ready to communicate His heart. You'll notice some themes are repeated and this is because some of us need to hear things over and over again until it touches our hearts. It has been quite a journey, and I learned a lot about Him and myself. He fathered me in a way that I had never known before. Looking back, it's hard to believe that He had this in store for me—but eyes have not seen, nor ears have heard what He has planned for those that love Him. I pray that you feel His love surround you as you read ahead.

So I kneel humbly in awe before the Father of our Lord Jesus, the Messiah, the perfect Father of every father and child in heaven and earth. And I pray that he would unveil within you the unlimited riches of his glory and favor until supernatural strength floods your innermost being with his divine might and explosive power. Then by constantly using your faith, the life of Christ will be released deep inside you, and the resting place of his love will become the very source and root of your life. Then you will be powered to discover what every holy one experiences, the great magnitude of the astonishing love of Christ in all its dimensions. How deeply intimate and far reaching is his love! How enduring and inclusive it is! Endless love beyond measurement that transcends our understanding, this extravagant love pours into you until you are filled to overflowing with the fullness of God! Never doubt Gods mighty power to work in you and accomplish all this. He will achieve infinitely more than your greatest request, your most unbelievable dream, and exceed your wildest imagination! He will outdo them all, for his miraculous power constantly energizes you. (Ephesians 3:14-20)

Paula Sellars

JANUARY

JANUARY 1

I understand your struggles, doubts and fears about seeing me as a loving Father who cares for all your needs. I understand your struggle with trusting me since it can be hard to trust the people around you that you *can* see. So, I am not *demanding* that you trust me. I am here to help you understand that I will help you, just like I helped the man with his sick boy that asked me to help his unbelief. What you desperately wanted in an earthly father, I can, and I want to give to you. And I will give you even more than what you are expecting. All I need from you is to be open to receiving my healing love. I long to be close to my children because I have so much to show them, so much to give them.

SCRIPTURES TO MEDITATE ON:

For God has proved his love by giving us his greatest treasure, the gift of his Son. And since God freely offered him up as the sacrifice for us all, he certainly won't withhold from us anything else he has to give. (Romans 8:32)

When he heard this, the boy's father cried out with tears, saying, "I do believe, Lord; help my little faith!" (Mark 9:24)

The Father said , my son, you are always with me by my side. Everything I have is yours to enjoy. (Luke 16:31)

JANUARY 2

I am so happy when you come see me, no matter what time of day or night it is. Somewhere along your journey, you have learned things about me that have distorted how you see me. And so, you thought this morning that because you did not spend time with me that I would not talk to you. Do you stop talking to your children when they don't talk to you? I love when you spend time with me, but I am not going to go away or stop talking to you throughout the day if you don't spend time with me in the morning. I encourage you to come see me because it is good for you and I love our times together.

SCRIPTURES TO MEDITATE ON:

This is love: He loved us long before we loved him. It was his love, not ours. (1 John 4:10)

So now I live with the confidence that there is nothing in the universe with the power to separate us from God's love. I'm convinced that his love will triumph over death, life's troubles, fallen angels, or dark rulers in the heavens. There is nothing in our present or future circumstances that can weaken his love. There is no power above us or beneath us – no power that could ever be found in the universe that can distance us from God's passionate love, which is lavished upon us through Lord Jesus, the Anointed One! (Romans 8:38-39)

JANUARY 3

I know about the times when you feel completely alone. I know at times these feelings can be very difficult and I know that they started at a very young age. It is hard for me to see my children go through this heartache and my arms long to scoop you up and rescue you, but I cannot just barge into your life like that. This is not the plan I had for you when I created you. I want you to know that I am here for you and that I want to help you to heal and break the power of that tormenting lie that you are alone. In those moments, I long to hold you close, especially in the night hours when fear rattled your little heart and there was no one there to comfort you. I want to hold you close and rock you whispering in your ear reassurance of my presence. Do not be afraid, my dear child, I will make everything ok.

SCRIPTURES TO MEDITATE ON:

And teach them to faithfully follow all that I have commanded you. And never forget that I am with you every day, even to the completion of this age. (Matthew 28:20)

Where could I go from your Spirit? Where could I run and hide from your face? If I go up to heaven, you're there! If I go down to the realm of the dead, you're there too! If I fly with wings into the shining dawn, you're there! If I fly into the radiant sunset, you're there waiting! Wherever I go, your hand will guide me; your strength will empower me. It's impossible to disappear from you or to ask the darkness to hide me, for your presence is everywhere, bringing light into my night. There is no such thing as darkness with you. The night, to you, is as bright as the day; there's no difference between the two. (Psalm 139:7-12)

JANUARY 4

I am so happy to see you. Please, come in and close the door. Come sit with me, there are many things that I want to share with you. There is much truth I want to reveal to you about our relationship, so that you feel the security I want you to have. I am happy to reassure your heart that I have room for each and every one of my children. I never want you to feel left out when you see what I am doing with others. I am not the kind of father that would only be involved with a select few of my children. Do not try to figure out how I am involved with each one but focus on our relationship. You will be able to experience my love personally and that will put your heart to rest.

SCRIPTURES TO MEDITATE ON:

Peter said, "Now I know for certain that God doesn't show favoritism with people but treats everyone on the same basis." (Acts 10:34)

Become intimate with him in whatever you do, and he will lead you wherever you go. Don't think for a moment that you know it all. (Proverbs 3:6)

Of course, we wouldn't dare to put ourselves in the same class or compare ourselves with those who rate themselves so highly. They compare themselves to one another and make up their own standards to measure themselves by, and then they judge themselves by their own standards. What self-delusion! (2 Corinthians 10:12)

JANUARY 5

I am so glad you came today. I have been waiting for you. I look forward to our one on one times together. I wanted to remind you to be watching for me, I don't want you to miss what I have for you. Just as a child doesn't hesitate to ask questions, I want you to feel free to ask me anything, and comfortable enough to talk to me about everything. I want you to know that I am true to my word. As time passes and you get to know me, you will understand this more and more. For I am your Father and it is in my heart to make these things happen for you. It brings me pure joy to see you blessed and happy, and it blesses me to see you walk out into all that I have for you.

SCRIPTURES TO MEDITATE ON:

"For I know the plans I have for you," declares the Lord, "plans to prosper you and not to harm you, plans to give you hope and a future." (Jeremiah 29:11 NIV)

Ask, and the gift is yours. Seek, and you'll discover. Knock, and the door will be opened for you. For every persistent one will get what he asks for. Every persistent seeker will discover what he longs for. And everyone who knocks persistently will one day find an open door. "Do you know of any parent who would give his hungry child, who asked for food, a plate of rocks instead? Or when asked for a piece of fish, what parent would offer his child a snake instead? If you, imperfect as you are, know how to lovingly take care of your children and give them what's best, how much more ready is your heavenly Father to give wonderful gifts to those who ask him? (Matthew 7:7-11)

JANUARY 6

I am your Father, who is capable, able and wanting to meet your needs. Children need the security of a father present. I have experiences for you that will help you to know the security of being a much loved child, the security that you longed for when you looked at others. You will learn that you can rely on me without fear of being let down. You will see when you turn to me I will always be there for you. When you are used to not having your needs met it becomes a way of life in which you ignore the feelings you have inside. When you come to me with your needs, you will find that I am a very attentive Father. A lot of healing will take place in your heart as I father you in ways that you have never known. I will make these lost years up to you, that is my promise to you. You have such a bright future to look forward to on this new journey with me.

SCRIPTURES TO MEDITATE ON:

I will be a true Father to you, and you will be my beloved sons and daughters, says the Lord Yahweh Almighty. (2 Corinthians 6:18)

I will repay you for the years the locusts have eaten—the great locust and the young locust, the other locusts and the locust swarm—my great army that I sent among you. (Joel 2:25 NIV)

JANUARY 7

When others speak negative things, I want you to only listen for my voice. My voice will build you up and make you feel cared for. My children don't always listen for my voice because they are not aware of how much I want to talk to them and think that they cannot hear me for themselves. There are moments in your daily life in which you forget that I am right there with you. I will always be here to love and care for you and that will never change. My Holy Spirit will help you know my voice and recognize the many ways that I am trying to speak to you, just as any loving father loves to talk to his kids.

SCRIPTURES TO MEDITATE ON:

Jesus, the Anointed One, is always the same—yesterday, today, and forever. (Hebrews 13:8)

My own sheep will hear my voice and I know each one, and they will follow me. (John 10:27)

JANUARY 8

My dear, dear child, I am not looking at life the same way that you do. I do not look at the outward appearance, but I look at the heart. I do not look at your flaws, but I look at you as my amazing, wonderfully one of a kind child of mine. I am not upset when you mess up and I know it is in those moments that you need reassurance that you will always have my love. I so enjoy watching the good plans I have for you unfold and to watch you discover who I am as your Father. When you call to me, I will be right there. You won't have to wonder where I am because I will not hide from you, especially when I see how much you need me. I will never let you down. I am a good listener and love when you come see me to share what is on your heart.

SCRIPTURES TO MEDITATE ON:

"For I know the plans I have for you," declares the Lord, "plans to prosper you and not to harm you, plans to give you hope and a future." (Jeremiah 29:11 NIV)

"For my thoughts are not your thoughts, neither are your ways my ways," declares the Lord. "As the heavens are higher than the earth, so are my ways higher than your ways and my thoughts than your thoughts." (Isaiah 55:8-9 NIV)

JANUARY 9

Yes, there is work I have for us to do together, but there is something you need to be convinced of first. Knowing my love from experience and not just from what you hear from others. Not knowing what it is like being my sons and daughters, you may do things for me for the wrong reasons. Too much emphasis is on the work that needs to be done and not enough on the relationship I want with my children. As I heal your heart, you will learn that I am not here to use you, but to love you as my child and to be present in your life. Anything you do will flow out of that love. I don't want you working for me to make me happy or earn my love. The enemy has tried to destroy you in your past with wearing you out enticing you to work hard taking advantage of your wounded heart but I am here to tell you that I am never going to let that happen. Be open to receiving my healing love, so that you can walk into your destiny, free of the little foxes that spoil the vine.

SCRIPTURES TO MEDITATE ON:

Every single moment you are thinking of me! How pre-cious and wonderful to consider that you cherish me constantly in your every thought! (Psalm 139:17)

You must catch the troubling foxes, those sly little foxes that hinder our relationship. For they raid out budding vineyard of love to ruin what I planted within you. Will you catch them and remove them from me? We will do it together. (Song of Solomon 2:15)

JANUARY 10

I look forward to showing you the kind of father I am, and I am so happy when you open your heart to me. You need my Holy Spirit because you only see in part, and have limited revelation about my love. My love is bigger than anything you know or see here, and there isn't anything I wouldn't do to reach you. Sometimes I see you watching fathers interact with their children and I see you longing to be that child. I can do this for you and even more than you could ever imagine. This is not just another teaching or another truth to receive before you go on your merry way. The reality is that you can really know me as your father. You can truly have this with me. This can happen for you, right here, right now.

SCRIPTURES TO MEDITATE ON:

Our present knowledge and our prophecies are but partial. (1 Corinthians 13:9)

But when the Father sends the Spirit of Holiness, the One like me who sets you free, he will teach you all the things in my name. And he will inspire you to remember every word that I've told you. (John 14:26)

JANUARY 11

Your emotions and your circumstances might try and tell you a different story and if you believe them it will make it even harder for you. I told you that when you look for me you will find me, and you will. I love you like no one has ever loved you and I will help you to know this. Pray for eyes to see and ears to hear what my Spirit wants to say to you about all this. I am the same loving Father to you that Jesus talked about when he was here, I never change, and neither will my love for you. It will bring you much comfort to believe this about me. Remember, faith is the substance of things not seen, so just because you can't see me doesn't mean you can't experience me. You can walk in a greater awareness of me in your daily life, even in the midst of all that is going on.

SCRIPTURE TO MEDITATE ON:

Now faith brings our hopes into reality and becomes the foundation needed to acquire the things we long for. It is all the evidence required to prove what is still unseen. (Hebrews 11:1)

JANUARY 12

I am the Father you always longed for. What you are not aware of is how much I want to father you. When you think about me this is what I want you to immediately connect to. I want to sit and have long talks together. I want to give you things you like. I want to help you feel safe. I want to be there for you when you hurt. I want you to know I would drop everything if you needed me. I want to be there with you in the fun times, the hard times and the good times. I want you to know me in this way. All the times you longed to have this, I longed even more to give this to you. Heaven rejoiced the day you realized that I am here to father you. I am the Father that Jesus talked about all the time and I am both his Father and yours. The closeness I have with my son Jesus, I want this with you.

SCRIPTURES TO MEDITATE ON:

"I myself said, 'How gladly I would treat you like my children and give you a pleasant land, the most beautiful inheritance of any nation.' I thought you would call me 'Father' and not turn away from following me." (Jeremiah 3:19 NIV)

Jesus cautioned her, "Mary, don't hold on to me now, for I haven't yet ascended to God, my Father. And he's not only my Father and God, but now he's your Father and your God! Now go to my brothers and tell them what I've told you, that I am ascending to my Father—and your Father, to my God—and your God!" Then Mary Magdalene left to inform the disciples of her encounter with Jesus. "I have seen the Lord!" she told them. And she gave them his message. (John 20:17-18)

JANUARY 13

All you have to do is ask me and I will show you who I am. I reveal my mysteries and show you my healing power, so I can also reveal to you who I am as your God and your Father. My Holy Spirit will help you to know and convince your spirit that you are my child. Your identity has been in many things but I want you to learn to relate to me as my sons and daughters. There is also the spirit of fatherlessness that tells my children that I do not care, but believe me when I say that he is the father of lies. Because of the pain around your earthly fathers you are more apt to listen to his lies about me. He is crafty and subtle in trying to get you to think that I am not here for you. This is why I tell you that I have good plans for you and I will not hurt you. I am here to father anyone who will be open to inviting me into their hearts and their homes. You are my child and my home is yours. Look for me today, and look for how I am loving you in a hundred different ways. I love when you notice that it is me coming to you trying to get your attention throughout the day.

SCRIPTURES TO MEDITATE ON:

My father and mother abandoned me. I am like an orphan! But you took me in and made me yours. (Psalm 27:10)

"For I know the plans I have for you," declares the Lord, "plans to prosper you and not to harm you, plans to give you hope and a future." (Jeremiah 29:11 NIV)

For the Holy Spirit makes God's fatherhood real to us as he whispers into our innermost being, "You are God's beloved child!" (Romans 8:16)

JANUARY 14

Dear child of mine, come to me expecting to receive from me. I am your Father who loves to give generously to his children. Be aware of your adult, analytical mind that gets in the way by trying to understand everything. I would like to see you just relax for a change, receive, and stop trying to figure this all out. Listen closely so you can hear me sing over you the way a mother sings her child to sleep. Everything is going to be ok; I will take good care of you. I have all the healing for your heart that you will ever need in order for you to learn to have that childlike trust again. What a wonderful place to live in, knowing that I will take care of all that concerns you. Think about what it would be like to not have a care in the world, knowing your Papa will always be a safe place for you, knowing you have a Papa that always wanted you.

SCRIPTURES TO MEDITATE ON:

Wisdom extends to you long life in one hand and wealth and promotion in the other. Out of her mouth flows righteousness, and her words release both law and mercy. (Proverbs 3:16)

Pour out all your worries and stress upon him and leave them there, for he always tenderly cares for you. (1 Peter 5:7)

So here's what I've learned through it all: Leave all your cares and anxieties at the feet of the Lord, and measureless grace will strengthen you. (Psalm 55:22)

Jesus taught his disciples, saying, "Listen to me. Never let anxiety enter your hearts. Never worry about any of your needs, such as food or clothing. For your life is infinitely more than just food or the clothing you wear. Take the carefree birds as your example. Do you ever see them worry? They don't grow their own food or put it in a storehouse for later. Yet God takes care of every one of them, feeding each of them from his love and goodness. Isn't your life more precious to God than a bird? Be carefree in the care of God! Does worry add anything to your life? Can it add one more year, or even one day? So if worrying adds nothing, but actually subtracts from your life, why would you worry about God's care for you? Think about the lilies. They grow and become beautiful, not because they work hard or strive to clothe themselves. Yet not even Solomon, wearing his kingly garments of splendor, could be compared to a field of lilies. If God can clothe the fields and meadows with grass and flowers, can't he clothe you as well, O struggling one with so many doubts? I repeat it: Don't let worry enter your life. Live above the anxious cares about your personal needs. People everywhere seem to worry about making a living, but your heavenly Father knows your every need and will take care of you. Each and every day he will supply your needs as you seek his kingdom passionately, above all else. So don't ever be afraid, dearest friends! Your loving Father joyously gives you his kingdom realm with all its promises!" (Luke 12:22-32)

JANUARY 15

First, I want to tell you how happy I am to see you. I do love when we are connecting so I can share with you as any concerned, loving father would talk to his children. There is so much teaching, so much information out there, but what you don't hear very much about is how much I want to father you. You need to know this more than anything else. There is much I want you to know about being my sons and daughters. I do believe you will like this place. Listen to my Holy Spirit; He will tell you what you need to know about me and what I want to say to you. I want you to hear me affirming you and encouraging you as I heal, nurture and restore you back to the person I made you to be. As you experience my love, you will see and feel something wonderful. Listen for my voice and listen to what I say about you.

SCRIPTURES TO MEDITATE ON:

"I promise that I will never leave you helpless or abandon you as orphans—I will come back to you!" (John 14:18)

But when the Father sends the Spirit of Holiness, the One like me who sets you free, he will teach you all things in my name. And he will inspire you to remember every word that I've told you. (John 14:26)

JANUARY 16

I just wanted you to call me 'Father.' Oh how I longed to take you under my wings. I want you to hear my heart and feel my love in Jeremiah 3:19 of how I am longing to father you. Many times I have cared for you, but you were not aware that it was me. I see you wondering if I am gone, if I am upset, but I am the one who is here to stay, and I do not want you to leave, or to get distracted. As your Father, I have so much to give you, but you are always gone before I can give it to you, trying to make it happen for yourself. I am the father that wants to be in your life, and I desire to give you the best. I can help you feel the security and safety that you never felt. I want you to feel cared for and even spoiled. I love to give to my children. So, freely and boldly come to me, call to me, the one who adores you more than you will ever know. Don't turn away from me, and don't let feelings of unworthiness keep you away.

SCRIPTURES TO MEDITATE ON:

So now we come freely and boldly to where love is enthroned, to receive mercy's kiss and discover the grace we urgently need to strengthen us in our time of weakness. (Hebrews 4:16)

So don't ever be afraid, dearest friends! Your loving Father joyously gives you his kingdom realm with all its promises! (Luke 12:32)

JANUARY 17

I am so glad you came. This is your home and I've always wanted you here with me. I want you to enjoy your life with me and let me carry all of your burdens. I am going to take care of everything, so you can go off and enjoy your day, or maybe have some fun for a change. You don't have to worry about a thing because your Father is home. You can count on me to be here every single time you need me. You will see over time that I will come through over and over and you will discover the truth about the kind of Father I am. My love will never waver for you and there is nothing and nobody that can ever separate us. Drink this truth, set your mind on what I am telling you and your heart will know my peace.

SCRIPTURES TO MEDITATE ON:

Hasn't he promised you, I will never leave you alone! And I will never lose my grip on your life. (Hebrews 13:5)

You will keep in perfect peace those whose minds are steadfast, because they trust you. (Isaiah 26:3 NIV)

Who could ever separate us from the endless love of God's Anointed One? Absolutely no one! For nothing in the universe has the power to diminish his love towards us. (Romans 8:35)

JANUARY 18

Isn't it wonderful that you do not have to figure this out on your own and you are never alone on this journey? Just like my son, Jesus, was with the disciples, so my Holy Spirit is right there with you. Pray for open eyes to see what I am doing all around you. I don't want you to miss out on this. I hope that you will stay here with me and not be distracted by the cares of this world. Many are not aware how much my Holy Spirit is there to help, guide and show them who I am. He will be honest with you and help you realize how present and how active I am in all the moments of your life. Be blessed today, my child, with knowing I have the healing you need. Be blessed today, my child, with eyes to see and ears to hear what I want to say to you, so that you can see me in places where you didn't notice me before.

SCRIPTURES TO MEDITATE ON:

But when the spirit of truth comes, he will guide you into all truth. (John 16:13)

But the Advocate, the Holy Spirit, whom the Father will send in my name, will teach you all things and will remind you of everything I have said to you. (John 14:26)

And Elisha prayed, "Open his eyes, Lord, so that he may see." Then the Lord opened the servant's eyes, and he looked and saw the hills full of horses and chariots of fire all around Elisha. (2 Kings 6:17 NIV)

JANUARY 19

I want you to have the freedom to ask me anything. I will never take from you, and I only take what you give to me, so it is your choice. When I ask you for your cares, it is your choice to give them to me or to carry them yourselves. Your day will be full of choices and I have strength, wisdom, and counsel for you if you choose to turn to me. I will never just take from you, but I do have a lot to give you. I have so much more to give you than what you are asking for, but for different reasons of your own you do not ask. I don't mind you asking and I love when you feel comfortable enough to talk to me about what you need. I really do care about the things that you like and the things that interest you. What kind of father would I be if all I talked to you about was what I wanted you to do for me, or how much you needed to change? I am with you when you go shopping, just as much as I am when you are doing my work.

SCRIPTURES TO MEDITATE ON:

And if anyone longs to be wise, ask God for wisdom and he will give it! He won't see your lack of wisdom as an opportunity to scold you over your failures but he will overwhelm your failures with his generous grace. (James 1:5)

JANUARY 20

I love being your Father. I want to help you to connect to this reality throughout your day. I encourage you to be mindful and watch for me. I have healing for that deep pain around your parents, that for different reasons were not able to be there for you. I don't want this to hurt you anymore, nor do I want to hurt you. I am a father that is moved by your pain. I want to help you. There needs to be an openness and a readiness on your part to receive. Don't be afraid, I am right here to help you trust what I am telling you. I wish you could see the smile you put on my face. We can move forward together as the close knit family that you always wanted.

SCRIPTURES TO MEDITATE ON:

My father and mother abandoned me. I'm like an orphan! But you took me in and made me yours. (Psalm 27:10)

The Lord is close to all whose hearts are crushed by pain, and he is always ready to restore the repentant one. (Psalm 34:18)

He heals the wounds of every shattered heart. (Psalm 147:3)

JANUARY 21

Just call out my name and I will leave wherever I am for you. I'll come running to see you again. All you have to do is call and your Abba Daddy will drop everything. Nothing is more near and dear to my heart than my children. I love the sound of your voice when I hear you call my name. I also know each one of your names and I recognize each one of my children's voices as they call out to me, just as a mother knows the sound of her child's voice in a crowd. It is my desire for you to hear me as much as I hear you, so we can sit and have long talks together. In any loving relationship, there needs to be a two-way conversation or it could be a very lonely one. I just want you to know that I am the kind of father that loves to talk to his kids. I tell you I am not quiet, distant and cold, but I am present, approachable and warm. Be bold, and do not hesitate to come to me. You put a smile on my face when you walk in, and I am always so happy to see you.

SCRIPTURES TO MEDITATE ON:

My own sheep will hear my voice and I know each one, and they will follow me. (John 10:27)

So now we come freely and boldly to where love is enthroned, to receive mercy's kiss and discover the grace we urgently need to strengthen us in our time of weakness. (Hebrews 4:16)

JANUARY 22

I am so much more involved in your life than you are aware of, guiding, opening and closing doors, and making things happen for you. I see you wondering if I will take the time to talk to you about things that are going on in your life, and I need you to know that I have all the time in the world for you. I also see my children walking around not grasping how much I want to be involved with their daily lives. This keeps them from thinking that they can talk to me about things that I want to help them with. They are not used to having someone love them as much as I do. The most loving person you know does not compare to me. "Ask me to show you and I will show you great and mighty things that you do not know about my love." (Jeremiah 33:3) There is so much you can experience with me and if you really want to know all you have to do is ask. It is a joy for me to reveal these things to you and I love to watch your expressions as this happens.

SCRIPTURES TO MEDITATE ON:

Call to me and I will answer you and tell you great and unsearchable things you do not know. (Jeremiah 33:3 NIV)

You will seek me and find me when you seek me with all your heart. (Jeremiah 29:13 NIV)

If you, imperfect as you are, know how to lovingly take care of your children and give them what's best, how much more ready is your heavenly Father to give wonderful gifts to those who ask him? (Matthew 7:11)

JANUARY 23

I am telling you that I can do so much more than you could ever ask or think, and you will see it unfold before your eyes. Whatever you are asking, whatever you are thinking, it is way beyond what you are comprehending at this moment. So, if you are asking me to father you, it would be beyond anything you are thinking of or expecting. I know you need a father and want to be fathered but its hard for you to believe that the longing of my heart is to father you. So many of my children are walking around with guarded hearts. Whenever parts of their hearts are closed, it will make it harder for them to see me and receive from me. But I have the answers, and I want to help. You just don't know how much I truly care about you. Yet, I don't mind telling you over and over until you are convinced.

SCRIPTURE TO MEDITATE ON:

Never doubt God's mighty power to work in you and accomplish all this. He will achieve infinitely more than your greatest request, your most unbelievable dream, and exceed your wildest imagination! He will outdo them all, for his miraculous power constantly energizes you. (Ephesians 3:20)

January 24

I want to remind you to get in the habit of coming to me about the things that are weighing on your heart. You will be comfortable with me, once you realize I am a safe Father. We can talk about whatever you want to talk about. You can ask me anything. You can also share things about yourself that you don't like, things you prefer to ignore because you don't know what to do with them. I encourage you to talk to me about this because these things do not shock me or change the way I feel about you. I would never shame you or make you feel bad. Turning to me is a good way of taking care of yourself. You will know healing as you experience my loving acceptance of you. Knowing how much I love you in spite of all your issues is not a familiar kind of love for you. You may have been called many things in your life, but I call you beautiful, healed, and whole. I call you, my child, to my arms, so I can hold and comfort you in the midst of your struggle with yourself.

SCRIPTURES TO MEDITATE ON:

So now we can come freely and boldly to where love is enthroned, to receive mercy's kiss and discover the grace we urgently need to strengthen us in our time of weakness. (Hebrews 4:16)

So, what does all this mean? If God has determined to stand with us, tell me, who then could ever stand against us? (Romans 8:31)

JANUARY 25

There is something I would like you to look at with me. I want you to know more about how I see you when you mess up. I see the struggle this can be, but this is the very place you need to experience my unconditional love. I want you to stop feeling bad because this is not from me. This struggle has become a way of life, you just accept it and agree with the voice of the accuser. Your life is so valuable, so precious to me and this is why I gave my son to die on the cross. I did not want to lose my children. Ask the Holy Spirit to make you aware when you go to that place and he will help you. My love will break through all those lies you learned to believe about me over the years of heartache. I will make my truth known to you how I feel so you can freely come to your Papa's waiting arms. I promise you that I will make my love known to you as you turn to me.

SCRIPTURES TO MEDITATE ON:

So now the case is closed. There remains no accusing voice of condemnation against those who are joined in life-union with Jesus, the Anointed One. (Romans 8:1)

Until finally, Jesus was left alone with the woman still standing there in front of him. So he stood back up and said to her, "Dear woman, where are your accusers? Is there no one here to condemn you?" Look around, she replied, "I see no one, Lord." Jesus said, "Then I certainly don't condemn you either. Go, and from now on, be free from a life of sin." (John 8:10-11)

January 26

I understand your struggle to believe that I love you as much as I do. It's hard for you to grasp that as your Father I would go to such lengths to give my Son for you just so that I could reach you. I was not upset with the man who came to me for healing for his son when he told me he believed but asked me to help his unbelief. I helped him and healed his son. I was not upset with his struggle to trust me. And now I will do the same for you. I will convince you, heal your heart and destroy that lie that tells you I don't care. You think you have to be good in order to please me; that you might get punished if you don't act right. Don't listen to the father of lies who wants to pull your attention away from me. I need you to come to me for help and healing. I know about your weaknesses. I know about your bitterness, your anger. I know about your bad attitude. I am not looking at that, I am looking at the child that I know so well, the child that I love. I am here to take you by your hand and guide you with my counsel.

SCRIPTURES TO MEDITATE ON:

When I saw all of this, what turmoil filled my heart, piercing my opinions with your truth. I was so stupid. I was senseless and ignorant, acting like a brute beast before you, Lord. Yet, in spite of all this, you comfort me by your counsel; you draw me closer to you. You lead me with your secret wisdom. And following you brings me into your brightness and glory! Whom have I in heaven but you? You're all I want! No one on earth means as much to me as you. Lord, so many times I fail; I fall into disgrace. But when I trust in you, I have a strong and glorious presence protecting me and anointing me. Forever you're all I need! (Psalm 73:21-26)

Love never brings fear, for fear is always related to punishment. But love's perfection drives the fear of punishment far from our hearts. Whoever walks constantly afraid of punishment has not reached love's perfection. (1 John 4:18)

JANUARY 27

My child, you are not used to having a father around to help you and this is why I keep reminding you to come to me for help. Many grow up learning to be independent because they had to take care of themselves. There is a fear that if you don't do something then your needs will not be met. There is a fear that others who are supposed to take care of you will not come through. You don't have to struggle alone anymore. You don't have to beg me for my love or for my help. I have been waiting to come into your world to show you just that. In every place where fear has hurt you, I want to come and father you there. No longer will the fears and lies push you around because you will know my love. I will make this happen for you. When I said in Jeremiah 3:19 that I just wanted you to call me Father, I meant that I want to father you. I want you to feel loved and cared for by me. Jesus told you to come see me and close the door because he knew how much I wanted to spend time with you, he knew my heart and wants you to know it too.

SCRIPTURES TO MEDITATE ON:

But whenever you pray, go into your innermost chamber and be alone with Father God, praying to him in secret. And your Father, who sees all you do, will reward you openly. (Matthew 6:6)

What is the value of your soul to God? Could your worth be defined by an amount of money? God doesn't abandon or forget even the small sparrow he has made. How then could he forget or abandon you? What about the seemingly minor issues of your life? Do they matter to God? Of course they do! So you never need to worry, for you are more valuable to God than anything else in this world. (Luke 12:7)

January 28

So, I was just wondering how you are doing today? It would be helpful for you to stop believing the lie that I am upset or going to leave when you think you are not doing the things you need to do to be accepted by me. Try to remember to quickly turn to me. I have what you need for your heart to heal and know my unconditional love. I love our times together, but if you don't take time to be with me, know that my love for you remains the same. I do not pull back from you. You are made in my image, but you and I have very different reactions, and responses to each other. I am here to help you get up and get on track when you mess up. Others have pulled away or got upset when you failed them, but I am not like man in that way. You are known, wanted and very special to me all the time. This is what I want you to remember when you feel bad about the way you think you should be.

SCRIPTURES TO MEDITATE ON:

God, you're such a safe and powerful place to find refuge! You're a proven help in time of trouble—more than enough and always available whenever I need you. (Psalm 46:1)

You kissed my heart with forgiveness in spite of all I've done. (Psalm 103:3)

JANUARY 29

My dear, dear child. How are you doing today with the things that are weighting on your heart? It is so easy to worry, but you carry all this stuff around when you don't have to, it is a waste of time and it is not good for you. Get in the habit of giving these things to me. You can leave all of this with me and I will take care of whatever it is. At first, it might be hard to comprehend why anyone would care so much that they would take your worries for you. I have a lot of grace to help you let go and release these things. Just think how wonderful it would be to be able to give your problems to someone that cares about you. Just think how wonderful it would be to be as carefree as a child, not having a care in the world because your heart knows you are so loved. I also want your heart to know that I am very attentive to you and what is going on in your life.

SCRIPTURES TO MEDITATE ON:

Are you weary, carrying a heavy burden? Then come to me. I will refresh your life, for I am your oasis. (Matthew 11:28)

Pour out all your worries and stress upon him and leave them there, for he always tenderly cares for you. (1 Peter 5:7)

JANUARY 30

There is so much I want to show you about my interaction with you. Any time you feel alone, I want you to realize that the presence of my love is everywhere, all around you every moment of the day and night. I love being close to my children so much that I would live in a tent just to be near them. When you were in the grocery store, I was right there next to you as you were comparing prices. When you were driving in your car, I was right there watching over you. When you were on the phone, I was right there wanting to talk to you as well. I was there at work with you when you were talking to someone about me and I wish you could have seen the smile on my face as I watched you. I was there cheering you on when you felt like you were having a bad day. Listen and watch for me, and you will see me for yourself. I love when you are aware of me coming to you in many different ways. I don't want you to believe that life has to always be so difficult. Just relax and enjoy the blessings I have in store for you. I am your greatest encourager.

SCRIPTURES TO MEDITATE ON:

It is impossible to disappear from you or ask the darkness to hide me, for your presence is everywhere, bringing light into my night. (Psalm 139:11)

Where could I go from your Spirit? Where could I run and hide from your face? (Psalm 139:7)

JANUARY 31

I want my children to know how much I want to talk to them as their Father. You see me with many titles, and hear me in many different ways, but coming to you as your Father who wants to talk to you, is beyond what you could imagine. Maybe you had a father here that didn't talk to you or was not present and now you see me this way. This is not the kind of father I am; I love to talk to my kids. You wait before me but are not expecting me to say anything or you think you have to wait forever before I will speak. Many think they just can't hear me, they don't know how special they are to me, so they don't have a lot of faith to believe that I want to talk to them. My plan was not to always talk to you through another person. There are many reasons why my children do not hear me, but I tell you that I have created you to hear my voice. I gave you my Holy Spirit to reveal to you the kind of father I am. My truth will set you free into a whole new place with me, a place where you can enjoy our times together knowing you have a Father that wants to be with you.

SCRIPTURES TO MEDITATE ON:

My own sheep will hear my voice and I know each one, and they will follow me. (John 10:27)

For if you embrace the truth, it will release more freedom into your lives. (John 8:32)

FEBRUARY

FEBRUARY 1

Do not let your heart be troubled dear one, by the events that happen unexpectedly in your relationships with others. These things will always try and get your focus off me when you start looking at them in the natural. They always look different when you are looking at them without my input or perspective. Bring these things to me so I can help you. Pray for those that you are struggling with. Pray and I will give you insight so that you know what I am trying to do here. Remember that I do not condemn you for your reactions. Know that my love is here for you in this place of struggling and remember that I am here to guide you as any loving father would help his child. I don't want you to struggle alone. Just as Jesus had compassion on them and healed them in John 14:14, so I have compassion for you, my dear child, to bring the healing you need in every area of your life.

SCRIPTURES TO MEDITATE ON:

"For my thoughts are not your thoughts, neither are your ways my ways," declares the Lord. "As the heavens are higher than the earth, so are my ways higher than your ways and my thoughts than your thoughts. (Isaiah 55:8-9)

Don't worry or surrender to your fear. For you've believed in God, now trust and believe in me also. (John 14:1)

FEBRUARY 2

My promise to you is to be all the things that I said I would be. One thing you can count on is when I say that I will not disappoint you. I am here to heal all the wounds of disappointment from others that you thought you could trust. When I tell you I will heal, I will do it. I will provide you with everything that you'll need to heal and feel whole. When I said I will never leave you, I meant it. This is my promise to you! I am not like man in that I would lie to you. Be comforted, my dear child, in knowing that I will always keep my word. I am your real Father and I am here to stay. As you experience this, you will be convinced of how important you are to me.

SCRIPTURES TO MEDITATE ON:

Here is what I learned from it all: Don't give up, don't be impatient; be entwined as one with the Lord. Be brave and courageous, and never lose hope. Yes, keep on waiting....for he will never disappoint you! (Psalm 27:14)

God is not human, that he should lie, not a human being, that he should change his mind. Does he speak and then not act? Does he promise and not fulfill? (Numbers 23:19 NIV)

So it is impossible for God to lie for we know that his promise and his vow will never change! And now we have run into his heart to hide ourselves in his faithfulness. This is where we established ahead of time—an unshakeable hope! (Hebrews 6:18)

FEBRUARY 3

I love when we are connecting and I love when I have your full attention. Pray for the eyes of your heart to be open to receiving, so that you can enter into all I have prepared for you. I will give you pictures of my love, so when you see a mother holding her baby close to her heart, this is me. When you see a father proudly smiling at his child, this is me. When you see a father helping his child clean up a mess they made, this is me. When you see a father loving his child while helping him clean up his favorite vase he broke, and in that moment when he cares more about his child than he does about the broken vase, this is me. When you see a father telling his son, "It's ok, good job son," after he missed the ball, this is me. The enemy has come to kill and destroy. But I have come to give you life, my child, to show you my healing love.

SCRIPTURE TO MEDITATE ON:

Love is large and incredibly patient. Love is gentle and consistently kind to all. It refuses to be jealous when blessing comes to someone else. Love does not brag about one's achievements nor inflate its own importance. Love does not traffic in shame and disrespect, nor selfishly seek its own honor. Love is not easily irritated or quick to take offense. (1 Corinthians 13:4-5)

FEBRUARY 4

I am aware of the difficult things you go through. I see you when you're feeling rejected, alone, and left out. Know that I will never do this to you. I do not like to see you mistreated by others. Try and remember, my child, that they also need my healing love. I do understand what you are going through because this is what my son endured. You are of so much value to me and I know this is what I need to convince you of. I don't want you to feel bad, I am not upset with you when you are reacting to a situation and when you are having difficulty believing in my love. I have the healing you need and will turn this around and use it for good. Don't think it is strange when you go through all kinds of things here, just know that I am working always to reach you. I love you, child of mine, you are near and dear to my heart.

SCRIPTURE TO MEDITATE ON:

My fellow believers, when it seems as though you are facing nothing but difficulties see it as an invaluable opportunity to experience the greatest joy that you can! (James 1:2)

FEBRUARY 5

Come, I have been waiting for you. I would like us to continue where we left off yesterday. Life is not just about difficult trials and hard times. Sometimes, people get stuck in that place and there is so much more I have for them. I like to encourage you to come and talk to me. I am a very good listener and very interested in what you have to say. Many look at me like all I want from them is to do my work. So they are busy about my business when I am longing to be close to them. There is more in my world than just work, there is also fun. Balance is good, understanding that there is a time for everything. I love when I hear your laughter, just like you love to hear your children laugh among themselves. I love to see you get excited about life and what I am doing for you. All you have to do is ask, and I will show you what I am really like. I want you to know me as I truly am. To many times I am portrayed as a serious, bossy, and uninterested God. Yet every ounce of compassion I feel is for my children.

SCRIPTURES TO MEDITATE ON:

For this is how much God loved the world—he gave his one and only, unique Son as a gift. So now everyone who believes in him will never perish but experience everlasting life. (John 3:16)

Ask, and the gift is yours. Seek, and you'll discover. Knock, and the door will be opened for you. (Matthew 7:7)

FEBRUARY 6

I just want to remind you before we start how much I love our times together. Just as you want to be with the people you care about, so I feel the same way about my children. It is natural to want to be with the people that you love. Healing your emotions has always been part of my plan for you, so that you can trust the love I have for you and I don't want to see you keep hurting. I also want to do this so that you have stability in your life as you move forward into the plans I have for you. I have had a plan all along for your life that you have not begun to realize yet. As your Father, I have a plan of just how I want to bless you. I want you not to lose hope about the future because I know just how I am going to make things happen for you.

SCRIPTURE TO MEDITATE ON:

"For I know the plans I have for you," declares the Lord, "plans to prosper you and not to harm you, plans to give you hope and a future." (Jeremiah 29:11 NIV)

February 7

I have made you to be able to hear my voice. What parent would not want their child to hear what they are saying? Most loving parents talk to their kids about their problems, their interests, and their day. My Holy Spirit can and will train you to hear my voice, not only as your God, but as your Father as well. This is so important and I want you to stay with me on this. It's to your benefit and others that you hear what I am saying, and besides, I love our one on one talks. I have heard you cry out to hear my voice, consider it done. Settle this in your heart and believe me when I tell you that I love when you come to me, I love talking to you, and not only at certain times. You can come to me anytime.

SCRIPTURES TO MEDITATE ON:

Do you know of any parent who would give his hungry child, who asked for food, a plate of rocks instead? (Matthew 7:9)

But when the Father sends the Spirit of Holiness, the one like me who sets you free, he will teach you all things in my name. (John 14:26)

FEBRUARY 8

When you woke up this morning and didn't feel that great about yourself because you messed up the day before, I was right there wanting to reassure you that I was not upset with you. When you realized there was a party and you weren't invited, I was right next to you wanting to hang out with you. When you were in a large gathering of people and felt alone, I was standing right there hoping you would notice me wanting to be with you. When others are in the limelight and you feel very small, I am right there calling you to come to me. I was with you in all the places that were difficult in your life, even when you were not aware of my presence. The story of your life with me goes on and will never end.

SCRIPTURES TO MEDITATE ON:

Every single moment you are thinking of me! How precious and wonderful to consider that you cherish me constantly in your every thought! O God, your desires toward me are more than the grains of sand on every shore! When I awake each morning, you're still with me. (Psalm 139:17-18)

He understands humanity, for as a Man, our magnificent King-Priest was tempted in every way just as we are, and conquered sin. (Hebrews 4:15)

FEBRUARY 9

I am always happy to see you. As you come and sit with me, I want you to enter into an awareness that I am listening to every word you say and even to the ones you don't say out of fear of what I might think. I want to heal any pain of not being heard, accepted, or understood. As you catch glimpses of my love, you think that it is too good to be true. You ask if anyone could really love you like this. My love is patient and my love is kind, I will wait as you are being convinced, until you can respond more fully to me. My love will bring comfort and healing to you that you can enjoy in this very moment. You do not have to wait and hope that I will answer. What mother would not run to her child that needs her, so I am always here for you when you need me.

SCRIPTURES TO MEDITATE ON:

Love is large and incredibly patient. Love is gentle and consistently kind to all. (1 Corinthians 13:4)

The Lord appeared to us in the past, saying: "I have loved you with an everlasting love; I have drawn you with unfailing kindness." (Jeremiah 31:3 NIV)

February 10

In case you were wondering, I have been working my will and purpose out for your life. I am involved so much more than you are aware of. I created Heaven and Earth, so you can know that I also have the ability to make things happen for you. Ask me anything, just ask and see what I will show you, I don't mind you asking and remember you are never a bother. As you experience my love, which you can, you will rest knowing everything will be ok. My plans are always good and full of surprises and I enjoy watching them unfold for you. Whatever you are thinking, it is so much more than that. You can experience 1 Corinthians 2:9, "What no eye has seen, what no ear has heard, and what no human minds have conceived…the things God has prepared for those who love Him." So just remember, it is going to be so much more than what you come up with and as you experience this with me you will know a blessing that you have never known before. This is my love for you.

SCRIPTURE TO MEDITATE ON:

"For I know the plans I have for you," declares the Lord, "plans to prosper you and not to harm you, plans to give you hope and a future. Then you will call on me and come and pray to me, and I will listen to you." (Jeremiah 29:11-12 NIV)

February 11

I understand and know it is hard for you to believe at times. How do you expect to just simply embrace my love for you when your heart has not received the tender love it needed to trust? There are many ways through which I can communicate just how important you are to me. I would go to the ends of the earth to convince you. My love is something you hear about, but it doesn't mean you fully grasp it or even grasp it at all, especially when you didn't grow up in a loving atmosphere. I want you to come to me and tell me how you feel and I promise I will always be there for you. My heart is so moved to help you, to reach you, and to let you know that I am here. Maybe you have heard it said to just get over it, but this is not what I am saying to you. My love for you will never make you feel bad about you. I am here to to give you the understanding and comfort that I always wanted you to have.

SCRIPTURES TO MEDITATE ON:

How great is our God! There's nothing his power cannot accomplish, and he has infinite understanding of everything. (Psalm 147:5)

As a mother comforts her child, so I will comfort you; and you will be comforted over Jerusalem. (Isaiah 66:13)

You keep every promise you've ever made to me! (Psalm 138:8)

FEBRUARY 12

You don't have to look anywhere else for the love that your heart is crying out for. You don't need outside sources to let you know you are okay. For many years, you have lived off of the approval of others to tell you that you were of any value. You found your importance in what you did or didn't do. You have been pushed around long enough. All that you didn't receive that you needed in order to love yourself, I have for you. As you recognize what is going on inside of you and turn to me, you will realize that I am the one that can give you what you need. As you experience my consistent unchanging love for you it will change your world. I have always had this for you. Be open and pray to become good receivers of a love that is greater that anything you have known here. It's time to start receiving from me.

SCRIPTURE TO MEDITATE ON:

Until then, there are three things that remain: faith, hope, and love—yet love surpasses them all. So above all else, let love be the beautiful prize for which you run. (1 Corinthians 13:13)

FEBRUARY 13

Please my child, do not try and figure all of this out on your own. You can only see in part until I show you the bigger picture. There is so much you don't understand about how I am so personally involved with all my children. Each one of you is so dear to my heart and that is why I don't like when you are so hard on yourself. I am a lot more understanding of you than you realize when you are struggling to believe this. I know I have told you many times, but I want to remind you that I am here for you. Turn to me as many times as you need to. My faithfulness to you reaches to the heavens, just think for a moment how big that is.

SCRIPTURES TO MEDITATE ON:

But you, O Lord, your mercy seat love is limitless, reaching higher than the highest heavens. Your great faithfulness is infinite, stretching over the whole earth. (Psalm 36:5)

Call to me and I will answer you and tell you great and unsearchable things you do not know. (Jeremiah 33:3 NIV)

FEBRUARY 14

My kids are expecting paper plates when I want to set out the royal china for them. They believe that they should be content with what they have so they don't ask me for special things. But my heart is to bless you. Some do not realize I have a Father's blessing for them, they don't know what it means, or what it looks like. You look at others, thinking they are blessed, but I would love to show you that I don't have favorites amongst my children. I am a fair and just God and Father, so do not think that you have to settle for paper plates. I am your Father who adores you and I want you to just rest and know that this is your portion to be blessed by me,. As you grow to know what kind of Father I am, you will be surprised at all the wonderful things I have for you.

SCRIPTURE TO MEDITATE ON:

The Lord bless you and keep you; the Lord make his face shine on you and be gracious to you; the Lord turn his face toward you and give you peace. (Numbers 6:24-26 NIV)

FEBRUARY 15

When you can see me in the middle of your storm, I will calm you down just like I did my disciples. When you see me and realize that I am not frazzled nor worried in the slightest, that in itself will calm you down. When you know that I am your God, your Father that deeply loves his children, you will know the security you need and that will change your world. Jesus slept in the boat during the storm because he knew me and knew that I would always take care of things. You can know this for yourselves as we spend time together and you learn that I am the same Father to you as I am to Jesus.

SCRIPTURE TO MEDITATE ON:

Suddenly a violent storm developed, with waves so high the boat was about to be swamped. Yet Jesus continued to sleep soundly. The disciples woke him up, saying, "Save us, Lord! We're going to die!" But Jesus reprimanded them. "Why are you gripped with fear? Where is your faith?" Then he stood up and rebuked the storm and said, "Be still!" And instantly it became perfectly calm. The disciples were astonished by this miracle and said to one another, "Who is this Man? Even the wind and waves obey his Word." (Matthew 8:24-27)

FEBRUARY 16

I really would like you to come and sit with me when you are feeling bad about yourself. I don't want you to go to that lonely place anymore where you hear the voice that tells you that you are bad. This is the time for you to experience me and this is where you learn to trust as I tenderly care for you. Come quickly you to be kind to yourself when you see your shortcomings and learn to receive my love in this place. I have been waiting for you, calling out to you to come to me so that I can give you the comfort you need. Just quiet yourself and listen so you can hear me calling to you. My desire has always been to be close to my children just as you long to be close to your own sons and daughters.

SCRIPTURES TO MEDITATE ON:

So now the case is closed. There remains no accusing voice of condemnation against those who are joined in life-union with Jesus, the Anointed One. (Romans 8:1)

All praises belong to the God and Father of our Lord Jesus Christ. For he is the Father of tender mercy and the God of endless comfort. (2 Corinthians 1:3)

FEBRUARY 17

If you could see how much I love you, you would never be afraid again. I am at the helm and have only your best interest in mind. I tell you 365 times in my Word not to fear because I always know the outcome, and you will see that you feared for nothing. I am your Father and there is nothing too hard for me. I can and will continue to reveal myself to you so that you can feel what every child needs to feel safe. My love can make you feel the warmth of a mother's arms. My love can make you feel the security that comes from knowing you have a dad that takes care of all your needs, not just physically but emotionally as well. I am your Father and you need to know that I adore you for the treasure you are. You will need my Holy Spirit to help you take this truth in, to help you know a love that you are not use to.

SCRIPTURES TO MEDITATE ON:

Love never brings fear, for fear is always related to punishment. But loves perfection drives the fear of punishment far from our hearts. (1 John 4:18)

This is just to wonderful, deep, and incomprehensible! Your understanding of me brings me wonder and strength. (Psalm 139:6)

And I will ask the Father and he will give you another Savior, the Holy Spirit of Truth, who will be to you a friend just like me—and he will never leave you. The world won't receive him because they can't see him or know him. But you will know him intimately, because he will make his home in you and will live inside you. (John 14:16-17)

FEBRUARY 18

There are many ways I would love to father you that you have not thought of. When your experiences with your father or mother were hurtful, it will distort how you see me. If you can't trust a father that you can see, how will you trust a father that you cannot see. I can help you to know that I am a Father who will never hurt you. Just as a doting father cares deeply for his children, so this is the picture of me that I want you to have. Many hope that they could be this lucky, but it is not about luck at all. This is a sure thing that you can rely on, a sure thing that I am going to do for you. I have so much more for my kids than they have begun to consider, that they have not yet tapped into. I love telling you that I love being your Father. XOXO

SCRIPTURE TO MEDITATE ON:

If you, imperfect as you are, know how to lovingly take care of your children and give them what's best, how much more ready is your heavenly Father to give wonderful gifts to those who ask him? (Matthew 7:11)

FEBRUARY 19

Watch out for distractions. They can be so subtle, and some are rooted in legitimate needs. They are everywhere, even in my Church. One of your most basic needs is to be able to attach and bond with mom and dad. When this is absent, and it is for many, it is so easy to find comfort in false refuges. The pain that comes from this is hidden and buried inside until something or someone triggers it. When you, my child, do not know how much you are loved and so valued by me, the orphan heart acts up with jealousy, judging, and self-hatred. I am not shocked nor upset and I do not love you any less for this, my heart goes out to you even more. Putting away childish tendencies is getting the healing for that little child inside of you that isn't convinced yet that they are lovable.

SCRIPTURES TO MEDITATE ON:

From a long distance away his father saw him coming, dressed as a beggar, and great compassion swelled up in his heart for his son who was returning home. So the father raced out to meet him. He swept him up in his arms, hugged him dearly, and kissed him over and over with tender love. (Luke 15:20)

I promise that I will never leave you helpless or abandon you as orphans—I will come back to you! (John 14:18)

FEBRUARY 20

Come in, I am so happy to see you. Let's just sit here for a while and just let me hold you. I love holding you close as your heart receives and drinks in my love. Sometimes moms and dads cannot be there for their child when they are crying out, but you will see I am always here when you are hurting. Many are looking for me and don't realize I am right here in front of them. There are many distorted views of me based on your experience with your earthly parents. Keep this in mind, my dear child, I am never too busy for you and I am not hard to find. I always look forward to being with you and being the father that you always wanted and needed. Just watch in the days ahead, as your heart is healed, revelation and truth will bring new life to you and help you to see me as I truly am.

SCRIPTURES TO MEDITATE ON:

The Lord is close to all whose hearts are crushed by pain, and he is always ready to restore the repentant one. (Psalm 34:18)

For if you embrace the truth, it will release more freedom into your lives. (John 8:32)

The same way a loving father feels toward his children—that's but a sample of your tender feelings toward us. (Psalm 103:13)

February 21

I know your greatest need is to be known and loved. Our brains have been wired to believe the lies about what we need and we go about trying to get our needs met in unhealthy ways. Our hearts are not in a receiving posture, but more guarded because of all the pain over the years. It is very sad for me that this goes on in your heart and you are not aware that this is the very thing that keeps you from me. I know how to heal you, break through any wall, and nurture you back to life. My love is more powerful than any of these orphan stronghold thoughts. My Holy Spirt will bring to life all that I am telling you. Just as my Spirit moved on you and changed your life instantly when you met me, I will continue to move. So I am still at work in your life to heal and move you from an orphan place into my home as sons and daughters.

SCRIPTURES TO MEDITATE ON:

Beloved friends, what should be our proper response to God's marvelous mercies? I encourage you to surrender yourselves to God to be his sacred, living sacrifices. And live in holiness, experiencing all that delights his heart. For this becomes your genuine expression of worship. Stop imitating the ideals and opinions of the culture around you, but be inwardly transformed by the Holy Spirit through a total reformation of how you think. This will empower you to discern God's will as you live a beautiful life, satisfying and perfect in his eyes. (Romans 12:1-2)

Jesus replied, "Loving me empowers you to obey my word. And my Father will love you so deeply that we will come to you and make you our dwelling place." (John 14:23)

FEBRUARY 22

Come in, my dear child. Try and stay in this moment with me. How I long to be with my children. There are so many distractions that pull you away from being in the moment with me. Many see me as their God but are not seeing me as their Father who wants to be with them. My children struggle with the reality that I am a compassionate Father who wants to be involved in the details of their lives. Our time is important to me. I just love being with you and I am not in a hurry when we are together. Why do you think Jesus wanted you to come see me? My son Jesus knew something about this time with me and that is why he urged you to come see me and close the door. He knew how much I wanted to spend time with you, to see me as the kind of father that interacts with his children. How good it would be for you to know me in this way.

SCRIPTURES TO MEDITATE ON:

We have come into an intimate experience with God's love, and we trust in the love he has for us. (1 John 4:16)

But whenever you pray, go into your innermost chamber and be alone with Father God , praying to him in secret. (Matthew 6:6)

FEBRUARY 23

You can call out my name and you know that wherever I am, I'll come running to see you again. Just like the father that ran to see his son returning home in the prodigal son story that my son Jesus told you, so I am always happy to see you. This is a picture of the kind of father I am and I want you to see me this way. I will always remember the day you turned to me. You were not aware of it, but we were all rejoicing on this side of heaven. I was waiting for that day. My heart was so happy to finally have you back with me. And now I bless you to walk out in all the wonderful plans I have for you. I bless you with the inner knowing deep in your heart that I am always with you. I bless you with continual revelation of my constant love for you as your Father. My love for you will never change, it is constant.

SCRIPTURES TO MEDITATE ON:

And teach them to faithfully follow all that I have commanded you. And never forget that I am with you every day, even to the completion of this age. (Matthew 28:20)

I the Lord do not change. So you, the descendants of Jacob, are not destroyed. (Malachi 3:6 NIV)

Every gift God freely gives us is good and perfect, streaming down from the Father of lights, who shines from the heavens with no hidden shadow or darkness and is never subject to change. (James 1:17)

FEBRUARY 24

How I long to gather you under my wings, as a mother hen gathers her chicks. My desire is to comfort, protect you, and to make you feel safe. I so long for you to know how much I want to do this for you. You can relax here where it is warm and nurturing. You can relax now because this is a safe place. Your Father is here, your Father is home. I can help you to receive a comfort that is safe, a comfort you can trust, a comfort that may not be familiar to you. Don't let feeling unworthy keep you away. Don't let your anger, pride and doubt keep you from this place. I invite you to come experience this depth of love that I have for you. Like John, I invite you also to come rest on my bosom.

SCRIPTURES TO MEDITATE ON:

So many times I have longed to gather a wayward people, as a hen gathers her chicks under her wings—but you were too stubborn to let me. (Matthew 23:37)

His massive arms are wrapped around you, protecting you. You can run under his covering of majesty and hide. His arms of faithfulness are a shield keeping you from harm. (Psalm 91:4)

FEBRUARY 25

When you hear the name 'Father,' it stirs many different emotions. I am sad for those who did not have a good experience with their fathers. I understand the struggle to trust when you did not have your dad there for you. I am here with the power to heal those wounds where fear came into your life. Let my truth speak to every part of your heart, every cell in your body that holds painful memories. Right now, in this moment I am here to help you to not be afraid. I ask you to open up your heart and receive my healing, nurturing love. As you let me help you, I will take care of those fears away. Just as I helped David with his fears when he cried out to me, so I will help you. I will not let them hurt you any longer, but I need you to let me help you. I reassure you that you are safe with me as you step out and become that trusting child again.

SCRIPTURE TO MEDITATE ON:

Can a mother forget the baby at her breast and have no compassion on the child she has borne? Though she may forget, I will not forget you! (Isaiah 49:15 NIV)

February 26

Come expecting and come with an open heart to receive. My thoughts and ways are not like yours, but I do want to share them with you. I want you to be successful and to feel good about yourself. I want you to be happy and to know it is ok for you to be happy when others are not. I want you to have this settled in your heart, that your relationship with me is more important than anything you could do for me. Sometimes my children are busy working for me, but they are not walking in the revelation of the relationship I want with them. When you realize that you can continually grow in the knowledge and experience of who I am, your life will become an adventure taking on a whole new meaning. I promise you it will be a lot more interesting to go on this journey together with me.

SCRIPTURES TO MEDITATE ON:

You are busy analyzing the scriptures, frantically poring over them in hopes of gaining eternal life. Everything you read points to me, yet you still refuse to come to me so I can give you the life you're looking for. (John 5:39)

As the heavens are higher than the earth, so are my ways higher than your ways and my thoughts than your thoughts. (Isaiah 55:9 NIV)

FEBRUARY 27

Until your heart is open to trust in the love I have for you, I will just keep reminding you that I am with you in this very moment. Please, think about this for a while. Your Father God is here right now, in this very moment with you. I am with you in all your moments and I love being your Father. I have happy thoughts when I think of you, and even when I am well aware of your shortcomings. I am with you today guiding you, revealing myself to you along the way. Watch for me because I connect to all my children in a very personal way that means something to each one individually. I love you being my child, know that my world is all about my children. Stay in this moment with me and ask me what I am doing, what I am thinking, I don't mind you asking. I will always be here for you and love when you come talk to me about whatever is on your heart .

SCRIPTURE TO MEDITATE ON:

Where could I go from your Spirit? Where could I run and hide from your face? If I go up to heaven, you're there! If I go down to the realm of the dead, you're there too! If I fly with wings into the shining dawn, you're there! If I fly into the radiant sunset, you're there waiting! Wherever I go, your hand will guide me; your strength will empower me. It's impossible to disappear from you or to ask the darkness to hide me, for your presence is everywhere, bringing light into my night. (Psalm 139:7-11)

February 28

I bless you, my child, to be able to receive and experience my love. I bless your eyes to see this incredible love I have for you. I bless your heart to be open so that it can be touched by my love. I bless you with knowing the height, depth, breath, and length of my love, to know the love of Christ that surpasses all knowledge. I pray that it would pass from your head and go right to your heart. I bless you with being able to get out of your own way, to rest and to not try to figure everything out. I bless your receivers, that everything inside of you will let go and trust my love. I bless all my children to know that I have this love for each one of them.

SCRIPTURE TO MEDITATE ON:

So I kneel humbly in awe before the Father of our Lord Jesus, the Messiah, the perfect Father of every father and child in heaven and on the earth. And I pray that he would unveil within you the unlimited riches of his glory and favor until supernatural strength floods your innermost being with his divine might and explosive power. Then, by constantly using your faith, the life of Christ will be released deep inside you, and the resting place of his love will become the very source and root of your life. Then you will be empowered to discover what every holy one experiences—the great magnitude of the astonishing love of Christ in all its dimensions. How deeply intimate and far-reaching is his love! How enduring and inclusive it is! Endless love beyond measurement that transcends our understanding—this extravagant love pours into you until you are filled to overflowing with the fullness of God! Never doubt God's mighty power to work in you and accomplish all this. He will achieve infinitely more than your greatest request, your most unbelievable dream, and exceed your wildest imagination! He will outdo them all, for his miraculous power constantly energizes you. Now we offer up to God all the glorious praise that rises from every church in every generation through Jesus Christ—and all that will yet be manifest through time and eternity. Amen! (Ephesians 3:14-21)

MARCH

MARCH 1

Be comforted in knowing I will never reject you or turn my back on you. I am here to heal the rejection that made you feel like something was wrong with you, that made you wonder why they don't like you. I bless you with knowing how much you have my approval. I know everything about you and I like who you are and think that you are pretty special. I do understand the pain of rejection and the lies you believed from that wound. I know about the sins in your life that you struggle with, the ones I want to help you with. If you were to ask me what my mission was, I would tell you that I am all about my kids, trying to reach them to convince them that they already have all my unchanging love. They don't have to do good, be good, or act just right to get my love. Don't be shy, and don't let anything hold you back from coming boldly to your Papa's throne room.

SCRIPTURE TO MEDITATE ON:

So now we come freely and boldly to where love is enthroned, to receive mercy's kiss and discover the grace we urgently need to strengthen us in our time of weakness. (Hebrews 4:16)

MARCH 2

My dear child. I want to remind you that I am always thinking about you. So many things compete for your attention, mostly in your thought life that try and fill up your day . Nothing here compares to what I have for you. The most enticing distraction, the biggest dream that you have, does not compare to what I am planning for you. You might think that what is going on here can be pretty exciting, and it is, but wait till you see what I have for you. My world is all about my children. What you feel for your children is a very small inkling of my huge love for you. I just want you to be at home with me as your Father . My love for you will wash away all those distorted images you have of me because of what was done to you over the years. Come, my child, it is time to receive the love that I have had for you all along. All the times you didn't know how I felt, my love was always there for you and it will never change.

SCRIPTURES TO MEDITATE ON:

Every single moment you are thinking of me! How precious and wonderful to consider that you cherish me constantly in your every thought! O God, your desires toward me are more than the grains of sand on every shore! When I awake each morning, you're still with me. (Psalm 139:17-18)

His unforgettable works of surpassing wonder reveal his grace and tender mercy. He satisfies all who love and trust him, and he keeps every promise he makes. He reveals mighty power and marvels to his people by handing them nations as a gift. All God accomplishes is flawless, faithful, and fair, and his every word proves trustworthy and true. They are steadfast forever and ever, formed from truth and righteousness. His forever-love paid a full ransom for his people so that now we're free to come before Jehovah to worship his holy and awesome name! (Psalm 111:4-9)

To truly know him meant letting go of everything from my past and throwing all my boasting on the garbage heap. It's all like a pile of manure to me now, so that I may be enriched in the reality of knowing Jesus Christ and embrace him as Lord in all of his greatness. (Philippians 3:8)

MARCH 3

I am so glad you came to see me today. I know you were busy, but I did miss our time together. I was still with you although you might not have been fully aware of me being there. I saw you leave the place you were at later than planned so I held the bad weather back for you. I love how grateful you are. Actually, I love everything about you. I so enjoyed the day I formed you in your mother's womb and looked forward to your birth. You see, I am the one who made your looks, your personality and I loved you then and I love you now. My Holy Spirit will help you to drink in this truth, and receive the love you always longed for. Remember, my dear child, when you leave our time to go about your day, I am always right there with you.

SCRIPTURES TO MEDITATE ON:

Have I not commanded you? Be strong and courageous. Do not be afraid; do not be discouraged, for the Lord your God will be with you wherever you go. (Joshua 1:9 NIV)

You formed my innermost being, shaping my delicate inside and my intricate outside, and wove them all together in my mother's womb. (Psalm 139:13)

MARCH 4

I would like to talk to you about an area that I see you struggling with, so let's look at this together. When you look at others and compare yourself, you are actually saying that I was unfair when I made my children, that I made some better than others. I know you didn't receive what some appear to have, but I will make that up to you. I know you think that I do more for others, this is another lie you have believed about me for a long time because of the pain around your dad . When feeling insecure or feeling jealous of someone, it's difficult to think straight, so you don't think to ask me for what you need or want. I want to Father you and pour out my love for you in this place. I would love for you just to be able ask me, so you can be aware of me answering you. Because of this wound you sometimes believe I don't even care. When you are jealous of others, you won't be able to see what I have for you, which is right there in front of you. I am not upset with your reactions, but I am here to take you by your hand and guide you with my counsel.

SCRIPTURES TO MEDITATE ON:

Peter said, "Now I know for certain that God doesn't show favoritism with people but treats everyone on the same basis." (Act 10:34)

When my heart was grieved and my spirit embittered, I was senseless and ignorant; I was a brute beast before you. Yet I am always with; you hold me by my right hand. You guide me with your counsel, and afterward you will take me into glory. (Psalm 73:21)

MARCH 5

Ask me anything, and don't ever think you are bothering me. Ask me anything, I am always here for you. I have compassion for my children who never learned to trust at an early age. As you see me doing things for you that are very personal to you and almost seemingly impossible at times, you will learn to trust me. Watch for me, and I will show you things you do not know about being fathered. I will help you feel the security you long for. I want to do this for you. I want you to know the security of how it feels when you are snuggled upon your Papa's lap. I want you to feel my love as I wrap my arms around you, knowing this love that I feel is for you. Maybe you did not have this, but I will get through to you just how special you are to me. Just know that your Papa will always be home for you, so you can rest now and enjoy being a much loved child of mine.

SCRIPTURES TO MEDITATE ON:

His massive arms are wrapped around you, protecting you. You can run under his covering of majesty and hide. His arms of faithfulness are a shield keeping you from harm. (Psalm 91:4)

Don't fear a thing! Whether by night or by day, demonic danger will not trouble you, nor will the powers of evil launched against you. (Psalm 91:6)

MARCH 6

You may not always understand what I am doing. I want you to believe that, more than anything else, I want a relationship with you. If this has not been your experience growing up, it may be hard for you to grasp. The things you go through try to tell you that there is something wrong with you, that I don't care about you. It's in your struggle, trials, and wilderness that you need to find out how much I am here to father you. There is only good that will come out of you getting to know me. Identity and security will be the fruit of you turning to me instead of false refuges. They only temporarily satisfy, and do not resolve the problem. My children are not believing how much I want to be with them just as they are, without anything to impress me with. Pray for open eyes to see my love, for open ears to hear me calling your name, and for an open heart to receive a love that is not based on anything you do.

SCRIPTURES TO MEDITATE ON:

You've gone into my future to prepare the way, and in kindness you follow behind me to spare me from the harm of my past. With your hand of love upon my life, you impart a blessing to me. This is just too wonderful, deep, and incomprehensible! Your understanding of me brings me wonder and strength. (Psalm 139:5-6)

Who could ever separate us from the endless love of God's Anointed One? Absolutely no one! For nothing in the universe has the power to diminish his love toward us. Troubles, pressures, and problems are unable to come between us and heaven's love. What about persecutions, deprivations, dangers, and death threats? No, for they are all impotent to hinder omnipotent love. (Romans 8:35)

MARCH 7

There are times when things are not going the way you would like and you are wondering where I am. It is easy to think that I am busy and not concerned with your many questions. As your heart learns that it can safely trust me you will know in these times that, just maybe, I have something planned that you didn't think of. Instead of believing I don't care, I would like for you to know that your Father God has a different plan that is going to be good and that I have good reasons for doing what I do. This is truth that will become part of you as I restore to you a childlike faith!! You will see each and every time that I do things in your best interests. When the heart is guarded, and the pain of the past has not been healed and comforted, it makes it harder to trust me. But I tell you, dear one, you can rest knowing I am here to take care of you. I am here to tell that little one inside that everything is going to be ok.

SCRIPTURES TO MEDITATE ON:

So above all, guard the affections of your heart, for they affect all that you are. Pay attention to the welfare of your innermost being, for from there flows the wellspring of life. (Proverbs 4:23)

But you, O Lord, your mercy-seat love is limitless, reaching higher than the highest heavens. Your great faithfulness is infinite, stretching over the whole earth. (Psalm 36:5)

Your love is so extravagant it reaches to the heavens, your faithfulness so astonishing it stretches to the sky! (Psalm 57:10)

MARCH 8

I will continue to show you the areas where you are not seeing me correctly because I do not want anything to hinder our relationship. I ask you to be open, so I can heal those wounds that keep you from me. I don't want them to hurt you any longer and it is my desire to be close to my children. I am waiting for the day that you are able to come to me and feel safe, to freely trust without all the struggling in your mind. Just as you long to comfort your child or comfort someone you love, so I long to give you the comfort you never received. I want to encourage you to have hope in a future with me, that I will give you all that you need. You will walk in a place of not worrying, carefree, and full of a security that is unshakeable. I am a good Father and I would never hurt you. I am always so happy to watch all this unfold for you.

SCRIPTURES TO MEDITATE ON:

As a mother comforts her child, so will I comfort you; and you will be comforted over Jerusalem. (Isaiah 66:13 NIV)

Love never brings fear, for fear is always related to punishment. But love's perfection drives the fear of punishment far from our hearts. Whoever walks constantly afraid of punishment has not reached love's perfection. (1 John 4:18)

You will be guarded by God himself. You will be safe when you leave your home and safely you will return. He will protect you now, and he'll protect you forevermore! (Psalm 121:8)

MARCH 9

I know you don't like some things about yourself, but I see them too, and I am not changing my mind about you. I believe that you are way too hard on yourself and expecting way more than I am. It makes me sad when you struggle with not liking yourself. Come to me with these things, so that I can help you. Remember, do not try and figure out how I could love you like I do. I just do, and I am patiently waiting for you to receive it. This is a where you need to experience my love more than any other time. This is a place where you will be convinced of my unconditional love. I am right there with you feeling for you when you are feeling bad about yourself. This is a common thing that goes on for my children, and that is why I gave the commandment for you to love you. It's a commandment because I am very serious about wanting you to love yourself the way I love you.

SCRIPTURES TO MEDITATE ON:

Love the Lord your God with all your heart and with all your soul and with all your mind and with all your strength. The second is this: "Love your neighbor as yourself. There is no commandment greater than these." (Mark 12:30-31 NIV)

He understands humanity, for as a Man, our magnificent King-Priest was tempted in every way just as we are, and conquered sin. So now we come freely and boldly to where love is enthroned, to receive mercy's kiss and discover the grace we urgently need to strengthen us in our time of weakness. (Hebrews 4:15-16)

MARCH 10

I want you to know that I'm the kind of father you can come to and ask anything. You are my child, so you have the freedom to come boldly before me and ask me anything. I don't mind; I like when you come to me. I also have a question for you. As your Father, as your God, what would you like for me to do for you? You might not be used to having someone care about what you want and so maybe you don't even bother asking or just don't think to ask. I would like for you to feel comfortable coming to me, to feel at home with me. I would like to encourage you to get in the habit of seeing me as your Father that you can freely share your heart with. I am always here, I have always loved you and that will never change.

SCRIPTURES TO MEDITATE ON:

I the Lord do not change. So you, the descendants of Jacob, are not destroyed. (Malachi 3:6 NIV)

So now we come freely and boldly to where love is enthroned, to receive mercy's kiss and discover the grace we urgently need to strengthen us in our time of weakness. (Hebrews 4:16)

MARCH 11

Bring your thoughts to me, even the unpleasant ones. Don't let them trouble you or keep you away from me. I want you to know that I am a kind Father and will only affirm, validate and encourage you. You have paid too much attention to the accuser, who has planted thoughts that are not even yours. Listening to his lies and accusations only brings discouragement. I want you to hear what I have to say about you. Could you imagine a mother forgetting her nursing child? I will never forget you. My thoughts of you are more than all the sand on the shores, impossible to count. I will never let anything separate us. These are the things I want you to remember when you are struggling with your thoughts. You really need to come to me, and know that I am always so happy when you do. I try to remind you of this because the tendency is to pull away when I am here with open arms for you my dear, dear child.

SCRIPTURES TO MEDITATE ON:

Every single moment you are thinking of me! How precious and wonderful to consider that you cherish me constantly in your every thought! O God, your desires toward me are more than the grains of sand on every shore! When I awake each morning, you're still with me. (Psalm 139:18)

So, what does all this mean? If God has determined to stand with us, tell me, who then could ever stand against us? For God has proved his love by giving us his greatest treasure, the gift of his Son. And since God freely offered him up as the sacrifice for us all, he certainly won't withhold from us anything else he has to give. Who then would dare to accuse those whom God has chosen in love to be his? God himself is the judge who has issued his final verdict over them— "Not guilty!" Who then is left to condemn us? Certainly not Jesus, the Anointed One! For he gave his life for us, and even more than that, he has conquered death and is now risen, exalted, and enthroned by God at his right hand. So how could he possibly condemn us since he is continually praying for our triumph? Who could ever separate us from the endless love of God's Anointed One? Absolutely no one! For nothing in the universe has the power to diminish his love toward us. Troubles, pressures, and problems are unable to come between us and heaven's love. What about persecutions, deprivations, dangers, and death threats? No, for they are all impotent to hinder omnipotent love, even though it is written: All day long we face death threats for your sake, God. We are considered to be nothing more than sheep to be slaughtered! Yet even in the midst of all these things, we triumph over them all, for God has made us to be more than conquerors, and his demonstrated love is our glorious victory over everything! So now I live with the confidence that there is nothing in the universe with the power to separate us from God's love. I'm convinced that his love will triumph over death, life's troubles, fallen angels, or dark rulers in the heavens. There is nothing in our present or future circumstances that can weaken his love. There is no power above us or beneath us—no power that could ever be found in the universe that can distance us from God's passionate love, which is lavished upon us through our Lord Jesus, the Anointed One! (Romans 8:31-39)

MARCH 12

One of your greatest battles, one of your greatest struggles, is going to turn out to be your greatest blessing as you experience me fathering you in that place. Whatever you missed out on, I will come to you and give you so much more than any earthly father could. I am here to Father you and bring you healing. Just as broken as you were, so your healing will be even greater. The enemy will take your past or present circumstances that you are not happy about and lie to you about me. My children get so convinced that I don't care because of what they are going through. I understand the struggle to trust me in that dark place, but if you turn to me I will give you the reassurance you need. You need to get out of your head and stop trying to figure this out or control the situation. In yourself, you are limited and cannot see the whole picture. I want to reassure my children that I am always right there with them even though they can't see me in the midst of their battle. You will look back one day and you will see and say to yourself, He was with me the whole time! Call out to me as David did, and I will answer your heart's cry.

SCRIPTURE TO MEDITATE ON:

I look up to the mountains and hills, longing for God's help. But then I realize that our true help and protection come only from the Lord, our Creator who made the heavens and the earth. He will guard and guide me, never letting me stumble or fall. God is my keeper; he will never forget nor ignore me. He will never slumber nor sleep; he is the Guardian-God for his people, Israel. Jehovah himself will watch over you; he's always at your side to shelter you safely in his presence. He's protecting you from all danger both day and night. He will keep you from every form of evil or calamity as he continually watches over you. You will be guarded by God himself. You will be safe when you leave your home and safely you will return. He will protect you now, and he'll protect you forevermore! (Psalm 121:1-8)

MARCH 13

I want you to freely come to me just as a child would run to his Papa's arms. Bring your problems, every one of them and place them down before me. Keep giving each burden to me, one at a time and then leave them with me. Don't take them back out of habit of carrying them for so long Why carry this if you don't have to? I know you are not used to having someone to care for you like this, so I do understand your struggle at times to let go of things. I am right here, let's do this together. You are not alone even though you might feel alone at times. I want to take the things you are carrying so you can experience what it feels like to be taken care of by me, my dear, dear child. This is how much I love you.

SCRIPTURES TO MEDITATE ON:

Pour out all your worries and stress upon him and leave them there, for he always tenderly cares for you. (1 Peter 5:7)

So here's what I've learned through it all: Leave all your cares and anxieties at the feet of the Lord, and measureless grace will strengthen you. (Psalm 55:22)

MARCH 14

I just want to remind you that you are not alone. Sometimes you go about your day as if you are all alone. You can't see me, but I like to show myself to you in many ways that will let you know I am here. If you could see into the unknown, you would see my angels all around you, protecting you wherever you go, and I, personally, am also constantly watching over you. If you are feeling alone and afraid, turn to me and I will quickly come to you with all the reassurance you need. I want you to feel fussed over, for you to know that there is a God in heaven that comes to you to Father you. I will never scare you or make you afraid. I speak only words that bring life and healing. I know what you have been through so I will patiently wait as I try to get through to you. We rejoice here on this side of heaven, watching as your heart heals and you are able to respond to me. You can hold on to the truth that you are so wanted and so loved by your Father God who never gives up on you.

SCRIPTURES TO MEDITATE ON:

Don't fear a thing! Whether by night or by day, demonic danger will not trouble you, nor will the powers of evil launched against you. (Psalm 91:6)

You will be guarded by God himself. You will be safe when you leave your home and safely you will return. He will protect you now, and he'll protect you forevermore! (Psalm 121:8)

MARCH 15

My kids have no idea how much I want to be with them. Many are not aware of how much they need a father and how I long to Father them. I want to come and wash off all the junk that was put on you over the years. I will wash off all shame, fears, and insecurities for you. I ask you to enter into this moment with me and receive my nurturing love as a weaned child that rests on her mother's breast. There are no fears or worries in this place. Let go of trying to figure out how to secure your world. Worry has become too big a part of your life, but my love will put your heart at rest. My dear child, because you are not used to being loved like this, pray for the healing you need so that you can receive, so your heart will be open, so that you will believe me when I tell you that you are lovable. It is my desire to bless my children way beyond what they are imagining or expecting.

SCRIPTURES TO MEDITATE ON:

Lord, my heart is meek before you. I don't consider myself better than others. I'm content to not pursue matters that are over my head—such as your complex mysteries and wonders—that I'm not yet ready to understand. I am humbled and quieted in your presence. Like a contented child who rests on its mother's lap, I'm your resting child and my soul is content in you. O people of God, your time has come to quietly trust, waiting upon the Lord now and forever. (Psalm 131:1-3)

Never doubt God's mighty power to work in you and accomplish all this. He will achieve infinitely more than your greatest request, your most unbelievable dream, and exceed your wildest imagination! He will outdo them all, for his miraculous power constantly energizes you. (Ephesians 3:20)

MARCH 16

If you watch, you will see that I am the one who will make things happen for you. I created heaven and earth, so you know that there is nothing too hard for me and I don't mind doing things for you. I want you to feel the freedom to come to me anytime with whatever is on your heart. You can know a lot about me from reading my word or from others, but I want you to have the experience of me directly fathering you, to make it real to your five senses. Even in your present struggle, I want you to know I am here for you, to comfort you, guide you, or give you whatever it is you need. Look for me, I am your Father who wants to be involved in your daily life. Just get used to the idea that you really have a father around. If I had to, I would move mountains just to reach you. I encourage you again to look for me, I am right here.

SCRIPTURES TO MEDITATE ON:

Every spiritual blessing in the heavenly realm has already been lavished upon us as a love gift from our wonderful Heavenly Father, the Father of our Lord Jesus—all because he sees us wrapped into Christ. (Ephesians 1:3)

Ask, and the gift is yours. Seek, and you'll discover. Knock, and the door will be opened for you. (Matthew 7:7)

So it is with your prayers. Ask and you'll receive. Seek and you'll discover. Knock on heaven's door, and it will one day open for you. Every persistent person will get what he asks for. Every persistent seeker will discover what he needs. And everyone who knocks persistently will one day find an open door. (Luke 11:9-10)

MARCH 17

Maybe you are not feeling your best today, but know that I haven't gone anywhere. You don't have to face difficult days alone when you have me. Faith is believing that I am as real as the person sitting next to you. Faith is believing everything I have told you will happen even though you don't know how, or even though you don't see it yet. I will help you to trust that. I am not like any father that you know here on earth. You can look forward to me showing you what I am like. My son Jesus came to reveal who I am and just as he said he would, he will continue to make me known to you. The more you find out about me, the more you will feel loved. Your world will become a bright and better place even in the midst of difficulties. There is new territory for you to explore with me, so let the adventure begin.

SCRIPTURE TO MEDITATE ON:

I have revealed to them who you are and I will continue to make you even more real to them, so that they may experience the same endless love that you have for me, for your love will now live in them, even as I live in them! (John 17:26)

MARCH 18

My child, I made you in love. Close your eyes, sit back and take this in. See me, your Father, creating you in your mother's womb. I created you in love, and all of this love is for you. This is where you come from, and this is who you were before you entered the world and got beat up. You accepted the lie that your worth is based on the world's idea of worth. You won't care what anyone thinks when you truly know HOW I FEEL about YOU. When this becomes your reality, you will be free to be who I created you to be. I bless you, my child, to be free in who you are; the interesting, incredible, and very special person that I made you to be.

SCRIPTURES TO MEDITATE ON:

You formed my innermost being, shaping my delicate inside and my intricate outside, and wove them all together in my mother's womb. I thank you, God, for making me so mysteriously complex! Everything you do is marvelously breathtaking. It simply amazes me to think about it! How thoroughly you know me, Lord! You even formed every bone in my body when you created me in the secret place, carefully, skillfully shaping me from nothing to something. You saw who you created me to be before I became me! Before I'd ever seen the light of day, the number of days you planned for me were already recorded in your book. (Psalm 139:13-16)

And he chose us to be his very own, joining us to himself even before he laid the foundation of the universe! (Ephesians 1:4)

MARCH 19

My child, did you know that I look forward to our time together? I want you always to know that I am happy to see you and love when you freely share your heart with me. Many things get in the way of my relationship with my children. When you grow up with criticism, you may think that I am looking at what is wrong in your life and constantly wanting you to change. You may get too focused on things you see that you don't like about yourself. I am not a serious, stern father, but many see me this way. I know you well, know everything about you and I believe in you. The thing I am serious about is how I feel about my kids and I want them to know that they have a Father who is committed to them. I am not focused on your mistakes, and I am not upset when you make them. Just as I am okay with your mistakes, I want you to be okay with you when you mess up. My world is full of life, laughter and good things to come. So, my dear child, go off today and enjoy knowing that your Papa God is always here for you.

SCRIPTURES TO MEDITATE ON:

Lord, you know everything there is to know about me. (Psalm 139:1)

If you hear my words and refuse to follow them, I do not judge you. For I have not come to judge you but to save you. (John 12:47)

MARCH 20

You really don't have to beg me for anything, and I don't want you to beg me. Just as you would not want your children to beg so I feel the same way. Many do this because they don't really know that I am a Father who loves to be generous to his children. What I want to give to you right now is my time, so together we can help the little child inside that feels so alone. She didn't know what to do with the pain and no one was there to help her, so we will go and tell her we are here for her and that everything is going to be ok. Just think how wonderful it will be to be at peace inside, that your heart can know that you have a Father that wants you. I also want you know there is no other place I would rather be than with my children. You will see the goodness of your Father in the land of the living.

SCRIPTURES TO MEDITATE ON:

Look with wonder at the depth of the Father's marvelous love he has lavished on us! He has called us and made us his own beloved children. (1John 3:1)

Yet I totally trust you to rescue me one more time, so that I can see once again how good you are while I'm still alive! (Psalm 27:13)

MARCH 21

There are so many things that I would love to talk to you about, but there is one specific thing on my heart that I want to share with you today. It's all about the love I feel for you, which is bigger than anything you have ever known here. Anything you might try to imagine; my love is bigger. You can say, "I know God loves me," but you have no idea what this love is that I am talking about. Be open for me to show you so much more. Right now I want to tell you about the things I love about you. I love everything about you. I love your smile, your laughter. I love the way you get excited about what I am doing in your life. I love the way you respond to me. I love the way you care about others. I am so proud that you keep getting up when you fall down. These are the things I am looking at and this is what I want you to see also.

SCRIPTURE TO MEDITATE ON:

So the young son set off for home. From a long distance away, his father saw him coming, dressed as a beggar, and great compassion swelled up in his heart for his son who was returning home. So the father raced out to meet him. He swept him up in his arms, hugged him dearly, and kissed him over and over with tender love. Then the son said, 'Father, I was wrong. I have sinned against you. I could never deserve to be called your son. Just let me be—. The father interrupted and said, 'Son, you're home now!' Turning to his servants, the father said, 'Quick, bring me the best robe, my very own robe, and I will place it on his shoulders. Bring the ring, the seal of sonship, and I will put it on his finger.

And bring out the best shoes you can find for my son. Let's prepare a great feast and celebrate. For this beloved son of mine was once dead, but now he's alive again. Once he was lost, but now he is found!' And everyone celebrated with overflowing joy. (Luke 15:20-24)

MARCH 22

The pain from the past has given my children many distorted, inaccurate views of me. They see me as a judge, and a distant angry God. Many do not see me as a loving Father who longs to be close to them, who brings comfort and healing to their pain. They think I will leave them, and that I will not come through. My truth is more powerful than any lie that you have been told about me. There are days when you might feel all alone because of what you are going through, and it might seem hard for you to connect to the truth that I am right there with you. Your emotions are an important part of you and how I made you to be, but when they are not healed they can take you to a familiar place of not feeling cared for. I will keep reminding you to ask me for help until you get in the habit of asking. Be encouraged, my child, I have healing for those broken places.

SCRIPTURES TO MEDITATE ON:

The Lord is close to all whose hearts are crushed by pain, and he is always ready to restore the repentant one. (Psalm 34:18)

He tends his flock like a shepherd: He gathers the lambs in his arms and carries them close to his heart; he gently leads those that have young. (Isaiah 40:11 NIV)

MARCH 23

Maybe there was no one there for you growing up to tell you how special you are, to make you feel lovable and wanted. The striving and struggling to be someone important, to be relevant, are rooted in not knowing how valuable and precious you are. I am the stability you are needing and looking for. When you are trying to make a name for yourself, trying to draw attention to yourself by who you know, or what you are doing, it would be good for you to stop there and realize that I am not in that. If you knew how uniquely special you are to me, you would have nothing to prove to yourself or anyone else. I want you healed and free to be able to live your life to its fullest and not be driven by those insecurities, by the lies, and comparisons with others. Remember, I left the ninety-nine sheep to go after the one. This is a picture of how important each one of you are to me.

SCRIPTURE TO MEDITATE ON:

"There once was a shepherd with a hundred lambs, but one of his lambs wandered away and was lost. So the shepherd left the ninety-nine lambs out in the open field and searched in the wilderness for that one lost lamb. He didn't stop until he finally found it. With exuberant joy he raised it up and placed it on his shoulders, carrying it back with cheerful delight! (Luke 15:4-5)

MARCH 24

I want to take you to a place that maybe you are not familiar with. Please, my child don't ever think that you are asking too much or bothering me. I want you to come to me. It's been said to practice my presence, but I want you to practice running to your Papa when you want something. My children barely believe I will give them what they need, much less ask me for what they want. Just try and imagine having all of your needs met, having someone fuss over you, never fearing rejection or disapproval. Try and imagine feeling so loved that you never have to struggle with fear or self-doubt. Try and imagine not having to worry about a thing because you are so secure in your Father God's plans for your life. You don't have to wish for this, it's already yours from your Papa God. He will even help you to trust it and receive it.

SCRIPTURE TO MEDITATE ON:

So don't ever be afraid, dearest friends! Your loving Father joyously gives you his kingdom realm with all its promises! (Luke 12:32)

MARCH 25

I want to come and sit with you, just because I love being with you. You don't have to talk if you don't want to and if you do, you don't have to be concerned with having to say anything clever or brilliant. You don't have to act a certain way like you do with others. You don't have to impress me, I already know you and love you. Maybe you are not used to having anyone take such an interest in wanting to hang out with you like I do, but I want this to be your reality, your very own experience with me so you can relax and enjoy our time together. Ask my Holy Spirit to help you to take this truth in. So, my dear child, remember my son is here praying for your precious heart, praying that your heart will be open to having an increased ability to receive a love that does not put demands on you, a love that always believes you, a love that will never leave.

SCRIPTURES TO MEDITATE ON:

You unveiled to Moses your plans and showed Israel's sons what you could do. (Psalm 103:7)

He tends his flock like a shepherd: He gathers the lambs in his arms and carries them close to his heart; he gently leads those that have young. (Isaiah 40:11 NIV)

MARCH 26

If you look at my son Jesus, you will see all that he did to convince his disciples. If you did not have a foundation that nurtured trust and have been beat up a little along the way, I am not demanding for you to trust me. I have healing for the hard soil of your hearts that grew distant from my love. Why would I demand trust when your ability to trust was destroyed by people that were supposed to nurture you but were too broken themselves? I tell you today, my dear child, that I will rain on that soil that was hard for a very long time. I do have answers for you that you have been waiting for as you struggled to believe that I was listening. You will see that I keep my word and I will come through.

SCRIPTURES TO MEDITATE ON:

But you, O Lord, your mercy-seat love is limitless, reaching higher than the highest heavens. Your great faithfulness is infinite, stretching over the whole earth. (Psalm 36:5)

MARCH 27

There are so many things I want to talk to you about, my child, but first I just want to sit with you and hold you. Relax and enjoy being loved. I want you to know just how much I enjoy being with you. I have all the time in the world for you and I want you to just rest knowing my love is safe. I don't mind taking whatever time it takes to convince you of how I feel about you. As you watch me come through over and over, your trust in me will grow. You don't have to be afraid any more. You don't have to worry about your needs not being met. I have always been here for you, but I need you to invite me into your life and into the areas that you hold tight. I will not barge my way in, out of respect for you and what you have been through. I am waiting patiently, until you realize that I am your Father who is for you, and I would never hurt you.

SCRIPTURES TO MEDITATE ON:

For the Lord is always good and ready to receive you. He's so loving that it will amaze you—-so kind that it will astound you! And he is famous for his faithfulness toward all. Everyone knows our God can be trusted, for he keeps his promises to every generation! (Psalms 100:5)

"For I know the plans I have for you," declares the Lord, "plans to prosper you and not to harm you, plans to give you hope and a future." (Jeremiah 29:11 NIV)

MARCH 28

I want you to be comfortable, to feel at home with yourself and with me. Just know that your Papa is always here for you. I am the one who will help you to love the person I created you to be. I am not upset with you when you don't like yourself, but it does make me feel sad for you. It is even possible that you might not even be in touch with the areas of yourself that you reject. No one knows you like I do and there are ways I can help you with this. When you come to me, I want you to know that you are known and wanted by me. I want you to be so used to coming to hang out with me that it comes as easily as breathing for you. Just as my son and I are close and know each other well, so I want this with you also. Be blessed, my child, with an increased revelation of my love for you.

SCRIPTURES TO MEDITATE ON:

For it was always in his perfect plan to adopt us as his delightful children, through our union with Jesus, the Anointed One, so that his tremendous love that cascades over us would glorify his grace…for the same love he has for his Beloved One, Jesus, he has for us. And this unfolding plan brings him great pleasure! (Ephesians 1:5-6)

I pray for them all to be joined together as one even as you and I, Father, are joined together as one. I pray for them to become one with us so that the world will recognize that you sent me. (John 17:21)

MARCH 29

My dear child, I want to let you know I am constantly thinking of you. If you were to try and count all the sand on the shore it would be impossible but this will give you an idea of how much I am thinking of you. Have you ever wondered what my thoughts were concerning you? I don't mind you asking, and I don't mind sharing my thoughts with you. All you have to do is ask and listen because I love to talk to my children. You need to get rid of any ideas that I am too busy to talk to you. I have been so ready and wanting to share my heart. Just as your love for your children is strong and comes so naturally, in spite of all the things you go through with them, your love for them is always there. How much more will my love be for you?

SCRIPTURES TO MEDITATE ON:

If you, imperfect as you are, know how to lovingly take care of your children and give them what's best, how much more ready is your heavenly Father to give wonderful gifts to those who ask him? (Matthew 7:11)

MARCH 30

Does your love change when your child messes up? Do you look at them differently? So, my love for you never changes. Remember how much I love you when you mess up, how much I love you in that place. If you don't think you are handling things well, whether you are right or wrong, my love is there and I would like you to learn to be kind to yourself. I want to help you, but you are too busy feeling bad. I am not disappointed or angry, only sad that you don't turn to me for help. I have all the help you need. I am here waiting for you to know that I always believe in you and will never give up on you, nor will I ever change my mind about you. Receive this amazing grace, my unfathomable love for you when you are ready. It will always be here for you, my dear child.

SCRIPTURES TO MEDITATE ON:

Every gift God freely gives us is good and perfect, stream-ing down from the Father of lights, who shines from the heavens with no hidden shadow or darkness and is never subject to change. (James 1:17)

"I the Lord do not change." (Malachi 3:6 NIV)

For the Lord is always good and ready to receive you. He's so loving that it will amaze you—-so kind that it will astound you! And he is famous for his faithfulness toward all. Everyone knows our God can be trusted, for he keeps his promises to every generation! (Psalms 100:5)

MARCH 31

The deepest longing, the deepest need of the human heart is to be loved. There are many things you turn to but nothing really works for long. My kids are very good at numbing their emotions, and ignoring their pain. So many are not in touch with their needs and are not aware that I am their devoted faithful Father that longs to care for them. The truth is I am the only one that can love you the way you need to be loved. When you turn to me, you will find out I am always here. My love will help you know that you are okay and that there is nothing to worry about. Because you are not used to being loved like this, you need to come to me daily to drink this in. Come and talk to me about what is going on with you; your needs, your thoughts, your fears, whatever is on your heart. I just want to remind you that I am here whenever you want to talk.

SCRIPTURES TO MEDITATE ON:

Don't be pulled in different directions or worried about a thing. Be saturated in prayer throughout each day, offering your faith filled requests before God with overflowing grat-itude. Tell him every detail of your life, then God's wonderful peace that transcends human understanding will make the answers known to you through JesusChrist. (Philippians 4:6-7)

Jesus replied, "If you only knew who I am and the gift that God wants to give you—you'd ask me for a drink, and I would give to you living water." The woman replied, "But sir, you don't even have a bucket and this well is very deep. So where do you find this 'living water'? Do you really think that you are greater than our ancestor Jacob who dug this well and drank from it himself, along with his children and livestock?" Jesus answered, "If you drink from Jacob's well you'll be thirsty again and again. (John 4:10-13)

APRIL

APRIL 1

Nothing is too hard for your Father. I created heaven and earth, so it is not hard for me to heal your heart and make my love known to you. There are all kinds of miracles that I am doing, and my love is behind each one. I want you to make the connection that it is me, your Father, doing this for you. So, I am here to tell you that my greatest desire is to reach my kids and help them feel secure in my love. The things that you are asking me for are not hard for me to do for you. It is my desire to make my love known to you in such a way that you never worry or fear anything again. I have the love for you that you felt like you always missed out on, the love you needed to help you face life. As you look to me, I will open a whole new world for you with experiences and places I want to take you. I encourage you to be open because I have very lovingly planned all this out, to refresh you, and to restore your hope.

SCRIPTURES TO MEDITATE ON:

"For I know the plans I have for you," declares the Lord, "plans to prosper you and not to harm you, plans to give you hope and a future." (Jeremiah 29:11 NIV)

"Ah, Sovereign Lord, you have made the heavens and the earth by your great power and outstretched arm. Nothing is too hard for you." (Jeremiah 32:17 NIV)

APRIL 2

I would like for you to grow in the awareness that I am with you in your inner struggles that you don't let anyone see. Please, don't spend a lot of time there when you can come to me for my help. I keep reminding you to do this because in the flesh there tends to be an independent, self-reliant challenge to work it out alone. This can become a habit if this is the only thing you knew growing up. It is a lot easier when you know someone that knows and cares enough about you to want to help. There is time wasted when you try to work through things without me. I realize that you just need to be reminded until you get used to having your Father around. You don't have to worry about me ever changing my mind about you or ever leaving you. I will always be here in all your moments, so you never have to wonder where I am. I am on this journey with you guiding you the whole way, so don't ever lose sight of this.

SCRIPTURES TO MEDITATE ON:

Am I only a God nearby, declares the Lord, and not a God far away? Who can hide in secret places, so I cannot see them?...do I not fill heaven and earth? declares the Lord? (Jeremiah 23:23-24)

Jesus, the Anointed One, is always the same—yesterday, today, and forever. (Hebrews 13:8)

APRIL 3

As you enjoy my blessings, which many times are more than you are anticipating, I see that sometimes you are unsure if you can trust it, or that you feel unworthy of what I have given to you. I am here to tell you, that I want to give these things to you and that I want you to relax and just receive them. It's not that you won't have your share of problems in this life, but I want you to believe that I have many good things in store for you also. Remember how much you want to bless your children. Well, I am your Father and I feel the same way. There is a place inside your heart, where I want to whisper to your inner child that I am here and everything is going to be ok. I speak to that child to lift their head and look to me. I want that child to know it is safe to let go now, that their Papa is home.

SCRIPTURE TO MEDITATE ON:

The Lord is close to all whose hearts are crushed by pain, and he is always ready to restore the repentant one. Even when bad things happen to the good and godly ones, the Lord will save them and not let them be defeated by what they face. God will be your bodyguard to protect you when trouble is near. Not one bone will be broken. (Psalm 34:18-20)

APRIL 4

What I have planned for you today is always more than what you are expecting. So it might be a good idea to ask me because your plans might seem good to you, but eyes have not seen, nor ears heard what I have in store for you, my dear, dear child. Don't rely on your natural limited thoughts, but on your Father God who adores you and would move mountains for you. When you are looking to me for guidance, you will see that I have a whole new world to open up to you. I have so much in store for my kids. While the enemy of your soul tells you that I do not care, I am here making all these incredible plans for you. So, whatever you are thinking, lay it down for a moment, look my way and allow me to show you things that you would have never dreamt of on your own. In the meantime, I will continue to remind you that I am always working on your behalf, behind the scenes, and cant wait to see your face as these things unfold.

SCRIPTURES TO MEDITATE ON:

This is why the Scriptures say: Things never discovered or heard of before, things beyond our ability to imagine—these are the many things God has in store for all his lovers. (1 Corinthians 2:9)

We have become his poetry, a re-created people that will fulfill the destiny he has given each of us, for we are joined to Jesus, the Anointed One. Even before we were born, God planned in advance our destiny and the good works we would do to fulfill it! (Ephesians 2:10)

You saw who you created me to be before I became me! Before I'd ever seen the light of day, the number of days you planned for me were already recorded in your book. (Psalm 139:16)

APRIL 5

How I longed to gather you under my wings as a mother hen gathers her chicks. This is how I feel about you when you are struggling and trying to work through it alone. I long to help you see that I am here wanting to bring you comfort and protection from the storm. I am here for you and I have the security that you need. You know that you can come talk to me anytime and I will be here every time. I want to help you work through this. I want you to give this over to me and let me carry it for you. You might be so surprised as you turn to me and find me in the midst of your struggles. Your faith will grow as you see how present I am for my children to help them with their every concern. You have no need to worry, I am very good at taking care of my kids. Just rest in the security and comfort of my love. Draw on my grace, it will help you to enter into rest. Your trust will grow also as you see me come through over and over for you.

SCRIPTURES TO MEDITATE ON:

So many times I have longed to gather a wayward people, as a hen gathers her chicks under her wings—but you were too stubborn to let me. (Matthew 23:37)

God, you're such a safe and powerful place to find refuge! You're a proven help in time of trouble—more than enough and always available whenever I need you. So we will never fear even if every structure of support were to crumble away. We will not fear even when the earth quakes and shakes, moving mountains and casting them into the sea. (Psalm 46:1-2)

APRIL 6

I ask you, my child, to be open to the possibilities of many things that I would like to show you. As your Father, I am coming to you to give you my blessings, but you need to be open to receiving it. Different things can get in the way and I don't want you to miss out on what I have for you. Pray to be good receivers. There are things like unbelief and feeling unworthy that can try and get in the way of what I have for you. My Holy Spirit is here to help convince you that I am your Father who loves you dearly. I know all about you and your struggles to believe that I could love you this much. I do love to watch your face light up as you realize what I am telling you is true. I remind you once again, we are on this journey together.

SCRIPTURE TO MEDITATE ON:

The mature children of God are those who are moved by the impulses of the Holy Spirit. And you did not receive the "spirit of religious duty," leading you back into the fear of never being good enough. But you have received the "Spirit of full acceptance," enfolding you into the family of God. And you will never feel orphaned, for as he rises up within us, our spirits join him in saying the words of tender affection, "Beloved Father!" For the Holy Spirit makes God's fatherhood real to us as he whispers into our innermost being, "You are God's beloved child!" And since we are his true children, we qualify to share all his treasures, for indeed, we are heirs of God himself. And since we are joined to Christ, we also inherit all that he is and all that he has. We will experience being co-glorified with him provided that we accept his sufferings as our own. (Romans 8:14-17)

APRIL 7

The way of faith and trust is so misunderstood. To have faith is believing what you don't see. But when you never learned to trust as a child, I will step in and show myself trustworthy. I want to come into your world showing you in so many different ways that I am here for you. When your heart was broken and you had to be strong, you got used to not being comforted and you might not really grasp what that feels like. But I tell you my child, every hurting place needs to be comforted. I am not demanding you to trust me when you have not had the nurturing that is necessary for trust to be there. David said he learned to trust at his mother's breast, so you see it is something you learn to do. I have this for you my dear child, I will make it up to you what you never received. Just remember I gave my son for you, so there is nothing I wouldn't do for you. I will even help you open your heart to trust that I have this for you.

SCRIPTURES TO MEDITATE ON:

For God has proved his love by giving us his greatest treasure, the gift of his Son. And since God freely offered him up as the sacrifice for us all, he certainly won't withhold from us anything else he has to give. (Romans 8:32)

I will repay you for the years the locusts have eaten—the great locust and the young locust, the other locusts and the locust swarm my great army that I sent among you. (Joel 2:25 NIV)

APRIL 8

You are not here by yourself. Many times you look at your life as if you were all alone. But you never are because I am always with you and I have been here all along. You don't see me, but I am present at all times. So don't try to always figure out how I do this, but try to remember what I am telling you and if you need me to, I don't mind reminding you.. I know about all the times you felt alone, but I promise you there are happy days ahead as you experience my faithfulness to you. I reassure you that I was always there when you were not aware of me. Pray for eyes to see, and ears to hear. Pray for your heart to be opened. I want you to know this comforting truth about me, that I am even faithfully with you when you are not turning to me. This is something my children have not fully grasped, that my faithfulness is bigger than life, that it reaches to the heavens.

SCRIPTURES TO MEDITATE ON:

But even if we are faithless, he will still be full of faith, for he never wavers in his faithfulness to us! (2 Timothy 2:13)

But you, O Lord, your mercy-seat love is limitless, reaching higher than the highest heavens. Your great faithfulness is infinite, stretching over the whole earth. (Psalm 36:5)

Higher than the highest heavens—that's how high your tender mercy extends! Greater than the grandeur of heaven above is the greatness of your loyal love, towering over all who fear you and bow down before you! (Psalm 103:11)

APRIL 9

In my world there is so much more than what you see here. I want to open your eyes to see the wonders of my love, to give you my perspective on things. You really do need my help to receive the love I have for you, a love that you don't have to work for, a love that is not based on your behavior. I am not going to love you more if you do good deeds like helping the poor. Again, I am not going to suddenly love you more because you are doing some type of great work for me. You don't have to earn my love because you already have it, and you have all of it. I don't want you working for me, I want your heart and I want a relationship. Anything you do will be birthed out of that. Jesus could only do what he saw me doing, so why would it be any different for you?

SCRIPTURES TO MEDITATE ON:

So Jesus said, "I speak to you timeless truth. The Son is not able to do anything from himself or through my own initiative. I only do the works that I see the Father doing, for the Son does the same works as his Father. (John 5:19)

For I'm not speaking as someone who is self-appointed, but I speak by the authority of the Father himself who sent me, and who instructed me what to say. (John 12:49)

APRIL 10

My ways are not yours, nor my thoughts yours. The way I love is so far beyond anything you know here. It is so much bigger than anything you could ever imagine in your wildest dreams, and I have all this love in my heart that I feel for you. You need to ask so that you will have a greater awareness when I am coming to you. I have been waiting to show you, waiting to tell you, waiting for you to ask me. My thoughts of you are constant. My thoughts are something that I would like to share with you. Whatever your ideas are of what I am like and what I have for you, it will always be so much more than what you are thinking. I want to care for you down to the smallest detail and want you to get use to having a doting Father around. Whatever your needs are, whether big or small, I want you to feel cared for by me.

SCRIPTURES TO MEDITATE ON:

"For my thoughts are not your thoughts, neither are your ways my ways," declares the Lord. "As the heavens are higher than the earth, so are my ways higher than your ways and my thoughts than your thoughts." (Isaiah 55:8-9 NIV)

Every single moment you are thinking of me! How precious and wonderful to consider that you cherish me constantly in your every thought! O God, your desires toward me are more than the grains of sand on every shore! When I awake each morning, you're still with me. (Psalm 139:17-18)

APRIL 11

You are made in my image, but I am not like man that I should lie. I am not like your father; I would never hurt you. I know about your pain when favoritism was shown, and this has influenced the way you see me. I am not like this and I will give you all the reassurance you need. It's going to be all right. I will make things better for you. I will make things happen for you. I want you to be able to enjoy my love, to not just hear the words, but to experience what I am telling you. There is more than enough of my healing love that flows from the cross and is here to mend the broken pieces of your heart. Let your earthly father go; he was a man suffering under the weight of his own pain. Just watch my dear, dear child, as I turn this around for you and use it for good.

SCRIPTURES TO MEDITATE ON:
You intended to harm me, but God intended it for good to accomplish what is now being done, the saving of many lives. (Genesis 50:20 NIV)

Peter said, "Now I know for certain that God doesn't show favoritism with people but treats everyone on the same basis." (Acts 10:34)

APRIL 12

You are always on my mind. That may be hard for you to believe, that the God of the universe, who made heaven and earth, is always thinking of you, but it is true. And since I can do all of that, I also know how to reach you and help you experience the love that I feel for you. Many times, you see the problems in your life as bigger than what they really are or even bigger than me. The issue is not the problem, the problem is your inability to be able to trust me for answers and to really believe that I will be there for you. I come to you, my dear child, and ask you if you are willing to take the risk with your heart? I am the safest one to do that with, the safest place to put your trust, how fragile or broken that might be, is with me. I am your Father who waits and longs to be close to you. I am your Father who will help you trust again.

SCRIPTURES TO MEDITATE ON:

Every single moment you are thinking of me! How precious and wonderful to consider that you cherish me constantly in your every thought! O God, your desires toward me are more than the grains of sand on every shore! When I awake each morning, you're still with me. (Psalm 139: 17-18)

APRIL 13

You are so welcomed in this place with me. I want you to feel that and experience the things in your life that you missed, that you longed for as a child. Don't think for one moment that I ever took my eyes off you. I was with you in every difficult place and nothing will be wasted of what you went through. For every painful memory, I have a new one for you that holds loving thoughts of all the wonderful plans I have for healing and restoring you. The thing I promise to restore is your ability to trust. You will learn to trust again as you find me coming to the guarded places of your heart where you let no one near. The sun will shine again, my rain will fall on the hard soil of your hearts and I wash off all your cares, as my love soothes all your pain. I promise you new freedom, new places. I will make it all new, and give to you all that I intended for you to have.

SCRIPTURES TO MEDITATE ON:

You can buy two sparrows for only a copper coin, yet not even one sparrow falls from its nest without the knowledge of your Father. Aren't you worth much more to God than many sparrows? So don't worry. For your Father cares deeply about even the smallest detail of your life. (Matthew 10:29-31)

You saw who you created me to be before I became me! Before I'd ever seen the light of day, the number of days you planned for me were already recorded in your book. Every single moment you are thinking of me! How precious and wonderful to consider that you cherish me constantly in your every thought! O God, your desires toward me are more than the grains of sand on every shore! When I awake each morning, you're still with me. (Psalm 139:16-18)

APRIL 14

I ask you to watch for me as my love comes to you today in many different ways. The love I want to show you is not what you are used to, so I know you are not sure what that looks like. You see the miracles that I can perform, but many do not see the love I have in my heart for them. Many say, "Yes, I know He loves me," but it is not a reality for them, it has not been something they have experienced in their hearts yet. In your limited thinking, you have no idea of all the ways I want to come to you to make you feel wanted and doted on by me. Just be open, and again I ask you to be in a receiving position in your heart. Of all the things I do in this world, loving you is my top priority. You see all the many wonderful things I can do, so why would I not want to come and make my love known to you? The day I look forward to with all my kids, is the day their hearts are open to see me as their real Father, the day they turn to me and call me 'Papa.'

SCRIPTURES TO MEDITATE ON:

And you are not to be addressed as 'father,' for you have one Father, who is in heaven. (Matthew 23:9)

I myself said, "How gladly would I treat you like my children and give you a pleasant land, the most beautiful inheritance of any nation. I thought you would call me 'Father' and not turn away from following me." (Jeremiah 3:19 NIV)

April 15

I ask you, my child, to trust me with what you are facing. I am aware of everything that is going on with you and I would love for you to come and talk to me about whatever it is that is on your heart. I look forward to talking to my children, and it saddens me to see that many struggle with this idea. I look forward to the day my kids have this increasing revelation of how much I want to interact with them. I want you to know that I am going to make things happen for you, that you are not alone in this life. I am always here, always loving you, always working behind the scenes on your behalf. I am involved a lot more than you realize. I know sometimes it feels like life is not fair to you, if you can try and relax, you will understand that you are only seeing part of the picture. I will show you that I am a good Father, and soon things will become clear as to what I am doing in your life.

SCRIPTURE TO MEDITATE ON:

Become intimate with him in whatever you do, and he will lead you wherever you go. Don't think for a moment that you know it all. (Proverbs 3:6)

APRIL 16

I saw you, and I watched you, waiting for the day I knew your heart would be open to see me as your Father. I waited, and I planned with great anticipation for that moment when you would know I was the Father that you always longed for. I also want you to know that you are the child that I have always wanted. I will make this truth known to you through my Holy Spirit. He is the one that will help convince you. Now, my child, I take you by your hand and open up a whole new world of my love. I will show you the kind of Father that I will be for you.

SCRIPTURES TO MEDITATE ON:

For the Holy Spirit makes God's fatherhood real to us as he whispers into our innermost being, "You are God's beloved child!" (Romans 8:16)

But when the truth-giving Spirit comes, he will unveil the reality of every truth within you. He won't speak his own message, but only what he hears from the Father, and he will reveal prophetically to you what is to come. (John 16:13)

APRIL 17

My dear, dear child, all this time you thought I would be hard to find. You thought you had to seek me out to find me, that I would hide myself. If you as a parent would be thrilled to see your children when they come, why wouldn't I be thrilled to see you when you come to see me? I am so misunderstood by my children as they view me through unhealed places in their hearts. I promise that many of the things that you have heard about me along the way are not true. The truth is that I am so present, and will run to you, not away. I will come to you just because I want to be with you. I want you to learn all about me being your father. Much attention is given to places in your faith walk, but very little is given to our personal relationship. As you experience me fathering you, you will learn to trust again, play again, and live the life I intended for you all along.

SCRIPTURE TO MEDITATE ON:

"I will be a true Father to you, and you will be my beloved sons and daughters," says the Lord Yahweh Almighty. (2 Corinthians 6:18)

APRIL 18

There is a place that I would like to take you, and hoping you will stay. It's a homey place, full of warmth, security, and comfort. I can't wait to see your expressions as you become acquainted with it. It is a place that I have just for you. It is a place called home, where you can discover what it is like to be my daughter, to be my son. There is a lot to learn about being my child, and I know that you will love what I have to show you. You will finally get to be carefree and know the love of a Father. You can rest your heart knowing that I have this for you. You have been many things, many titles, but how much do you know about living daily with a heart of a son or daughter? I hope you will start looking forward to living this way and experiencing the benefits and blessings that come with being my child. It's a new life and it's a new day. Welcome home.

SCRIPTURE TO MEDITATE ON:

With my whole heart, with my whole life, and with my innermost being, I bow in wonder and love before you, the holy God! Yahweh, you are my soul's celebration. How could I ever forget the miracles of kindness you've done for me? You kissed my heart with forgiveness, in spite of all I've done. You've healed me inside and out from every disease. You've rescued me from hell and saved my life. You've crowned me with love and mercy. You satisfy my every desire with good things. You've supercharged my life so that I soar again like a flying eagle in the sky! (Psalm 103:1-5)

APRIL 19

I always welcome you, dear child, into my heart, into my home. I see you feeling uncomfortable but I hope you just keep coming and watch. One day you will let go of the orphan clothes you wore for such a long time. I will continually convince you until you know how much I want you with me, until you are convinced just how lovable you are to me. Your new clothes are laying out for you whenever you are ready to put them on. I realize many things will be new for you since you didn't have a father that you related to, so you don't always know what to expect from me. Just know that I look forward to showing you the kind of Father I want to be to you.

SCRIPTURE TO MEDITATE ON:

For the Holy Spirit makes God's fatherhood real to us, as He whispers into our innermost being, "You are God's beloved child!" (Romans 8:16)

APRIL 20

I see you looking at the things that are wrong in your life and I see how this troubles you. These things that you don't like, you are spending way too much time thinking about. I really don't have any problems with the way you are. I do not get upset over spilled milk. I am not surprised by your mess ups and I do not think differently of you because you reacted poorly to a situation. You are always okay in my sight. You can't change who you are, only I can. So learn to embrace your weaknesses because that is where you will find me. When you are weak, I am strong. It is not a bad thing to feel weak when you turn to me and discover that I am there for you with my strength and grace.

SCRIPTURES TO MEDITATE ON:

The extraordinary level of the revelations I've received is no reason for anyone to exalt me. For this is why a thorn in my flesh was given to me, the Adversary's messenger sent to harass me, keeping me from becoming arrogant. Three times I pleaded with the Lord to relieve me of this. But he answered me, "My grace is always more than enough for you, and my power finds its full expression through your weakness." So I will celebrate my weaknesses, for when I'm weak I sense more deeply the mighty power of Christ living in me. So I'm not defeated by my weakness, but delighted! For when I feel my weakness and endure mistreatment— when I'm surrounded with troubles on every side and face persecution because of my love for Christ—I am made yet stronger. For my weakness becomes a portal to God's power. (2 Corinthians 12:7-10)

I hear the Lord saying, "I will stay close to you, instructing and guiding you along the pathway for your life. I will advise you along the way and lead you forth with my eyes as your guide. So don't make it difficult; don't be stubborn when I take you where you've not been before. Don't make me tug you and pull you along. Just come with me!" (Psalm 32:8-9)

APRIL 21

Don't try and understand this love I have for you, it surpasses knowledge and you only see in part. I can reveal my love to you but don't try and figure it out with your mind and a heart that struggles to trust. With your mind you think, "How can he love me after failing so many times?", or you think you have to be good so I will be pleased with you. This is the way of the world and you can see your mind gets in the way here. When your heart is guarded, it will always question everything, and believe the lie that you are unloveable. Just try and relax and receive my love, I know how to get through to you. I know all about you and my love for you will never change. It is constant, loyal and committed.

SCRIPTURES TO MEDITATE ON:

Then you will be empowered to discover what every holy one experiences—the great magnitude of the astonishing love of Christ in all its dimensions. How deeply intimate and far-reaching is his love! How enduring and inclusive it is! Endless love beyond measurement that transcends our understanding—this extravagant love pours into you until you are filled to overflowing with the fullness of God! (Ephesians 3:19)

Trust in the Lord completely, and do not rely on your own opinions. With all your heart rely on him to guide you, and he will lead you in every decision you make. Become intimate with him in whatever you do, and he will lead you wherever you go. Don't think for a moment that you know it all. (Proverbs 3:5-6)

APRIL 22

I encourage you to get your eyes on me today and the relationship that I want with you. I don't come and go, I am here to stay. I have planned for us to be together and I want you to know that this is what I want. I want to be with you. I am not like your earthly father, I want to be involved in your life. Ask me to show you, but you need to ask or else you will not be watching for me to answer you. I will show up in ways that just might surprise you. I bless you, dear one, with a heart that will be receptive to all I have for you, for a heart that will recognize me as your God who wants to father you. I bless you with feeling the security that is found as you discover just how much I love you.

SCRIPTURES TO MEDITATE ON:

The Lord bless you and keep you; the Lord make his face shine upon you and be gracious to you: the Lord turn his face toward you and give you peace. (Numbers 6:24-26)

Don't be obsessed with money but live content with what you have, for you always have God's presence. For hasn't he promised you, "I will never leave you alone, never! And I will not loosen my grip on your life!" (Hebrews 13:5)

APRIL 23

Just to remind you that you are not in this life alone. Just keep looking to me for whatever it is that you need. I see and hear the cry of your heart. Once you can learn to be as a child, with a childlike trust, you will be able to leave everything in my hands knowing your Papa is very good at taking care of everything that concerns you. Just entertain the thought of what it would be like to be carefree, not having a thing to worry about. But what you really need to know experientially, is that you really are my child and I love to watch you come to life as I bring healing to your heart. This is not work for me, and I do take it serious about coming to you to help you to trust me. The love you are longing for is not in a distant land, or in a certain place, it is right here, right now, it's right in front of you and I want you to know it.

SCRIPTURE TO MEDITATE ON:

So do not fear, for I am with you; do not be dismayed, for I am your God. I will strengthen you and help you; I will uphold you with my righteous right hand. (Isaiah 41:10 NIV)

APRIL 24

There are times when I am blessing my children and they don't realize it is me blessing them, therefore they are not receiving the fullness of the blessing. I know it is because you are not used to being blessed by your earthly father in this way and you are not sure what to expect from me. I want to remove the dust from your 'father filters' so you can see me as I truly am, so you can see me as your Father who is loving you right now in this very moment. I know you have known pain and experienced some difficult days, but I am here to tell you that you will see the goodness of the Lord in the land of the living. I look forward to my children connecting with me wanting to bless them, to have the security of me being so involved in their lives. I run to you with a heart full of love just like the father who ran to his prodigal son.

SCRIPTURES TO MEDITATE ON:

From one man, Adam, he made every man and woman and every race of humanity, and he spread us over all the earth. He sets the boundaries of people and nations, determining their appointed times in history. He has done this so that every person would long for God, feel their way to him, and find him—for he is the God who is easy to discover! (Acts 17:26-27)

Yet I totally trust you to rescue me one more time, so that I can see once again how good you are while I'm still alive! (Psalm 27:13)

APRIL 25

I want to give to you the comfort that every child needs from a Father. I am right here longing to comfort you, to give you my time and attention. Maybe you are not used to experiencing comfort and you just haven't thought about it too much. Maybe you had to face difficult times alone, but know it was hard watching you go through that when you didn't know me. I long to father you and want you to know me this way. My people don't always see me as a nurturer, but this is the heart of who I am. I love to hold you, I love to talk to you even about the littlest of things. I love to fuss over you like a doting mother. I love when you ask me about things and wonder what I am thinking. I long to hold you close when you are hurting. I hope that you will learn to turn to me and not to other things or people. I will give you the security your heart longs for.

SCRIPTURES TO MEDITATE ON:

All praises belong to the God and Father of our Lord Jesus Christ. For he is the Father of tender mercy and the God of endless comfort. He always comes alongside us to comfort us in every suffering so that we can come alongside those who are in any painful trial. We can bring them this same comfort that God has poured out upon us. (2 Corinthians 1:3-4)

Don't be obsessed with money but live content with what you have, for you always have God's presence. For hasn't he promised you, "I will never leave you alone, never! And I will not loosen my grip on your life!" (Hebrews 13:5)

APRIL 26

I invite you to come to this resting place with me. It is so easy to get caught up in carrying burdens and taking on responsibilities that I have not given you. You fill your life with all these cares that take your attention away from the relationship I want with you. So again, I invite you to come away with me and let go of all the troubles of this life. When you taste and see that I am a good Father, you will naturally want more of who I am and what we can have together. I am so safe and present. I am all that your heart longs for. I bless you with knowing that it is ok to rest, it is ok to be happy and receive all of the wonderful things I have for you.

SCRIPTURE TO MEDITATE ON:

He offers a resting place for me in his luxurious love. His tracks take me to an oasis of peace, the quiet brook of bliss. That's where he restores and revives my life. He opens before me pathways to God's pleasure and leads me along in his footsteps of righteousness so that I can bring honor to his name. (Psalm 23:2-3)

APRIL 27

If you only knew how present I am in your world, and even in this present moment in time. If you only knew that I think about you more than all the sand granules on the shores, impossible to count. I am right here as you are reading this. If you only knew how my heart longs to be a Father to you. If you could believe this about me, your life would be so different. It would be more like the life you always wanted and didn't think you could have. Maybe you don't know this because of what you have gone through, but if you turn to me and ask for help in believing, I can do this for you and so much more. I helped the man that asked me to help his unbelief and I will help you also. I ask you to be open to all the places I want to take you and the things I want to show you about my love that you have not experience yet. There is so much more of my love available to you than you could ever dream possible.

SCRIPTURES TO MEDITATE ON:

When he heard this, the boy's father cried out with tears, saying, "I do believe, Lord; help my little faith!" (Mark 9:24)

Call to me and I will answer you and tell you great and unsearchable things you do not know. (Jeremiah 33:3 NIV)

APRIL 28

I hear you, I see you, I know your name and I know you like no one else does. I know everything about you, even things you would rather hide and pretend they are not there. I know where you live, I know your habits, and even the way you like to do things. I love your smile, I love your laugh; actually, I love everything about you. What I want to bring to your attention is what you don't know about me. You know that I am God your Father, that my son Jesus went to the cross for you, and that my Holy Spirit is here to help you. What you don't know is just how much I love you. Receive the healing I have for you, and let it wash over you. Let my Holy Spirit speak to your heart about my love, to help you know that it is bigger than anything you are thinking, anything that you have ever experienced. So, I ask you to relax and enjoy being my sons and daughters for a change.

SCRIPTURES TO MEDITATE ON:

For the Holy Spirit makes God's fatherhood real to us as he whispers into our innermost being, "You are God's beloved child!" (Romans 8:16)

Lord, you know everything there is to know about me. You perceive every movement of my heart and soul, and you understand my every thought before it even enters my mind. You are so intimately aware of me, Lord. You read my heart like an open book and you know all the words I'm about to speak before I even start a sentence! You know every step I will take before my journey even begins. You've gone into my future to prepare the way, and in kindness you follow behind me to spare me from the harm of my past. With your hand of love upon my life, you impart a blessing to me. This is just too wonderful, deep, and incomprehensible! Your understanding of me brings me wonder and strength. (Psalm 139: 1-6)

APRIL 29

I would like for us to sit together for a while. You don't have to talk if you don't want to and if you do, you don't have to say anything clever or brilliant. You don't have to act a certain way around me like you do with others. You don't have to impress me, I already know how interesting you are because I made you that way. I want you to know the unconditional love that I feel when I see you with all your flaws and quirks. I don't want you to worry or be concerned if you still feel and think orphaned thoughts and ways. I will do everything that I need to do to help you know the love I have in my heart for you. I understand your struggles and your doubts and I will help you the same way you would want to help your own children. You have had to endure some painful situations, but once you get to know me the way I truly am, and I become bigger in your life than your past or this present day, it will put your heart at rest!

SCRIPTURE TO MEDITATE ON:

And I will ask the Father and he will give you another Savior, the Holy Spirit of Truth, who will be to you a friend just like me—and he will never leave you. The world won't receive him because they can't see him or know him. But you will know him intimately, because he will make his home in you and will live inside you. (John 14:16-17)

APRIL 30

I will never give up on you and I will never forget about you. Though a mother could forget her nursing child, I could never forget you. I see how you long to know me and that makes me happy. I want to encourage you to trust that I will make myself known to you. I want you to know my heart, that I am a good Father who takes care of His kids. Whatever you are facing today, just remember all the times I came through for you and know that I will do it again. You will see for yourself over time that I am a good Father and will always be good to you. The more you experience this over time, the more secure you will feel in my love for you.

SCRIPTURES TO MEDITATE ON:

Call to me and I will answer you and tell you great and unsearchable things you do not know. (Jeremiah 33:3 NIV)

Can a mother forget the baby at her breast and have no compassion on the child she has borne? Though she may forget, I will not forget you! (Isaiah 49:15 NIV)

MAY

MAY 1

Look around you today and be watchful, so you don't miss my love coming to you in many different ways, sometimes through the simplest things. I will show up to let you know I am here with you. I love when you notice that it is me trying to reach you and I love watching your reaction. Watch for me and when you realize it's me, just sit there, take it in and enjoy what I am doing for you. I enjoy our times together and hope that you don't run off or get so quickly distracted. I will always tell you until you are convinced that you are lovable, and that I love being with you. You will discover as we hang out together how much better you will feel. This is the place where you will find your true identity, the person I created you to be before anyone else told you who you were. Just receive this love, a love that you do not have to earn, nor try to impress me. It's already all yours, my dear child, and I bless you to be happy and enjoy.

SCRIPTURES TO MEDITATE ON:

Don't be pulled in different directions or worried about a thing. Be saturated in prayer through out each day, offering your faith filled requests before God with overflowing gratitude. Tell him every detail of your life, then God's wonderful peace that transcends human understanding, will make the answers known to you through Jesus Christ. (Philippians 4:6-7)

But whenever you pray, go into your innermost chamber and be alone with Father God, praying to him in secret. And your Father, who sees all you do, will reward you openly. (Matthew 6:6)

MAY 2

Let your thoughts be filled with the truth that I am speaking into your life. I am excited for you and I am also very much at peace about your life and what I have planned. Don't dwell on the things which are temporary or the things that are not going to really matter in the end. When you wake in the morning, be intentional about being with me and learning how to be my child. I will show you how to live carefree and I will help you to know my blessing in your life. I know how to open the doors that you need to go through, so trust me and my timing. Even though things look cloudy right now, you will look back and understand later what I was doing. I will encourage your heart along the way. I just ask you to trust me in where I have you right now.

SCRIPTURES TO MEDITATE ON:

Our present knowledge and our prophecies are but partial. (1 Corinthians 13:9)

Pour out all your worries and stress upon him and leave them there, for he always tenderly cares for you. (1 Peter 5:7)

May 3

Be open to the "so much more." I want you to know that with me you will always have two shoes. The other shoe will not drop, and I will heal all your disappointments that cause you to fear that you cannot trust when good things happen for you. There is always more with me. During the healing process, I will encourage your heart to believe this. There is no need to be begging or crying out for my blessing because it is in my heart to bless you. There is no need for you to feel like you have to deal with your problems alone. You say you know I am here, but you still think independently as I stand by watching and waiting for you to finish trying to work it out without me. I am not upset with you when you struggle through by yourself. I just want you to be aware of this when it happens because I am always here for you.

SCRIPTURES TO MEDITATE ON:

I look up to the mountains and hills, longing for God's help. But then I realize that our true help and protection come only from the Lord, our Creator who made the heavens and the earth. (Psalm 121:1-2)

So don't ever be afraid, dearest friends! Your loving Father joyously gives you his kingdom realm with all its promises! (Luke 12:32)

MAY 4

Put aside all those thoughts in your head that want to figure everything out, that want to understand it all. Instead, look to me for revelation about who I am as your Father. I am not like any Father that you know here on earth, and because that is the only thing you know, you have a clouded image of who I really am. You don't have to work at this alone, I want to show you and I am longing for you to know. I want you to be at home with me and be secure in my love for you when you are amongst all your brothers and sisters. I not only have revelation for you, but I will also give you ears to hear me speak to you as a loving Father would talk to his children. And I hear you say, would I really do this for you, do I really care about you this much? I say to you, watch and see what I will do for you, because eyes have not seen, nor have ears heard what I have in store for you.

SCRIPTURE TO MEDITATE ON:

This is why the Scriptures say: Things never discovered or heard of before, things beyond our ability to imagine—these are the many things God has in store for all his lovers. (1 Corinthians 2:9)

MAY 5

Since you are not used to being anyone's daughter or son, you are in for a blessed adventure as I show you the kind of relationship we can have. I want to give to you the security a child feels when they have a daddy at home who dotes over them. As I father you, your heart will grow to know what it feels like to be a child that has all their needs met without even asking. As you feel my smile of approval that is always there for you, you will see how lovable you truly are. I love being your Dad, and I love who you are. All the things you felt that you missed out on, that you longed for from your dad, I will make up to you, and be that for you. Don't think that you have to wait for that day to come, I want to do this for you now. I want to father you now, today, in this very moment in time.

SCRIPTURE TO MEDITATE ON:

To the fatherless he is a father. To the widow he is a champion friend. To the lonely he gives a family. To the prisoners he leads into prosperity until they sing for joy. This is our Holy God in his Holy Place! But for the rebels there is heartache and despair. (Psalm 68:5-6)

MAY 6

I want to tell you about the longing of my heart. That longing is for you. You might not see me as an emotional Father, but I am very emotional when it comes to you. I have provided much healing for my kids, not just for their health, but also for their hearts so they can see me as a loving Father. When you need healing around your father, it blocks you from seeing my care for you. I understand your struggles to believe that I could love you this much. It is also easy to misread your circumstances and believe the lie that I don't care about what you are facing. I long to bring you the healing you need in order for you to trust again. Just try and imagine this place, a place of total peace where everything inside of you feels cared for, and a place where you know everything is going to be okay because your Father is right there for you. Oh how I would love to take you to this place where you don't have a care in the world.

SCRIPTURES TO MEDITATE ON:

Trust in the Lord completely, and do not rely on your own opinions. With all your heart rely on him to guide you, and he will lead you in every decision you make. (Proverbs 3:5)

So many times I have longed to gather your wayward children together around me, as a hen gathers her chicks under her wings—but you were too stubborn to let me. (Luke 13:34)

MAY 7

Many of my children love to work for me and try very hard to be a good Christian trying to please me. While this may seem right and a good thing to do, there needs to be an equally important time and place for our relationship, a place where you can discover how to be with me as my sons and daughters. Just as you want to be with someone you love, so I want to be with you. There are many reasons why we want to be with someone, but my main reason for wanting to be with you is that I love you. I want you to freely come to me so you can find out for yourself that I am not a distant authoritative Father, stern and unapproachable. That is the lie the enemy has whispered to my children over the years. I always look forward to our times together. You can approach me anytime, day or night. This is the imprint I want to leave on your heart of me. I am your Father that has always been here waiting for you.

SCRIPTURE TO MEDITATE ON:

So now we come freely and boldly to where love is enthroned, to receive mercy's kiss and discover the grace we urgently need to strengthen us in our time of weakness. (Hebrews 4:16)

MAY 8

I am here to help you believe that I am your Father, who wants you in his life. I am so moved to father you every time I look at you. Just as you believed the lie that your life was not important because you did not have the love of a father, so I will make my truth known to you that I always wanted you in my life. I will never leave you in that place where you feel uncared for. When this truth comes to your heart, you will discover a whole new world as you continually experience my love for you. Your past will no longer dominate your thoughts and your memories will no longer push you around emotionally. I promise you that I will come to you and you will know that you have a Father that you always daydreamed about, a Father that you always wished you had.

SCRIPTURE TO MEDITATE ON:

I will be a true Father to you, and you will be my beloved sons and daughters," says the Lord Yahweh Almighty. (2 Corinthians 6:18)

May 9

I love you being my sons and daughters. Just stay with me for a while and let this sink in. It's so easy to get busy on the inside, so preoccupied with so many things. You are not expecting me to come to you in the midst of your busy day, but I want you to see for yourself, that I am trying to communicate to you that you are a much-loved child of mine. I can help you with this. This is truth, and this is the reality I want you to have. I am here to affirm you, to bring you the comfort you need, and to care for you in ways that will surprise you at times because you didn't think those things mattered to me. I want you to feel cared for in every area of your life. I know you, my child, like no one else does and I always look forward to and enjoy our times together.

SCRIPTURE TO MEDITATE ON:

Lord, even when your path takes me through the valley of deepest darkness, fear will never conquer me, for you already have! You remain close to me and lead me through it all the way. Your authority is my strength and my peace. The comfort of your love takes away my fear. I'll never be lonely, for you are near. (Psalm 23:4)

MAY 10

Sometimes when struggling with problems you forget in that moment that you are not alone. You don't like the way you are reacting to a situation, and feeling bad keeps you from turning to me for help. Don't work through these things by yourself when I am here to help you. You can't change who you are, so bring these things to me and talk to me about them. Try to remember to not let fear and condemnation keep you away. You will find comfort when you realize how much I accept you in these places. You might have a hard time with yourself and others might condemn you, but I never will. Another reminder, my child, is that I am always here for you. Every single time you turn to me I will be here and even when you don't think to turn to me, I will still be here. There is so much I want to give you, so I encourage you to be open to receiving from me.

SCRIPTURES TO MEDITATE ON:

So now the case is closed. There remains no accusing voice of condemnation against those who are joined in life-union with Jesus, the Anointed One. (Romans 8:1)

This is just too wonderful, deep, and incomprehensible! Your understanding of me brings me wonder and strength. (Psalm 139:6)

MAY 11

You may not be used to having a father that is so involved in your life the way I want to be. If your father was away a lot or not present for you, this is how you will view me as well. Maybe not on a conscious level, but you will have a tendency to interact with me in that same way. While it is good for you to quiet your soul before me, I also love talking to you and love making things happen for you. I see my children coming before me and just waiting, but not really believing that I want to talk to them. When a child comes to talk to his dad, most loving dads would drop everything and respond with open arms. He would not place the child on hold, making them wait. Jesus told the story about a father and his sons in Luke for a very good reason. He wanted to give you a picture of the kind of father I am, the kind of father that would run to his child when he saw him coming. The kind of father that loves unconditionally.

SCRIPTURE TO MEDITATE ON:

Then Jesus said, "Once there was a father with two sons. The younger son came to his father and said, 'Father, don't you think it's time to give me the share of your estate that belongs to me?' So the father went ahead and distributed among the two sons their inheritance. Shortly afterward, the younger son packed up all his belongings and traveled off to see the world. He journeyed to a far-off land where he soon wasted all he was given in a binge of extravagant and reckless living. With everything spent and nothing left, he grew hungry, for there was a severe famine in that land. So he begged a farmer in that country to hire him. The farmer hired him and sent him out to feed the pigs. The son was so famished, he was willing to even eat the slop given to the pigs, because no one would feed him a thing. Humiliated, the son finally realized what he was doing and he thought, 'There are many workers at my father's house who have all the food they want with plenty to spare. They lack nothing. Why am I here dying of hunger, feeding these pigs and eating their slop? I want to go back home to my father's house, and I'll say to him, "Father, I was wrong. I have sinned against you. I'll never be worthy to be called your son. Please, Father, just treat me like one of your employees."' So the young son set off for home. From a long distance away, his father saw him coming, dressed as a beggar, and great compassion swelled up in his heart for his son who was returning home. So the father raced out to meet him. He swept him up in his arms, hugged him dearly, and kissed him over and over with tender love. Then the son said, 'Father, I was wrong. I have sinned against you. I could never deserve to be called your son. Just let me be.' The father interrupted and said, 'Son, you're home now!' Turning to his servants, the father said, 'Quick, bring me the best robe, my very own robe, and I will place it on his shoulders. Bring the ring, the seal of sonship, and I will put it on his finger. And bring out the best shoes you can find for my son. Let's prepare a great feast and celebrate. For this beloved son of mine was once dead, but now he's alive again. Once he was lost, but now he is found!' And everyone celebrated with overflowing joy. Now, the older son was out working in the field when his brother returned, and as he approached the house he heard the music of celebration and dancing. So he called over one of the servants and asked, 'What's going on?' The servant replied, 'It's your younger brother. He's returned home and your father is throwing a party to celebrate his homecoming.' The older son became angry and refused to go in and celebrate. So his father came out and pleaded with him, 'Come and enjoy the feast with us!' The son said, 'Father, listen! How many years have I been working like a slave for you, performing every duty you've asked as a faithful son? And I've never once disobeyed you. But you've never thrown a party for me because of my faithfulness. Never once have you even given me a goat that I could feast on and celebrate with my friends like he's doing now. But look at this son of yours! He comes back after wasting your wealth on prostitutes and reckless living, and here you are throwing a great feast to celebrate—for him!' The father said, 'My son, you are always with me by my side. Everything I have is yours to enjoy. It's only right to celebrate like this and be overjoyed, because this brother of yours was once dead and gone, but now he is alive and back with us again. He was lost but now he is found!'" (Luke 15:11-32)

MAY 12

It is a good thing to learn and grow in knowledge, but many have not learned a crucial part of life, that is learning to love yourself. Did you ever think about why I made this the second commandment? In my world, there is forgiveness, patience, kindness and acceptance. This is what I want you to have in your world. I don't want you going back to the place of self-rejection and listening to the voice that condemns you. Another important thing to learn is to listen to my voice, the voice that tells you that you are my much-loved child. Remember, my love is bigger than anything you know here. I am not looking for people with titles, money, looks, nor talents, but for a heart that is open to me being their Father.

SCRIPTURES TO MEDITATE ON:

Love is large and incredibly patient. Love is gentle and consistently kind to all. It refuses to be jealous when blessing comes to someone else. Love does not brag about one's achievements nor inflate its own importance. Love does not traffic in shame and disrespect, nor selfishly seek its own honor. Love is not easily irritated or quick to take offense. Love joyfully celebrates honesty and finds no delight in what is wrong. Love is a safe place of shelter, for it never stops believing the best for others. Love never takes failure as defeat, for it never gives up. Love never stops loving. It extends beyond the gift of prophecy, which eventually fades away. It is more enduring than tongues, which will one day fall silent. Love remains long after words of knowledge are forgotten. Our present knowledge and our prophecies are but partial, but when love's perfection arrives, the partial will fade away.

When I was a child, I spoke about childish matters, for I saw things like a child and reasoned like a child. But the day came when I matured, and I set aside my childish ways. For now we see but a faint reflection of riddles and mysteries as though reflected in a mirror, but one day we will see face-to-face. My understanding is incomplete now, but one day I will understand everything, just as everything about me has been fully understood. Until then, there are three things that remain: faith, hope, and love—yet love surpasses them all. So above all else, let love be the beautiful prize for which you run. (1 Corinthians 13:4-13)

And the second is this: 'You must love your neighbor in the same way you love yourself.' You will never find a greater commandment than these. (Mark 12:31)

MAY 13

I understand that you know many things, and continue to increase in knowledge, but what do you do with all this when so much emotional turmoil goes on inside? Usually it is easy to stay busy and focus on what's in your head instead of what's in your heart. You can tell yourself all the things you know to be true and that can help some or you can turn to temporary false comforts and that can also help in the moment. But your deepest need is to be fathered, to be mothered, to be comforted. Many do not have the experience of having a secure, comforting surrounding, but this is what your heart is looking for and you just haven't connected to this unmet need yet. I am here to give to you all that was taken from you over the years. I will affirm you, take good care of you, and hold you close to my heart.

SCRIPTURES TO MEDITATE ON:

He tends his flock like a shepherd: He gathers the lambs in his arms and carries them close to his heart; he gently leads those that have young. (Isaiah 40:11)

I will repay you for the years the locusts have eaten—the great locust and the young locust, the other locusts and the locust swarm—my great army that I sent among you. (Joel 2:25 NIV)

MAY 14

It is true, I am right here. It is true, I am your Father who is right here, right now in this very moment. You don't have to wonder where I am because I will be here when you need me. I will always be here, and I want you to feel the security of knowing that. You don't have to go searching for me, hoping you will find out where I am because I am always here with you. It is also true that I am your Father who loves to talk to you. It is not just about changing and the work you want to do for me. I love to talk to you about you. Just as a devoted father here on earth is interested and cares about what is going on with his children, so you have my full attention. When my son was here, his heart was for my people. He was not trying to become rich and famous, he was in the present moment, he was all about reaching my children for me. I tell you, my child, to get used to having your Father around, and not just any Father, but one who loves you so much that I would give my son up to have you back with me.

SCRIPTURES TO MEDITATE ON:

For this is how much God loved the world—he gave his one and only, unique Son as a gift. So now everyone who believes in him will never perish but experience everlasting life. (John 3:16)

He has done this so that every person would long for God, feel their way to him, and find him—for he is the God who is easy to discover! (Acts 17:27)

MAY 15

I want to take you on this journey with me and look into the world of a little child. I will help you see this as you try and imagine what it would be like to be in a home full of love and laughter. Warm colors fill the rooms, with an aroma coming from the kitchen of your favorite meal being cooked. You can hear the noise of the saw out in the barn. Your dad is making you a rocking chair because he knows how much you love to rock. You are out on your tree swing feeling the warm summer breezes blow through your hair. The best thing yet, is that you don't have a care in the world, nor concerns about what others think of you. You are at total peace with your world. Mom and Dad are always home, and all of your needs are met. You don't have to worry about a thing today, tonight, or tomorrow. To be free of all responsibilities and free of the caretaker role that you learned to walk in most of your life. Now its time for you to skip, laugh, jump up and down, and role in the grass being free to be a child. This is what I have for you and you will know this even though this time has passed. Don't try and figure out how this will happen; only I know how to do this. You really don't have a thing to worry about, because I am going to take care of everything for you.

SCRIPTURE TO MEDITATE ON:
*I will repay you for the years the locusts have eaten—
the great locust and the young locust, the other locusts
and the locust swarm—my great army that I sent
among you.* (Joel 2:25 NIV)

MAY 16

I see you thinking about many things, but I tell you to give your mind a rest. I already know how I am going to do this for you. Remember all of the times in the past, how I worked things out when you had no idea how it was going to happen. I will do that again, but in the meantime, until I open doors that you need open, learn to rest in knowing that I am a good Father who will never forget about you and who always has a plan. How many times have you looked back and said, "Oh, that's what He was doing?" I do understand, it is not always easy waiting and not knowing, especially when you are not feeling secure in my love. But know that I am all about my children and helping them. As you see me come through time and time again, you will learn that I am your Father who you can safely rely on.

SCRIPTURE TO MEDITATE ON:

Because of the Lord's great love we are not consumed, for his compassions never fail. They are new every morning; great is your faithfulness. (Lamentations 3:22-23 NIV)

MAY 17

I love out times together, and so happy to reveal the truth to you about me being your Father. I know it's hard for you to believe this, but I am asking you to position your heart to be blessed by me. Many of my children have no idea of how much I want to bless them because of what they have been through; they think that just getting by is what life is about. You may be expecting life to be hard or feeling that you are unworthy on a subconscious level, but you have no idea of the blessings that are in store for you. You think you know what my blessing might be, but it is so much more than what anyone is thinking. You don't have to work hard trying to be blessed, trying to make your life better, I already have this for you. David learned to trust and I will help you learn to trust. I will show you its safe to jump, and I will help you to be open to receiving what I have for you.

SCRIPTURE TO MEDITATE ON:

Look at the nations and watch—and be utterly amazed. For I am going to do something in your days that you would not believe, even if you were told. (Habakkuk 1:5 NIV)

MAY 18

If you woke up one day and found out that you came from royalty, I am sure that would make you look at yourself differently. You might see yourself as being pretty special. Even if that were not the case, the truth is you were always special because you are my child. I created you, have always loved you, and you will always belong to me. I wanted you in my life, and there was never a time that I didn't. I have never changed my mind about you, even when you were ignoring me and living a life apart from me. So, I bless you my child to enjoy your life knowing you're my child. There are things I would love to give you, but you need to be open to receiving. This is when you need to come like a little child because they are very good are receiving. Put your adult posture aside that goes into, "I will take care of everything myself" mode. I encourage you to relax, open your arms, open your heart and receive.

SCRIPTURE TO MEDITATE ON:

But you are a chosen people, a royal priesthood, a holy nation, God's special possession, that you may declare the praises of him who called you out of darkness into his wonderful light. (1 Peter 2:9)

MAY 19

I am not only your Father, I am a present Father, who is present in every way that you need me to be for you. I am mentally present, for my thoughts are always on you. I am emotionally present longing to take you under my wings. There are fathers who are in the house, but do not interact with their children. If your father didn't talk to you very much and he didn't feel your pain, this will interfere with the way you see me. I am to the most extreme that you can go to opposite of this kind of fathering. I can help you to know the truth about me and you never have to worry that I will not be here for you, because there is no force in heaven nor earth that could ever separate us. I will never let that happen.

SCRIPTURES TO MEDITATE ON:

Every single moment you are thinking of me! How precious and wonderful to consider that you cherish me constantly in your every thought! O God, your desires toward me are more than the grains of sand on every shore! When I awake each morning, you're still with me. (Psalm 139:17-18)

So, what does all this mean? If God has determined to stand with us, tell me, who then could ever stand against us? (Romans 8:31)

MAY 20

Be comforted in knowing that I am always here if you need to talk or need me to listen. If you have questions or just need advice, I am here. You can talk to me anytime. I see you trying to work things out on your own, so unaware that I am right here hoping that you will remember to turn to me. I love helping my children and my heart is always moved when you come to me. There is so much that goes on in this world that grabs for your attention and tries to keep you away from me. But, you also have learned over the years an independence that keeps you from me as well. So I am thrilled when you turn to me and I can have some time with you. I am sad that my children think that all I want them to do is work for me. My relating to you as your Father is my main concern that I want to communicate to you. I want you to know there is so much more you can have in your relationship with me.

SCRIPTURES TO MEDITATE ON:

My help comes from the Lord, the Maker of heaven and earth. He will not let your foot slip....he who watches over you will not slumber. (Psalm 121:2-3)

I promise that I will never leave you helpless or abandon you as orphans—I will come back to you! (John 14:18)

MAY 21

I want to show you a glimpse of what is going on at my end, from the place where I see you. I am so happy about my children and love to celebrate who they are. I am not angry like many see me. So much of this life has given them a distorted view of me and now they don't realize that I am a happy God that enjoys His children. My world is full of life, laughter and compassion like you have never known or experienced yet. I am not troubled, but at total peace. There is one emotion that you are familiar with that I know, and it is sadness. I feel much sadness that my children do not know me as a devoted, understanding, and compassionate Father. I long to be this for them and because of their experience with their earthly father, they can't see me as I am. I am here waiting for the moment when their hearts turn to me to father them. You only have to ask, and I will show you.

SCRIPTURE TO MEDITATE ON:

Call to me and I will answer you and tell you great and unsearchable things you do not know. (Jeremiah 33:3 NIV)

MAY 22

I would like for you to continue discovering daily how I feel about you. As you grow secure in my love, knowing that your Father is always here and you are always ok in my eyes, you will not be being tossed around emotionally by other's reactions toward you. You measure your value by how others treat you. I don't want you to have to live this way and I can help you love yourself, so others will not define you. I want you rooted and grounded in my truth, my unconditional love that constantly tells you that you are okay no matter what issues you may face or have. The message you got from others is that you were not okay, even if you were not having issues. You didn't get the affirmation you needed when you needed to hear comforting words of reassurance, but instead you heard a, "What is wrong with you?" message in words or looks. You throw parties for birthdays, I throw parties for my children when their eyes are opened to my love for them as their Father.

SCRIPTURES TO MEDITATE ON:

Turning to his servants, the father said, 'Quick, bring me the best robe, my very own robe, and I will place it on his shoulders. Bring the ring, the seal of sonship, and I will put it on his finger. And bring out the best shoes you can find for my son.' (Luke 15:22)

Then, by constantly using your faith, the life of Christ will be released deep inside you, and the resting place of his love will become the very source and root of your life. (Ephesians 3:17)

MAY 23

As I watch my children from heaven, I see them so troubled with the cares of this world. They struggle with trusting me, wondering if I really care for them and if I care enough to be involved with whatever they are facing. And then at times, they are so focused on what is happening in their lives that they are not connecting to the reality of how present I am in helping them work through their dilemmas. They are so caught up with feeling alone and worried and they have no idea of how much I want them to know that I am here for them. They don't see me, all they see is what is in front of them, forgetting how big I am and how much I can move mountains for them. They are not able to trust me coming through for them because of so many disappointments. My child, I have healing for you so you can find out once and for all that you can trust the heart of your Father God. It's in my heart to help my children. My child, you are in my heart and I will never stop at trying to reach you.

SCRIPTURE TO MEDITATE ON:

So don't ever be afraid, dearest friends! Your loving Father joyously gives you his kingdom realm with all its promises! (Luke 12:32)

MAY 24

Just as I expressed my unconditional love to my sons in the prodigal father story, so this is a picture of what my loves looks like for you. I am not looking at what is wrong with you, I am just so happy to have you in my life as my children. I am your Father who gets very excited about you, just as you see in the prodigal story the excitement I felt when I ran to my son when he came home. It's been ingrained in my children to believe they have to act right, do good works, and be the ideal Christian to be loved by me. What needs to be experienced is my love for you when you are honest about your weaknesses, when you mess up. Just as a child trusts the heart of his dad who daily cares for him, so I look forward to you knowing this about me. This is the new imprint I want to leave on your heart. Many think they know, but they don't fully comprehend the relationship I am after with them. If you don't know this, your Christian walk will take a lot of work, a lot of your energy and result in little to no relationship with me.

SCRIPTURE TO MEDITATE ON:

This is what the Lord says: "Let not the wise boast of their wisdom or the strong boast of their strength or the rich boast of their riches, but let him boast about this:that he understands and knows me, that I am the Lord, who exercises kindness, justice and righteousness on earth, for in these I delight." declares the Lord. (Jeremiah 9:23-24 NIV)

MAY 25

I do not change from one day to the next. You can count on my love always being there for you. Just ask me to show you the kind of daughter/son relationship I want to have with you. This is the day I have been waiting for. I know you are not used to being fathered, you might not know what to expect, nor what you can have with me. I will father you in ways that you have longed for and meet all your unmet needs from childhood to present. I know you struggle to believe me for this, but just ask and be ready for the journey of your life. I will touch your heart in ways that no one else can. You will be surprised as I help you with things that you had to face alone, things that you carried that were put on you that you should have never had to deal with at a young age. You will be surprised as you watch me take care of these things. It's time for you to lay all this down and let me care for you. I will help you to trust me in this place where you need to be fathered and I will not let you down.

SCRIPTURES TO MEDITATE ON:
God is not human, that he should lie, not a human being, that he should change his mind. Does he speak and then not act? Does he promise and not fulfill? (Numbers 23:19 NIV)

Jesus, the Anointed One, is always the same—yesterday, today, and forever. (Hebrews 13:8)

Every gift God freely gives us is good and perfect, stream-ing down from the Father of lights, who shines from the heavens with no hidden shadow or darkness and is never subject to change. (James 1:17)

MAY 26

I see your thoughts, I see you trying to understand, trying to process everything in the midst of all the mind-boggling stuff. I am right here wanting you to turn to me for help. All you have to say is, "Papa, help." Try and be aware of getting caught up in the cares of this world. There is so much going on in my world, so much I want to share with you, but if you are too busy and bogged down with all these other concerns, you won't hear what I am trying to say to you. There is much going on around you, but there is so much going on here where I am also, and I don't want you to miss out on all that I have for you. Remember past events and how I always surprised you with outcomes that you were not expecting, and I can do that again. There were things that happened that you didn't understand, don't let some of these disappointments keep you from coming to me. My thoughts for you are always good, and I will never hurt you. You will know this as you get to know me that my heart is always for you.

SCRIPTURES TO MEDITATE ON:

"For I know the plans I have for you," declares the Lord, "plans to prosper you and not to harm you, plans to give you hope and a future." (Jeremiah 29:11 NIV)

Become intimate with him in whatever you do, and he will lead you wherever you go. Don't think for a moment that you know it all. (Proverbs 3:6)

MAY 27

There's a tendency to shy away from me when you think of your God being your Father. Maybe not always on a conscious level, but the thought of me being your Father stirs up all kinds of emotions. Jesus is a friend of sinners, so you naturally feel close to him, but as soon as you realize that his Father is your Father, you start feeling distant. Anything that is unresolved with your father here will affect how you think and how you feel about me. It will interfere with what you will be able to receive from me. There is so much I want to show you about what I have for you in our relationship, so it is important to have healing and forgiveness toward your father and mother. If you are not sure, ask me and I will show you that I have whatever it is you need to bring about your healing. I am always here to help you work through and process the things you need to face, and I will counsel you with my eye on you.

SCRIPTURES TO MEDITATE ON:

I hear the Lord saying, "I will stay close to you, instructing and guiding you along the pathway for your life. I will advise you along the way and lead you forth with my eyes as your guide. So don't make it difficult; don't be stubborn when I take you where you've not been before. Don't make me tug you and pull you along. Just come with me!" (Psalm 32:8-9)

He heals the wounds of every shattered heart. (Psalm 147:3)

This is love: He loved us long before we loved him. It was his love, not ours. He proved it by sending his Son to be the pleasing sacrificial offering to take away our sins. (1 John 4:10)

MAY 28

Did you know my child, that you have learned to live with many unmet needs that you are not in touch with? So you could be feeling something and not know exactly what it is you need, but I do and I can help you. It might be hard for you to believe that I am here to meet those needs no matter how big, how little, or how impossible it looks to you. I saw you as a little girl who needed her daddy to notice her, to make her feel pretty. I saw a little boy who needed his dad to just give him that affirming smile that lets him know that he is okay when he didn't make the team. In John 5:17, Jesus said that he and his father were always at work even to this very day. When my son was with you on earth, he was always working to reach you for me. I am not working to build mansions and a fortune for myself, but I am working to reach you, to bring you healing, and to convince you that you are no longer orphans, you belong to me. I am your Father and my home is yours, this is where I spend my time, this is where my heart is.

SCRIPTURES TO MEDITATE ON:

Jesus replied, "Loving me empowers you to obey my word. And my Father will love you so deeply that we will come to you and make you our dwelling place." (John 14:23)

MAY 29

I want my kids to feel the freedom to approach me at all times. You will discover nothing but acceptance and that will make you feel at home with me. I like when you can honestly talk to me about the unpleasant things in your life that you don't like to look at nor talk about. Whatever your need is, whatever you are facing, I am here to help. When you are feeling uncertain about me or feeling insecure about yourself, that is when I want you to learn how safe it is to open your heart to receive from me. Put yourself in the receiving position and learn to be good at receiving. If you are feeling unworthy I will help you with that also. Whatever you are giving out of, it should be from an overflow of my love that you are experiencing when you come to me.

SCRIPTURES TO MEDITATE ON:

Our love for others is our grateful response to the love God first demonstrated to us. (1 John 4:19)

So now we come freely and boldly to where love is enthroned, to receive mercy's kiss and discover the grace we urgently need to strengthen us in our time of weakness. (Hebrews 4:16)

So if you feel restless or uneasy because you think you should be doing more for me, make sure you don't do anything from that place. I know you were raised believing you had to do things to get approval and you had to be good to get attention. I do not expect nor demand that you have to do anything for me to love you or think well of you. With me you don't have to be concerned with any of that. What I long to have with you is a close relationship where you feel free to come and talk to me anytime. I have said in my Word how important relationship is to me, but many do not grasp this truth, they are not able to hear me. I come to you to love you and show you what we can have together. It's important for you to know this love that I have for you more than you know anything else, more than knowledge, more than the world you live in, and more than anyone you know.

SCRIPTURE TO MEDITATE ON:

Until then, there are three things that remain: faith, hope, and love—yet love surpasses them all. So above all else, let love be the beautiful prize for which you run. (1 Corinthians 13:13)

I will give them a heart to know me.
(Jeremiah 24:7)

MAY 31

I am constantly working to reach my children and I will never stop until I get their attention. If you sit down and think over your life time, you would be able to pinpoint all the times that you knew it was me trying to rescue you from danger, making things happen for you and you wondered how it happened. Think about my son when he came into this world, I sent him as a baby because I knew it would help you to get a picture of who I am. I could have let him be born in a castle, and he could have hung out with the rich and famous. He was and still is a picture of who I am. Before he went to the cross, he washed the disciples feet; he was not having a pity party about the suffering he was about to endure. When Jesus was on the shore making breakfast for the disciples after he died on the cross, another picture of my love. I will never stop trying to reach my children and I will never give up on you.

SCRIPTURES TO MEDITATE ON:

Jesus answered his critics by saying, "Everyday my Father is at work, and I will be too!" (John 5:17)

"You have sent messengers to John, and what he testified about me is true." (John 5:33)

JUNE

JUNE 1

I know you have been busy lately, preoccupied with many things. But I am still here waiting and wanting to be with you. Don't let feeling bad keep you from me. I love our times together and I look forward to being with you and sharing our hearts with each other. Think on the different times in my word where my children were not acting right and I did not shame nor scold them. I offered them my love and encouragement and that is what I offer you. I did not scold Peter when he denied me, and I did not scold nor shame the younger brother when he returned home, nor the older brother when he was jealous. Sadly, my children see me as ready to judge, ready to punish, a ready to correct Father and I am nothing at all like what they are expecting. Ask me and I will show you more than miracles, I will show you my love in ways that you have never known.

SCRIPTURE TO MEDITATE ON:

Then Jesus said, "Once there was a father with two sons. The younger son came to his father and said, 'Father, don't you think it's time to give me the share of your estate that belongs to me?' So the father went ahead and distributed among the two sons their inheritance. Shortly afterward, the younger son packed up all his belongings and traveled off to see the world. He journeyed to a far-off land where he soon wasted all he was given in a binge of extravagant and reckless living. With everything spent and nothing left, he grew hungry, for there was a severe famine in that land. So he begged a farmer in that country to hire him. The farmer hired him and sent him out to feed the pigs. The son was so famished, he was willing to even eat the slop given to the pigs, because no one would feed him a thing. Humiliated, the son finally realized what he was doing and he thought, 'There are many workers at my father's house who have all the food they want with plenty to spare. They lack nothing. Why am I here dying of hunger, feeding these pigs and eating their slop? I want to go back home to my father's house, and I'll say to him, "Father, I was wrong. I have sinned against you. I'll never be worthy to be called your son. Please, Father, just treat me like one of your employees."' So the young son set off for home. From a long distance away, his father saw him coming, dressed as a beggar, and great compassion swelled up in his heart for his son who was returning home. So the father raced out to meet him. He swept him up in his arms, hugged him dearly, and kissed him over and over with tender love. Then the son said, 'Father, I was wrong. I have sinned against you. I could never deserve to be called your son. Just let me be.' The father interrupted and said, 'Son, you're home now!' Turning to his servants, the father said, 'Quick, bring me the best robe, my very own robe, and I will place it on his shoulders. Bring the ring, the seal of sonship, and I will put it on his finger. And bring out the best shoes you can find for my son. Let's prepare a great feast and celebrate. For this beloved son of mine was once dead, but now he's alive again. Once he was lost, but now he is found!' And everyone celebrated with overflowing joy. Now, the older son was out working in the field when his brother returned, and as he approached the house he heard the music of celebration and dancing. So he called over one of the servants and asked, 'What's going on?' The servant replied, 'It's your younger brother. He's returned home and your father is throwing a party to celebrate his homecoming.' The older son became angry and refused to go in and celebrate. So his father came out and pleaded with him, 'Come and enjoy the feast with us!' The son said, 'Father, listen! How many years have I been working like a slave for you, performing every duty you've asked as a faithful son? And I've never once disobeyed you. But you've never thrown a party for me because of my faithfulness. Never once have you even given me a goat that I could feast on and celebrate with my friends like he's doing now. But look at this son of yours! He comes back after wasting your wealth on prostitutes and reckless living, and here you are throwing a great feast to celebrate—for him!' The father said, 'My son, you are always with me by my side. Everything I have is yours to enjoy. It's only right to celebrate like this and be overjoyed, because this brother of yours was once dead and gone, but now he is alive and back with us again. He was lost but now he is found!'" (Luke 15:11-32)

JUNE 2

My dear child, watch out for the distractions that keep you from me. These things in themselves seem innocent, but they keep you from me and use up your time. I don't want you to miss out on what I want to show you. Watch out also for the restlessness that takes place on the inside of you when you come to spend time with me. This is where you will have to labor to enter the rest by laying it all down, all the busyness, burdens and cares. Your trust will grow over time as you will see that I will take good care of you. I see that many times you think you are in this alone, because this is what you are use to, but I am always with you. I am with you in the good times and the bad. I do love when you come to me and I have your attention. Ask for reassurance for whatever it is you need, I will help you trust me.

SCRIPTURES TO MEDITATE ON:

So then we must give our all and be eager to experience this faith-rest life, so that no one falls short by following the same pattern of doubt and unbelief. (Hebrews 4:11)

We look away from the natural realm and we fasten our gaze onto Jesus who birthed faith within us and who leads us forward into faith's perfection. His example is this: Because his heart was focused on the joy of knowing that you would be his, he endured the agony of the cross and conquered its humiliation, and now sits exalted at the right hand of the throne of God! (Hebrews 12:2)

JUNE 3

My desire to father you is way beyond what you are hoping or expecting. When I look at you, I long to reassure your troubled heart that I know you need a father. I see your hurt and your struggles from not having a father that was there for you to nurture and bless you. I want you to experience my heart felt longing to father you. I will give you eyes to see where I am caring for you since you are not sure what to look for. I will give you ears to hear so that you know that it is your father who is talking to you. I will give you a heart to know me not just as your God, but also as your Father. There is so much to look forward to in our lives together. I can tell you right now that you will not be disappointed in this adventure with me. My plans are so good that you might have a hard time believing what I have in store for you if I told you.

SCRIPTURES TO MEDITATE ON:

I will give them a heart to know me, that I am the Lord. They will be my people, and I will be their God, for they will return to me with all their heart. (Jeremiah 24:7 NIV)

Lovers of God have been given eyes to see with spiritual discernment and ears to hear from God. (Proverbs 20:12)

Look at the nations and watch—and be utterly amazed. For I am going to do something in your days that you would not believe, even if you were told. (Habakkuk 1:5 NIV)

JUNE 4

Every one of those troubling thoughts, every one of those fears, every concern bring to me. It is good for you to come and bear your soul. I want to minister to your heart the comfort it needs, that you would know that it is I, your Papa, who is holding you. I want you to experience my love when you feel like you failed again for the hundredth time. I want you to even experience my love when you are strug-gling to believe what I am telling you. I will help you when you are feeling bad and are struggling with forgiving your-self. I want you to take it serious about forgiving yourself. I want you to know that when I look at you I see you, my daughter, my son, and I am not looking at what is wrong with you. Just receive and enjoy the love that flows out of my heart to you. I want to make my love and truth about how I long to father you a reality in your daily life. I believe in you, I respect you, and I am not upset with you.

SCRIPTURE TO MEDITATE ON:
Give us even more greatness than before. Turn and com-fort us once again. My loving God, the harp in my heart will praise you. Your faithful heart toward us will be the theme of my song. Melodies and music will rise to you, the Holy One of Israel. I will shout and sing your praises for all you are to me—Savior, lover of my soul! I'll never stop telling others how perfect you are while all those who seek my harm slink away ashamed and defeated! (Psalm 71:21-24)

JUNE 5

The truth is I am here to father you day and night. You might say, "Yes I know this!" but is it truly your experience? You don't have to beg or plead with me to know me. I am right here waiting to show you who I am, who I want to be for you, just how much I want to father you. It's okay, you can truly relax, don't worry that you will ever lose my love or that I will ever change the way I feel about you. Even if you are not acting right, making a bad choice, not turning to me, I will never stop loving you. Even if you never change, my love for you remains. This is the experience I want you to have with me. You will know a love that you never imagined existed. You have some ideas, but there is so much more of my love that you will know as you turn to me and I open up windows of revelation for you.

SCRIPTURES TO MEDITATE ON:

Jesus, the Anointed One, is always the same—yesterday, today, and forever. (Hebrews 13:8)

I the Lord do not change. So you, the descendants of Jacob, are not destroyed. (Malachi 3:6)

Then you will be empowered to discover what every holy one experiences—the great magnitude of the astonishing love of Christ in all its dimensions. How deeply intimate and far-reaching is his love! How enduring and inclusive it is! Endless love beyond measurement that transcends our understanding—this extravagant love pours into you until you are filled to overflowing with the fullness of God! (Ephesians 3:18-19)

JUNE 6

I want to go into your past and touch the places, from the time you were a baby, where you needed comfort, where there were no bonding or healthy attachments. Places that you don't remember that have made you feel unlovable. I will come to those places where you attached yourself to false comforts, where you didn't know what else to do and turned to whatever you could to feel better. Nothing is too hard for me, and as your Father I can go into your past to bring healing and restore to you all that the enemy tried to take from you. I will come to you and give you what you didn't receive so you can know that your world will be okay. I do all kinds of miracles, so this is not too hard for me to make happen for you.

SCRIPTURE TO MEDITATE ON:

Send me a miraculous sign to show me how much you love me, so that those who hate me will see it and be ashamed. Don't they know that you, Lord, are my com-forter, the one who comes to help me? (Psalm 86:17)

JUNE 7

I would like for you to think about what a loving father naturally does. He naturally protects you without you asking him. Most fathers enjoy talking to their children and they know they can freely talk to him without wondering will he be silent, will he be too busy, will he want to talk to me? Most fathers naturally love to be close to their children, so they will want to spend time with them, doing things their children love to do. It is naturally in a loving father's heart to want to give generously to his kids, to bless them, to want to see them happy. Loving fathers will be sensitive to their children's feelings and care about listening to their thoughts and ideas. This is just a small inkling of what I am like as your Father. As your heart receives my healing, it will be opened to a whole new place of knowing a love that you have never known, and discovering your identity as my sons and daughters.

SCRIPTURES TO MEDITATE ON:

If you, imperfect as you are, know how to lovingly take care of your children and give them what's best, how much more ready is your heavenly Father to give wonderful gifts to those who ask him? (Matthew 7:11)

JUNE 8

When you are not used to receiving the blessing from anyone, it might be hard for you to comprehend the blessing that I have for you. I am waiting to bless you, waiting for your heart to be open to me. You have no idea just how wonderful it is. I am here to tell you, my child, that I want you to have this, to relax, receive and enjoy it. I understand your struggle to believe me when I tell you that I have wonderful things for you. You know much about the hardship and suffering in this life, and that has been more real to you than anything else, but I have so much more for you in the way of blessings. Don't be afraid, I will help you with all that I am telling you so that you can trust that I have only good thoughts and good plans for you. I want you to feel secure in knowing I am a Father who takes good care of His children.

SCRIPTURE TO MEDITATE ON:

So don't ever be afraid, dearest friends! Your loving Father joyously gives you his kingdom realm with all its promises! (Luke 12:32)

JUNE 9

I know many of my children are not familiar with a loving father-daughter/son relationship. Fathers have a great impact on how you feel about yourself . I see you wondering, I see your thoughts about how does it feel, what does it look like to have a father in your life. I know the very idea of having a father stirs up many unwanted memories and interferes with the way you see me. I will never demand that you to trust me. I understand and will work with you to show you that I am a very different kind of father. I will show you what it is like to have a Father in your life that wants to be involved with everything that concerns you. When you know the truth about me and I give you a heart to know me, you can finally enjoy being my sons and daughters.

SCRIPTURES TO MEDITATE ON:

Call to me and I will answer you and tell you great and unsearchable things you do not know. (Jeremiah 33:3)

"I will be a true Father to you, and you will be my beloved sons and daughters," says the Lord Yahweh Almighty. (2 Corinthians 6:18)

I will give them a heart to know me, that I am the Lord. They will be my people, and I will be their God, for they will return to me with all their heart. (Jeremiah 24:7)

JUNE 10

I do not condemn you. Be mindful of what happens when you are feeling bad to see who it is condemning you. It is not me and I would like for you to be aware of what is happening. I told you if your heart condemns you, I never will. I am not here to make you feel bad. There are enough forces at work trying to separate you from me, when you are not living up to what you are expecting of yourself. But in reality, you can do nothing apart from me. Jesus only did what he saw me doing, and he knew I would be right there for him to strengthen him and I will do the same for you. One thing I want to make clear, is that I will never condemn you. My heart longs for you to know the complete opposite of that, and that is how much I accept you when you fail. Take time to ask my Holy Spirit to make this real to you the next time you fall short and listen for my voice instead of the voice of the accuser.

SCRIPTURES TO MEDITATE ON:

So now the case is closed. There remains no accusing voice of condemnation against those who are joined in life-union with Jesus, the Anointed One. (Romans 8:1)

Whenever our hearts make us feel guilty and remind us of our failures, we know that God is much greater and more merciful than our conscience, and he knows every-thing there is to know about us. (1 John 3:20)

JUNE 11

Feeling condemnation clouds your thinking and distracts you from the truth of what I am saying about you. All through my Word, I tell you many times how I never condemn you and you might just pass right over it not being aware of how you have grown accustomed to feeling bad. When you are struggling with sin, and you are messing up, this is the very moment I would like you to turn to me and stay with me. It is here that I can help you believe how much I love you, how much I believe in you.. Stay with me, don't let these troubling emotions pull you away from me and isolate you from others. This is the place you will find out all about my commitment to you and this is something I do not want you going another day without knowing. I see your heart and I know it is a heart that loves me, and this is what makes me a very happy Papa.

SCRIPTURE TO MEDITATE ON:

Lord, so many times I fail; I fall into disgrace. But when I trust in you, I have a strong and glorious presence protecting and anointing me. Forever you're all I need! (Psalm 73:26)

JUNE 12

There are things I want you to know about me as your Father. Did you know I love fussing over you and care about all your needs? Do you know I value what you have to say and I know your voice well? Did you know that when we are together, I don't care about rushing off because I love being with you and treasure our time together? Did you know I know your favorite meals, and I know the things about you that make you feel loved the most? Did you know you can come to me any time and I will never turn you away? I want you to see me in all of your life, even the little things that you think I don't notice about you. You are my child and I am so aware of you and all that concerns you. I look forward to the day where you feel free to run and just jump onto my lap and call me your Papa.

SCRIPTURE TO MEDITATE ON:

Lord, you know everything there is to know about me. You perceive every movement of my heart and soul, and you understand my every thought before it even enters my mind. You are so intimately aware of me, Lord. You read my heart like an open book and you know all the words I'm about to speak before I even start a sentence! You know every step I will take before my journey even begins. (Psalm 139:1-4)

JUNE 13

You are relying too much on your own thoughts when you are comparing yourself to others. When you go to that place, you go alone, and you end up believing lies that keep you from having a healthy perspective. I don't want you to going there anymore. When comparing yourself, you will never have an accurate picture of what you come up with. This is not good for you. I would never be unfair in what I give to each one of my children. You started feeling this when you did not have your needs met early in life and when there was nobody there to tell you how special you were. You needed to hear words that would speak life, destiny and blessing over you. Look for me today and listen carefully, you will hear me calling your name and speaking these very words over you. I want you expecting more because there is always more I have for you.

SCRIPTURES TO MEDITATE ON:

Your words are so powerful that they will kill or give life, and the talkative person will reap the consequences. (Proverbs 18:21)

Of course, we wouldn't dare to put ourselves in the same class or compare ourselves with those who rate themselves so highly. They compare themselves to one another and make up their own standards to measure themselves by, and then they judge themselves by their own standards. What self-delusion! (2 Corinthians 10:12)

JUNE 14

Just as you long to be fathered, so I long to father you. Some of my children are walking around not even aware of how much they need a father and mother's comfort in their lives, but I am. They didn't have it and have no idea what it is like and what it is they need. It would be easy to miss me coming to you as your Father because you do not know what that looks like since you have not had the expe-rience of an earthly father who nurtures and comforts you. So when I am coming to my children to bless them, they don't see it as me coming to them, they call it a good day, or just lucky. Pray that the eyes of your heart will be opened, so you can see the kind of Father I want to be to you. When you see what I am really like, I know it will be easier for you to receive me as your Father. You are so worth waiting for.

SCRIPTURE TO MEDITATE ON:

I pray that the light of God will illuminate the eyes of your imagination, flooding you with light, until you experience the full revelation of the hope of his calling—that is, the wealth of God's glorious inheritances that he finds in us, his holy ones! (Ephesians 1:18)

JUNE 15

I want you to be able to walk with a deep sense inside of how much I value you as my child. I know it is hard to comprehend that someone could love you so much that they would give up their child for you, but I knew this would be the way to reach you and convince you of how much I love you. This was the only way I could have my children back in my life like it was in the beginning with Adam and Eve. I was not angry when they had to leave the garden, my heart was breaking knowing we would not be together the same way we had been. The enemy has tried to destroy the image of a father here on earth so that my children would have a distorted view of what I am like. My son came into the world to show you that I am your Father, but many cannot see this because of their father pain. If you ask my Holy Spirit, he will show you. You need to find this out for yourself from my Holy Spirit because no man can reveal me as your Father. Come in and see me, my child, and close the door. There is much I want to talk to you about and there is much that I want to show you. I look forward to being with you and can't wait to see the look on your face when you realize all that I am telling you.

SCRIPTURE TO MEDITATE ON:

But whenever you pray, go into your innermost chamber and be alone with Father God, praying to him in secret. And your Father, who sees all you do, will reward you openly. (Matthew 6:6)

JUNE 16

Just as the lies that have hurt you all this time, my truth is more powerful than any lie that has ever hurt you. I tell you that you are lovable. I tell you that you are never alone, and these are words of life I speak over you from my heart. I said I would never leave you and you can know this truth because I will help you to know it. I also know why you struggle with believing in me after being left behind in many situations, and this is where you started to believe that you were all alone and unlovable. Jeremiah 33:3 says, "Ask me and I will show you things you know not." So I encourage you to ask me and I will show you that I am your Father that will never leave you and who knows just how lovable you are. It will bring comfort to your heart as I make myself known to you, as you learn the truth about me. As the truth sets you free, we rejoice and celebrate this side of heaven as we watch you coming into new places that you have not yet discovered.

SCRIPTURE TO MEDITATE ON:

For if you embrace the truth, it will release more freedom into your lives. (John 8:32)

JUNE 17

Jesus is telling and wanting you to go see your Father and close the door. He wants you to go. He is saying that he knows that I want to spend time with you, that I want to see you. He knows how great it will be for you to come see me because of what he already knows and has already experienced with me. He wants you to be blessed as well. He knows that you need this time alone with me. He knows that I created the universe, and I created you, but I am telling you that I want you to know that the universe would not be the same without you in it. I want to let you know how important you are to me. Only good will come out of our time together. Ask me, and I will show you what kind of Father I am, what kind of Father I want to be to you.

SCRIPTURE TO MEDITATE ON:

"Call to me and I will answer you and tell you great and unsearchable things you do not know." (Jeremiah 33:3 NIV)

JUNE 18

Good morning, my dear child. I was waiting for you to wake up, so I could talk to you about your day. I have noticed how quickly you can move into focusing on your problems and let that fill your time. You know it uses your energy to worry or try to figure it all out and I see you at times turning to false comforts out of habit. So, I have an exercise that will help you, and I think you should take advantage of this. Practice casting all of your cares on me and I will give grace to help you release them. Another part of the exercise is that each time you pick them back up, lay them back down. Just enjoy how good it feels to give your cares to a father that cares deeply for you, and then run off and enjoy your day. When you give them to me know that they are in good hands, know that I will take good care of you. The more you see how reliable I am, the more it will put your heart at rest. You have a good Father who takes His kids seriously. I am fully present and completely devoted to you.

SCRIPTURE TO MEDITATE ON:

Pour out all your worries and stress upon him and leave them there, for he always tenderly cares for you. (1 Peter 5:7)

JUNE 19

I call you my child and I call you worthy. I call you blessed and I call you lovable. I call you healthy and whole, and I call you to life. These are the things you need to hear. I want you to be aware of your needs and see me as a dedicated Father that is meeting them. You have grown out of touch with what you need and just got used to living this way. As I call you to life you will be blessed to experience being cared for just because you are loved. I want to care for you without you even asking. There is a lot that goes on in my world that I want my children to see. I am actively involved even though you might not see me this way. I was involved all through the bible and that hasn't changed, so that means I am still involved with you. Ask for eyes to see, and a healed heart, so that you can let go of things that get in the way.

SCRIPTURES TO MEDITATE ON:

I am convinced that my God will fully satisfy every need you have, for I have seen the abundant riches of glory revealed to me through the anointed one, Jesus Christ! (Philippians 4:19)

The Lord is close to all whose hearts are crushed by pain, and he is always ready to restore the repentant one. (Psalm 34:18)

JUNE 20

I am so happy to see you, my child. I just want to remind you that I am still thinking of you and that I am will take care of your healing. Healing not just for your body, but also for your heart. I want you to know the comfort of my arms around you holding you close. You have no idea how I long to hold you close in that time. I see over the years how you have learned to bury your pain, not knowing what to do with it. The heart is so neglected and that is where the issues of life come from. Whatever part of your heart hurts, that part you won't be able to give to me and it will interfere with you relating to others. You will hold back from the closeness you desire and need. Don't be afraid, I am right here to help you. I am your father that is present, involved and dedicated to my kids. As you experience me in your daily lives as reliable and faithful to you, that is what will help you to open your heart again. My faithfulness is bigger than life itself.

SCRIPTURES TO MEDITATE ON:

But you, O Lord, your mercy-seat love is limitless, reaching higher than the highest heavens. Your great faithfulness is infinite, stretching over the whole earth. (Psalm 36:5)

So above all, guard the affections of your heart, for they affect all that you are. Pay attention to the welfare of your innermost being, for from there flows the wellspring of life. (Proverbs 4:23)

Beloved friend, I pray that you are prospering in every way and that you continually enjoy good health, just as your soul is prospering. (3 John 1:2)

JUNE 21

I hear your questions, I see your thoughts. I am so aware of everything about you and what is going on in your life. I see you wondering how I am going to father you from heaven. I see you wondering what my love is really like, and how much of it you can really experience and know. I tell you, if you are looking for it here, you will see dribbles of it here and there, but my love is like nothing you have ever seen or imagined. Try to be aware of putting me in a box thinking you know what it is, because it is bigger than anything you could think of. Don't look to man for it but look to me only. My Holy Spirit is here to reveal it to you. I can use man to show my love, but it is not so common here. I see that you are having a hard time comprehending the love I showed you at the cross when I gave up my son, but I can help you to believe that this was done for you. Do not rely on your own mind to figure this out but look to me and I will open your eyes to see a love that you are not used to seeing.

SCRIPTURES TO MEDITATE ON:

Trust in the Lord completely, and do not rely on your own opinions. With all your heart rely on him to guide you, and he will lead you in every decision you make. Become intimate with him in whatever you do, and he will lead you wherever you go. Don't think for a moment that you know it all. (Proverbs 3:5-6)

For this is how much God loved the world—he gave his one and only, unique Son as a gift. So now everyone who believes in him will never perish but experience everlasting life. (John 3:16)

JUNE 22

Others might have a hard time with your failures, and so may you, but I do not. I have no problem with you when I see these things in your life that you do not like. I want you to experience my total acceptance of you in this place of struggling. I ask you to be aware of closing your heart to me, instead of coming close to my waiting arms of comfort. Just as your focus is not on your children's faults or mistakes, so my attention is on the awesome person that I made you to be. Do not listen to the lie that you are all alone when you feel this way because you are not, I am always with you. So, I ask you to be aware of how you react to yourself and to just learn to receive your Papa's love. Just relax and enjoy the love that is in my heart when I look at you. I will help you to receive my love when you are feeling unworthy, all you have to do is ask.

SCRIPTURE TO MEDITATE ON:

Love is large and incredibly patient. Love is gentle and consistently kind to all. It refuses to be jealous when blessing comes to someone else. Love does not brag about one's achievements nor inflate its own importance. Love does not traffic in shame and disrespect, nor selfishly seek its own honor. Love is not easily irritated or quick to take offense. Love joyfully celebrates honesty and finds no delight in what is wrong. Love is a safe place of shelter, for it never stops believing the best for others. Love never takes failure as defeat, for it never gives up.
(1 Corinthians 13:4-7)

JUNE 23

I have given you an imagination so I would like you to use it to imagine this. See me as your Father who is so happy to see you coming home that I run to you and I am not looking at your sins like you are. You can see that just the sight of you thrills my heart. Try and imagine that you are this important to me, that I would love you like this. Try and imagine me sending out orders to my workers to get a lavish party set up for you, just to show you how special you are to me. Imagine me giving you my ring as a promise to you that I will always love you and every time you look at it you will be reminded of my love. This is the safe place that I want you to know and experience, not just in your imagination. This is the place I have for you as my sons and daughters, the place that I want you to call home.

SCRIPTURES TO MEDITATE ON:

Jesus replied, "Loving me empowers you to obey my word. And my Father will love you so deeply that we will come to you and make you our dwelling place. (John 14:23)

So the young son set off for home. From a long distance away, his father saw him coming, dressed as a beggar, and great compassion swelled up in his heart for his son who was returning home. So the father raced out to meet him. He swept him up in his arms, hugged him dearly, and kissed him over and over with tender love. (Luke 15:20)

JUNE 24

My dear child, come to me when you are afraid, you will find I will always be here to take you under my wings. I am not a demanding Father, but fully understanding of you and the person you are. So I am not demanding that you trust me when your heart needs healing. When I say I am close to the broken hearted, I come close to comfort and heal. I know how to reach you, to bring you healing, and to show you that I am your Father who is worthy of your trust and your heart, but this will all come in time. You will know how very special you are to me as you experience my acceptance of where you are at. My children put heavy yokes on themselves and each other that are not from me. I am excited as I watch you grow in making the connection that I truly am your Father and that you know deep in your heart that you belong to me.

SCRIPTURE TO MEDITATE ON:

For all that I require of you will be pleasant and easy to bear. (Matthew 11:30)

JUNE 25

I hear the cry of your heart and I hear every word that comes out of your mouth. To be heard is a deep human need. I am listening to my children on my end, but many are not always sure if I am really listening, not realizing how important they are to me. You might be zealously praying, or you might be just going on about many things not aware that I am right here in this moment listening. There is a tendency to get intercession mixed up with begging. Intercession is Spirit-led, begging comes from an orphan wound. I do not want my kids begging me when my heart delights to bless and make things happen for them. I just want to be your Father, to connect with you. Just like you, I too have to be patient, waiting for my children to heal and open up to me.

SCRIPTURE TO MEDITATE ON:

You are so intimately aware of me, Lord. You read my heart like an open book and you know all the words I'm about to speak before I even start a sentence! You know every step I will take before my journey even begins. (Psalm 139:3-4)

JUNE 26

I want you to know how much I want you to have your healing so that you feel comfortable coming to me, and your life can return to the wonderful plans that I had for you from the start. I know all that you have been through and how hard it has been. When you are feeling bad and wondering where I am, all you need to do is ask me. I will let you know that I am still here, that I am still thinking about you, and every time you ask me the answer will always be the same. I am not planning on ever leaving your side. I am as close to you as a baby is to its mother, and even closer than that, and that will never change. Think about how I know everything about you and even things you wished that I hadn't, and that doesn't change the way I feel about you. I will always want to be near you. In a world that is full of constant changes, know that there is nothing that will ever get me to change the way that I love you.

SCRIPTURES TO MEDITATE ON:

Now He comes closer, even to the places where I hide. He gazes into my soul, peering through the portal as He blossoms within my heart. The one I love calls to me. (Song of Solomon 2:9-10)

God, you're such a safe and powerful place to find refuge! You're a proven help in time of trouble—more than enough and always available whenever I need you. (Psalm 46:1)

JUNE 27

My children have no idea just how much I love them. They know a few things about me and have experienced degrees of my presence and they say they know my love, but in the deepest part of their hearts there is unrest. Look for me in those places where you have many questions, where you are troubled. In the midst of feeling alone in your struggles, I will bring to you a supernatural security. When you know how much I love you, the things that use to bother you will no longer have an effect on you. You will no longer be afraid of the many things that came into your life as a child. And now till this day these fears try to push you around and dictate your life. You don't always recognize them because once again, you grew up with fear and it has become a way of life. My love goes beyond anything you know here, so just ask my Spirit to show you, and he will reveal who I am. You will experience a love that will secure your world!

SCRIPTURE TO MEDITATE ON:

We have come into an intimate experience with God's love, and we trust in the love he has for us. God is love! Those who are living in love are living in God, and God lives through them. (1 John 4:16)

JUNE 28

Did you ever just think about how much I am here in the moment with you? How I am right here in this place at this very moment? Well, it is true, and there is no other place I would rather be. You can read this with your mind, but you need the eyes of your heart opened to see and experience me for yourself. You need to get out of your head, and ask me to show you just how guarded your heart is with me. Many times I see you wanting to come near but you only go so far. I also want you to stop trying to figure it all out before you can accept this incredible love that I offer you. I know for many of my children they just cannot believe that someone could love them as much as I do. I want you to know the lengths that I went through to communicate my love. Nothing in this life is more true than the love that I expressed for you at the cross, where my son endured unbelievable pain because he knew that was the only way to get you back to me.

SCRIPTURES TO MEDITATE ON:

We look away from the natural realm and we fasten our gaze onto Jesus who birthed faith within us and who leads us forward into faith's perfection. His example is this: Because his heart was focused on the joy of knowing that you would be his, he endured the agony of the cross and conquered its humiliation, and now sits exalted at the right hand of the throne of God! (Hebrews 12:2)

Trust in the Lord completely, and do not rely on your own opinions. With all your heart rely on him to guide you, and he will lead you in every decision you make. (Proverbs 3:5)

JUNE 29

If you did not get what you needed early in life you are going to have a hard time believing how valuable a person you are. You have believed lies about yourself for a very long time, lies that tell you that your life doesn't matter. You have run around trying to prove that you are of worth by doing things that you think will make you feel relevant. People you know and things you do only give a temporary feeling of significance, but it doesn't last. I created you and I know how to bring about what you need to fill all those empty lonely places from your past. The truth that I speak over you and into you is that your life does matter, so much more than you could ever possibly imagine. So don't run around trying to impress man because I am the only one that can meet the deepest longing of your heart. I am your Father who is willing, able and wanting to do this for you.

SCRIPTURE TO MEDITATE ON:

You can buy two sparrows for only a copper coin, yet not even one sparrow falls from its nest without the knowledge of your Father. Aren't you worth much more to God than many sparrows? (Matthew 10:29)

JUNE 30

O how I long to take you under my wings and have you stay here with me! When you are hurting and not used to being comforted, you go to a sad and lonely place. I want you to be aware of my arms longing to comfort you. You don't have to be strong anymore, you don't have to be afraid anymore, you don't have to face life alone anymore. It's okay, just relax and receive, you don't have to do anything or be anything to get me to love you or help you. All I want you to do now is just receive all the security you should have had as a child, and all that I long to give you. I want you to experience my longing to take you under my wings and care for you, something maybe you are not familiar with. I encourage you to come to me for my help in the area of receiving and opening your heart to me. I will help you to know that I am faithful, that I am safe, and that I have a love for you like no other. I long to take you under my wings and help you feel what you have been longing for.

SCRIPTURE TO MEDITATE ON:

He tends his flock like a shepherd: He gathers the lambs in his arms and carries them close to his heart; he gently leads those that have young. (Isaiah 40:11 NIV)

JULY

JULY 1

What do you think will happen when you come to see me and close the door? Think about this. You come to see your Father because Jesus said to come and see me. He knew something that he wanted us to know. So you are coming in to see me and you are closing the door. How does that make you feel knowing that I am here waiting for you? If the thought of that stirs up any uncomfortable emotions, just realize that those emotions stem from any unhealed pain in your earthy relationships. I come to you in the midst of your brokenness and pain to bring you healing, to bring to you all that you lost over the years. I want you to feel comfortable coming to me, to freely and boldly come to me. Think about my son. I did this for you so you know there isn't anything I wouldn't do to reach your heart.

SCRIPTURES TO MEDITATE ON:

The Lord is close to all whose hearts are crushed by pain, and he is always ready to restore the repentant one. (Psalm 34:18)

So now we come freely and boldly to where love is enthroned, to receive mercy's kiss and discover the grace we urgently need to strengthen us in our time of weakness. (Hebrews 4:16)

The Father now judges no one, for he has given all the authority to judge to the Son. (John 5:22)

JULY 2

I can see that as you are experiencing me more and more as your Father, that you get a little afraid that it might be too good to be true. The things that you felt you missed out on and now long for, you can really have with me. Bring this fear to me and meditate on my truth. I see you have been listening to lies about me, yourself and others because of the hurts in your past. I am not only here for you now in this moment, but here to stay and here to heal all those places that left you feeling orphaned. I also see your heart and I know that it is a heart that is for me. Don't you worry, I know just what to do to convince you of how much you mean to me.

SCRIPTURES TO MEDITATE ON:

For the Father tenderly loves you, because you love me and believe that I've come from God. (John 16:27)

So now we come freely and boldly to where love is enthroned, to receive mercy's kiss and discover the grace we urgently need to strengthen us in our time of weakness. (Hebrews 4:16)

JULY 3

I want you to live and I want your heart to heal so you can walk in the fullness of all that I have for you. Not knowing what to do with the pain over the years has caused you to bury it deep inside. This was well hidden and you just coasted through life, ignoring and forgetting the pain. But all the outward signs are there showing the condition of your heart. Being on guard to protect yourself, keeping a certain amount of distance from others, and relying too much on yourself instead of me, your Father. You are going through life not understanding what is really taking place in your heart and why. It's important for you to look at this so I can bring the healing to those broken places, so I can give you the comfort you never received. Maybe you haven't thought too much about being comforted, but everyone needs this, no matter how old you are.

SCRIPTURES TO MEDITATE ON:

So above all, guard the affections of your heart, for they affect all that you are. Pay attention to the welfare of your innermost being, for from there flows the wellspring of life. (Proverbs 4:23)

I will give them an undivided heart and put a new spirit in them; I will remove from them their heart of stone and give them a heart of flesh. Then they will follow my decrees and be careful to keep my laws. They will be my people, and I will be their God. (Ezekiel 11:19-20 NIV)

He heals the wounds of every shattered heart. (Psalm 147:3)

JULY 4

Do you know I am sitting right here in this very moment with you? And do you know how much I enjoy being with you? Please take time to think on this for a while and let it sink in that I am very serious about wanting you to believe this. I think you are an amazing child of mine and so love being around you. My children are not aware of how present I am for them. There is more of an awareness of their surroundings, their struggles, and what's in front of them. Many are not aware of how much I want to father them. I left my Holy Spirit for you, and he will help you to know about me and teach you all things. He will also bring you the comfort you need. See this, my dear child, as my way of caring for you.

SCRIPTURES TO MEDITATE ON:

And I will ask the Father and he will give you another Savior, the Holy Spirit of Truth, who will be to you a friend just like me—and he will never leave you. The world won't receive him because they can't see him or know him. But you will know him intimately, because he will make his home in you and will live inside you. (John 14:16-17)

But when the truth-giving Spirit comes, he will unveil the reality of every truth within you. He won't speak his own message, but only what he hears from the Father, and he will reveal prophetically to you what is to come. (John 16:13)

JULY 5

You have learned well over the years to take care of yourself. You also learned to guard your heart, and you learned to do both well, so much that it keeps you from coming to and relying on me. It hasn't been easy, but you made it through, you did well to adjust to whatever pain you had to deal with. But now, my dear child, I am here to let you know I will take good care of you if you let me. You don't need to be strong anymore. I will be strong for you. I encourage you to let go and relax for a change. You will see for yourself that I will come through, that I am here for you in ways that you never realized before now. I want you to find the comfort you need from me and not the things you used to turn to.

SCRIPTURES TO MEDITATE ON:

But he answered me, "My grace is always more than enough for you, and my power finds its full expression through your weakness." So I will celebrate my weaknesses, for when I'm weak I sense more deeply the mighty power of Christ living in me. So I'm not defeated by my weakness, but delighted! For when I feel my weakness and endure mistreatment—when I'm surrounded with troubles on every side and face persecution because of my love for Christ—I am made yet stronger. For my weakness becomes a portal to God's power. I have become foolish to boast like this, but you have forced me to do it, when you should have boasted in me instead. For there is nothing I lack compared to these "super-apostles" of yours, even though I am nothing. (2 Corinthians 12:9-11)

He offers a resting place for me in his luxurious love. His tracks take me to an oasis of peace, the quiet brook of bliss. That's where he restores and revives my life. He opens before me pathways to God's pleasure and leads me along in his footsteps of righteousness so that I can bring honor to his name. (Psalm 23:2-3)

July 6

I want to remind you once again that my relationship with you is more important than anything you could ever do for me here. You are my children; my very own family and I don't want you to be running around working for me when you don't know me as your Father. If you don't know me as your Father, how will you know how I feel about you or what I am telling you to do for me. Many know about me, but do not know me personally. My love goes way beyond your human understanding. There is on going revelation, on going bonding and growing together. My children put much emphasis on working for me, spiritual gifts, and being a good Christian, but I tell you this day that I want to be close to you. I just want to have my family together again.

SCRIPTURES TO MEDITATE ON:

I have made you known to them, and will continue to make you known in order that the love you have for me may be in them and that I myself may be in them. (John 17:26)

On the day of judgment many will say to me, 'Lord, Lord, don't you remember us? Didn't we prophesy in your name? Didn't we cast out demons and do many miracles for the sake of your name?' (Matthew 7:22)

JULY 7

Please, don't ever think that I wouldn't want to talk to you. I see you struggling so much within yourself when you don't have to. Maybe you are not aware yet how much I am here to help you. Please, don't ever think that I am too busy for you. Please, don't ever think that you couldn't come to me, that you are bothering me. I would drop everything for you. You have learned independence well, but I speak healing to the heart of that child whose needs were unmet, who learned early in life how to survive. There is a lot of pain in the world, but I have a lot of healing for my children. Even in this moment, just soak in the healing I have for you. I love to see your face light up as your childlike trust is restored and you realize that you can truly, finally rest in my arms.

SCRIPTURES TO MEDITATE ON:

Love never brings fear, for fear is always related to punishment. But love's perfection drives the fear of punishment far from our hearts. Whoever walks constantly afraid of punishment has not reached love's perfection. (1 John 4:18)

Who could ever separate us from the endless love of God's Anointed One? Absolutely no one! For nothing in the universe has the power to diminish his love toward us. Troubles, pressures, and problems are unable to come between us and heaven's love. What about persecutions, deprivations, dangers, and death threats? No, for they are all impotent to hinder omnipotent love. (Romans 8:35)

JULY 8

I want to speak to that lie that keeps nagging you and telling you that you are not okay. I want to speak to your heart to pull your attention to me and off others and what they think. Do you have any idea that you can know me as your loving, doting Father who will give you just what you need in the midst of all your struggling with yourself? I want to make this your reality. I am the one who will father you back to life. When you are driven to prove to yourself that you are okay, hiding from others because your heart needs more healing to handle their criticism, I will be right here to let you know that I think you are pretty special. I want you to be kind to yourself as you heal, as I restore you back into the person I originally created you to be, before the world beat you up and told you who you were. Be encouraged, my child, as you also realize that you are not alone in this, there are so many others that have the same painful struggles.

SCRIPTURE TO MEDITATE ON:

We all experience times of testing, which is normal for every human being. But God will be faithful to you. He will screen and filter the severity, nature, and timing of every test or trial you face so that you can bear it. And each test is an opportunity to trust him more, for along with every trial God has provided for you a way of escape that will bring you out of it victoriously. (1 Corinthians 10:13)

JULY 9

I love when you come to see me. I love our time together because I love being with you and I will keep telling you this until you believe me. We don't have to talk about ministry, problems or anything else unless you want to. My hope for you, my dear child, is that you will receive this truth into your heart of how much I enjoy you, how I see you as the very special, beautiful, and the kind person that I made you to be. Just as any good parent loves being with their children, so that is a small picture of what kind of Father I am. I feel that I can't say it enough just how I feel about you and just how I love being around you. The truth is that I am so much more involved with you then you realize, even after you leave our time together.

SCRIPTURE TO MEDITATE ON:

But whenever you pray, go into your innermost chamber and be alone with Father God, praying to him in secret. And your Father, who sees all you do, will reward you openly. (Matthew 6:6)

JULY 10

My dear child, I ask you today to consider these things that I want to share with you. I really don't want you to focus on what you don't like about yourself. You are spending your time in a place that makes you sad and I am not even looking at those things. Let me remind you of the things I love about you. I love your laughter, and the excitement in your eyes when you realize that I am answering you. I love the way you respond to me when I am trying to get your attention. I love that you want to please me, even though I am already pleased with you. I love that when you get back up after you fall, as soon as you see my affirming smile that tells you I believe in you. I love the person I created you to be and I want you to love her/him too. Self-rejection and self-hatred is not what I want for you. I ask you to receive from me all that it is you need to help you see yourself the way I see you. I loved you before you knew me and when your life was messy I went after you. This should show you how much I love you, and I don't want you stressing about getting it right.

SCRIPTURES TO MEDITATE ON:

But Christ proved God's passionate love for us by dying in our place while we were still lost and ungodly! (Romans 5:8)

For the Father tenderly loves you, because you love me and believe that I've come from God. (John 16:27)

JULY 11

I want you to know how happy I am to see you when you walk through that door. Ask me for the eyes to see and the ears to hear, so you can experience this with me. Ask me for a heart that is healed and responsive to me. I have all of this for you, and long to comfort all the pain you are feeling. I see at times you struggle with believing that I am the kind of father that waits for you to respond, the kind of father that will never give up on you. I said in my word that I would give them a heart to know me, so know that I am working this exact thing in you. I see your heart and I hear your crying out on the inside for answers. I tell you that you have been heard by your Father, who is always listening, even before you speak.

SCRIPTURES TO MEDITATE ON:

I will give them a heart to know me, that I am the Lord. They will be my people, and I will be their God, for they will return to me with all their heart. (Jeremiah 24:7 NIV)

I will give them an undivided heart and put a new spirit in them; I will remove from them their heart of stone and give them a heart of flesh. Then they will follow my decrees and be careful to keep my laws. They will be my people, and I will be their God. (Ezekiel 11:19-20 NIV)

July 12

My dear, dear child, I have been watching you praying and worrying, and fretting and wondering. When you look at your circumstances, you lean toward your natural thinking and start worrying. I am not upset with you because you worry, but I want you to know that you are wasting your time as you will see up ahead that I have been working behind the scenes the whole time, and all that fretting was for nothing. At times it may seem like nothing is happening, but I remind you now and will keep reminding you that I am a good Father. Just learn to rest my child in the truth that I am big enough to make things happen for you. If you only knew the love that I feel in my heart, you would not concern yourself with so many things that consume your time and energy. I am always here, you are never a bother, so get into the habit of turning to your Father who is always happy to see you.

SCRIPTURE TO MEDITATE ON:

So then, forsake your worries! Why would you say, 'What will we eat?' or 'What will we drink?' or 'What will we wear?' (Matthew 6:31)

JULY 13

Of all the things you can know about me, the thing that I want you to clearly know is that I want you to freely come to me at any time. You don't have to impress me with anything, and you don't have to be concerned about what I am thinking if you had a bad day and you are not handling things well. I see those things, but I am more interested in you and our time together. Don't let anything get in the way or hold you back from coming to see me. I will keep talking to you about this for as long as it takes, until you can trust what I am telling you. The greatest display of love that you have ever witnessed here in this life, will give you only a small picture of what my great big love looks like.

SCRIPTURES TO MEDITATE ON:

For the greatest love of all is a love that sacrifices all. And this great love is demonstrated when a person sacrifices his life for his friends. (John 15:13)

For he enjoys his faithful lovers. He adorns the humble with his beauty and he loves to give them the victory. (Psalm 149:4)

JULY 14

I do appreciate that you want to do something for me, but there is something you need to know before you get busy doing my work. You learned a long time ago that others were pleased when you did your work well, especially when others benefited from the fruit of your labor. Maybe this was the only time you were affirmed and noticed. So now you have learned that doing good works is a way to get your needs met and you have bought into the lie that this is what you need to do to be okay and accepted. Now I am here to convince you that you are so loved without doing a thing for me. You need to know this, or you will be doing things for the wrong reasons. You need to know that I love you no matter what your accomplishments are, even if you never did a thing for me. Anything you do can come out of your relationship with me. I am after my children to be close to them, not to use them. Pray to know this truth, that each one of you has a special place in my heart.

SCRIPTURES TO MEDITATE ON:

Don't set the affections of your heart on this world, or in loving the things of the world. The love of the Father and the love of the world are incompatible. For all that the world can offer us, the gratification of our flesh, the allurement of the things of the world, and the obsession with status and importance, none of these things come from the Father but from the world. (1 John 2:15-16)

On the day of judgment many will say to me, 'Lord, Lord, don't you remember us? Didn't we prophesy in your name? Didn't we cast out demons and do many miracles for the sake of your name?' (Matthew 7:22)

JULY 15

I want you to know you are first and foremost my top priority. Know that the things that are troubling you, I already have it all taken care of. Once you are convinced that I am a good Father whose concern is for his children, your heart will be able to rest just as a child rests in his mother's arms. My heart is for my kids and I will never stop caring for you. If there is any pain from your earthly parents, it will keep you from seeing all that I am for you, all that I want to give you. It will hinder that part of your heart that needs to trust me, and just make it harder for you to rest in what I am telling you. I encourage you to come and talk freely to me about all that is troubling you, your fears, your insecurities, or whatever it is that you need to talk about . Just rest, my dear child, it's going to be okay.

SCRIPTURE TO MEDITATE ON:

For it was always in his perfect plan to adopt us as his delightful children, through our union with Jesus, the Anointed One, so that his tremendous love that cascades over us would glorify his grace—for the same love he has for his Beloved One, Jesus, he has for us. And this unfolding plan brings him great pleasure! (Ephesians 1:5-6)

July 16

Come sit next to me and listen closely, my dear child. I want to share my heart with you about the way you see yourself. Many things were spoken over you, labels put on you that were not from me. I know who you are because I made you, so let me tell you what I see. I know just how unique and very interesting you are. I would not have made you any other way than the person I had in mind when I created you, and I love the person. Don't listen to those voices from the past that tried to hurt you. I am here for you in this moment to break the power of those words spoken over you. I speak life over all those broken places and I bless you my dear child with a healed heart that can freely give itself to me and others and so that you may receive all that I have for you.

SCRIPTURES TO MEDITATE ON:

I, even I, am he who comforts you. Who are you that you fear mere mortals, human beings who are but grass. (Isaiah 51:12 NIV)

The Lord is close to all whose hearts are crushed by pain, and he is always ready to restore the repentant one. (Psalm 34:18)

JULY 17

I am happy that you now know that I am your real Father. Just as a loving parent knows what is best for his child, so I know what is best for you. So when I tell you to be still and know that I am God, it would be very good for you to be still and become aware of me and who I am for you. When you are still, you will see more of me and less of your problems here in front of you. Always remember, my dear child, that before you were born I loved you. I am waiting for your heart to know and experience this truth. I encourage you to listen to your heart and let go of trying to figure this all out on your own, especially since you do not see the whole picture of what I am doing at the time. When you can know your heart, you will walk into the much fuller life that I have always planned for you.

SCRIPTURES TO MEDITATE ON:

Above all else, guard your heart, for everything you do flows from it. (Proverbs 4:23)

Yet I totally trust you to rescue me one more time, so that I can see once again how good you are while I'm still alive! (Psalm 27:13)

JULY 18

I know that you are not used to being loved the way I love you, but when you get a taste of my love you will know that it is exactly what your heart needs. I am here and always have been to heal the broken places, to heal the broken trust and restore to you the years that you have lost, the years that the locusts ate. I will father you in ways that you have never known, and I will love you the way you should have been loved. I will do this for you! You wonder how, but your Father happens to be God and as you look to me I will give you all that you missed out on and more. I ask you to consider these things that I am telling you, for I speak this to you from my heart.

SCRIPTURES TO MEDITATE ON:

To the fatherless he is a father. To the widow he is a champion friend. To the lonely he gives a family. To the prisoners he leads into prosperity until they sing for joy. This is our Holy God in his Holy Place! But for the rebels there is heartache and despair. (Psalm 68:5-6)

My father and mother abandoned me. I'm like an orphan! But you took me in and made me yours. (Psalm 27:10)

Drink deeply of the pleasures of this God. Experience for yourself the joyous mercies he gives to all who turn to hide themselves in him. (Psalm 34:8)

JULY 19

I hear you asking me to speak to you, but I see you struggling to believe that you will be able to hear me. The things that you have believed about me are getting in the way of your ability to hear my voice. When I do speak and you hear me, you are always surprised, but if you think about it, I am your Father so why would I not want to speak to you? So my children talk to me and don't really expect me to answer. They are not expecting me to talk to them the way a loving father talks to his kids. The truth is, I love talking to my children about anything and everything. Ask me to help you to see me differently, to see me as I truly am. I need you to invite me because I will not just barge into your life knowing that you have been hurt by others who have done that. So, I wait patiently for you, my dear child. And remember my Son is right here praying for you.

SCRIPTURE TO MEDITATE ON:

I pray that the Father of glory, the God of our Lord Jesus Christ, will impart to you the riches of the Spirit of wisdom, and the Spirit of revelation to know him through your deep intimacy with him. I pray that the light of God will illuminate the eyes of your imagination, flooded you with light, until you experience the full revelation of the hope of his calling, that is, the wealth of God's glorious inheritances that he finds in us his holy ones. (Ephesians 1:17-18)

JULY 20

I know that there have been many things that you have had to face in your life that were not easy. There is one thing that will help you and that is to know that I always wanted you. I formed you in your mother's womb, and you are always in my thoughts. I think about how you are doing in your struggles and I am just waiting here for you to turn to me for help. But in this moment, if there was one thing I would want to convince you of, it is how much you are wanted, how much I am here to care for you, to make you feel special, and to make you know my favor. I want you to know this more than anything you could ever experience or learn about in this life here. When I think of you, my heart overflows with joy, and there is no other place I would rather be than with you.

SCRIPTURE TO MEDITATE ON:

Before I formed you in the womb I knew you, before you were born I set you apart; I appointed you as a prophet to the nations. (Jeremiah 1:5 NIV)

JULY 21

The truth, my child, is that I have not forgotten you. In the waiting, you might get tempted to believe that lie, but I am in the waiting and at work and you will see eventually that there was a purpose for the things that happened. When you don't see me and know what I am doing, I see you being tempted to believe that you are not important to me, or that I am not listening to you. But I don't mind reassuring my children because I know how hard it can be for them. You only see in part, but one day you will look back and see what I was doing behind the scenes for you. Maybe you were hurt by others forgetting you, but my promise to you is that I will never forget you.

SCRIPTURES TO MEDITATE ON:

See, I have engraved you on the palms of my hands, your walls are ever before me… (Isaiah 49:16)

Can a mother forget the baby at her breast and have no compassion on the child she has borne? Though she may forget, I will not forget you! (Isaiah 49:15 NIV)

JULY 22

Look for me throughout your day and you will be surprised at all the places you see me where you hadn't noticed before. Look for me coming to you not just as your God, but also as your Father. I come to you in your quiet time, but I don't leave you there. I am always with you, even though you might not be connected to that reality. My care is constant and I will heal your father wound that keeps you from trusting this. I will heal the wound that tells you that I will not be here for you. The father wound keeps you from fully taking in my blessing. I can do things for you that you specifically ask for, but you will not see it as my love coming to you if your heart is not fully open. So remember, my child, to look for me, for I will show up in ways so that you know it is me. My heart is always longing to come to you, just to be with you and I love when you are aware and respond to me.

SCRIPTURES TO MEDITATE ON:

This is what the Scriptures say: Things never discovered or heard of before, things beyond our ability to imagine—these are the many things God has in store for all his lovers. (1 Corinthians 2:9)

So, what does all this mean? If God has determined to stand with us, tell me, who then could ever stand against us? (Romans 8:31)

JULY 23

When I tell you to not rely on your own understanding, but to trust with your heart, I am saying here that your eyes are seeing, but the heart is not really hearing me. I tell you that you can't trust me with your mind, only with your heart. Your mind wants to understand everything to feel secure and be in control when there is pain hidden in the deep places of your heart. I am aware of your heart and the broken places, the pain of rejection, the pain of isolation, and when I tell you that I am close to the broken hearted, it is hard for you to take that in. The more your eyes are open and healing comes to your heart, the more you will be able to take in all that I am telling you, and the more you will be able to grasp the reality of how much you are loved.

SCRIPTURES TO MEDITATE ON:

Become intimate with him in whatever you do, and he will lead you wherever you go. Don't think for a moment that you know it all. (Proverbs 3:6)

So now we come freely and boldly to where love is enthroned, to receive mercy's kiss and discover the grace we urgently need to strengthen us in our time of weakness. (Hebrews 4:16)

JULY 24

I know you keep struggling to understand my love for you, but I ask you to get out of your head because there is way too much chattering going on in there. I came after you when you were in sin, I loved you then and I love you now. I know all about you, your weaknesses, your flaws, and even the things you don't want others to know, and still none of that changes the love that I have for you. Many times, you have been hard on yourself when I was not even the slightest bit upset with you. I just patiently wait as you grow and heal for the moment when you will be able to move closer to me. I just ask one thing of you in this moment, and that is for you to be open to my healing love as it comes to you, so that you can see me as your Father that runs to you when I see you coming.

SCRIPTURES TO MEDITATE ON:

The Father now judges no one, for he has given all the authority to judge to the Son. (John 5:22)

But Christ proved God's passionate love for us by dying in our place while we were still lost and ungodly! (Romans 5:8)

JULY 25

My children have all kinds of ideas about me. Many times they think I don't care if I don't answer them a certain way. Nothing could be more farther from the truth. When you start to believe that I am good all the time, you will know than that there is a very good reason behind everything I do concerning you. I long for you to hear me singing over you, wanting to calm your fears about me and about life. I long for you to know I hear every word that you speak, and I know the very sound of your voice when you call to me. Just know and be comforted in knowing that I will come through no matter how things look at the moment. This is the kind of Father I am, and this is the kind of Father I want you to know.

SCRIPTURE TO MEDITATE ON:

The Lord your God is with you, the Mighty Warrior who saves. He will take great delight in you; in his love he will no longer rebuke you, but will rejoice over you with singing. (Zephaniah 3:17 NIV)

July 26

I am the God who made heaven and earth, but I am also your Father. I see you looking at me many times wondering what I am doing, wondering if I am too busy to take time for you. I am waiting for you to receive from me all that I have for you. I see you struggling to believe that I have all the time in the world for you and all the rest of my children. Maybe some of your struggle is with the idea that your God is your Father, who knows everything about you and still wants to be with you. Try and get out of the habit of trying to understand it all, trying to make sense of what is going on, and for a change just receive. Open up your heart and receive from your Father who adores you. You will see in time you can trust what I am offering to you!

SCRIPTURES TO MEDITATE ON:

Father, I ask that you allow everyone that you have given to me to be with me where I am! Then they will see my full glory—the very splendor you have placed upon me because you have loved me even before the beginning of time. (John 17:24)

This is what the Lord says—your Redeemer, who formed you in the womb: I am the Lord, the Maker of all things, who stretches out the heavens, who spreads out the earth by myself. (Isaiah 44:24 NIV)

JULY 27

I have been loving you all along, but until the places in your heart are open and healed it will be very easy to miss. I see you asking, "What Lord, what places in my heart?" Ask me and I will show you the places that you are not aware of, places where pain, fear, and rejection are hiding. I don't want these things hurting you any longer, and I don't want them to get in the way of our relationship. The healing and restoration I have for you is something I take very seriously, and I have very carefully planned. The greater the pain, the greater is the healing and my loving acceptance is for you. Wherever you are, my love is always trying to reach you.

SCRIPTURES TO MEDITATE ON:

Catch for us the foxes, the little foxes that ruin the vineyards, our vineyards that are in bloom. (Song of Solomon 2:15 NIV)

But I will restore you to health and heal your wounds. declares the Lord. (Jeremiah 30:17)

JULY 28

Just as Jesus was full of emotion for my children, so this is a picture of me and how I feel about you. I am not disconnected and distant, but right there with you as you go through this life. I see your sad times, your disappointments, and your fears about who really cares about you. There is a love that I have for you that you have not begun to even realize. My love will never let you go and it is stronger than death (Song of Solomon 8:6). You will be just as excited as I am when you realize how I long to father you and share a deeper closeness. I am safe, my dear child, and I will never hurt you. When you are afraid, just remember my Son and what I had to let him go through in order to reach you.

SCRIPTURE TO MEDITATE ON:

When Jesus looked at Mary and saw her weeping at his feet, and all her friends who were with her grieving, he shuddered with emotion and was deeply moved with tenderness and compassion. He said to them, "Where did you bury him?" "Lord, come with us and we'll show you," they replied. Then tears streamed down Jesus' face. (John 11:33-35)

JULY 29

I want to remind you it's my Father's heart that is always trying to reach you to let you know I am here. I want you to know that while I am your God, it is important for you to realize that I am also your Father. As your Father, I want you to see my heart is to bless you beyond what you may have considered. Maybe you are one of my children that never received this from their natural father, so you have no idea what it is, you don't have a frame of reference. Try to imagine that you really do have a Father who loves you and is doing all He can to reach you with this truth. Don't be afraid to come to me and ask for my blessing, I am so ready to pour out on you a blessing that is bigger than life. Just as Jabez was not afraid to ask me to bless him and enlarge his territory, so I ask you to come to me with the same boldness.

SCRIPTURE TO MEDITATE ON:

With my whole heart, with my whole life, and with my innermost being, I bow in wonder and love before you, the holy God! Yahweh, you are my soul's celebration. How could I ever forget the miracles of kindness you've done for me? You kissed my heart with forgiveness, in spite of all I've done. You've healed me inside and out from every disease. You've rescued me from hell and saved my life. You've crowned me with love and mercy. You satisfy my every desire with good things. You've supercharged my life so that I soar again like a flying eagle in the sky! (Psalm 103:1-5)

July 30

Now that you are getting to know me, that I am your real Father, I would like for you to know that you can come to me anytime. It would be good for us to talk about your fears, since they have interfered with your life. I am here to free you from your fears like I did my son David. I can only help you if you are willing to talk to me. Don't be afraid, I will never shame you for what you feel. Maybe you are afraid to let others see you out of fear of rejection, if they knew how you really felt, and what you are really thinking, you are certain they will react to you. You can tell me anything, I will always accept you. My people are so afraid to let others see their true selves. You never need to be afraid with me, I want you to feel at home with me, knowing you can run to your Papa whenever you need me.

SCRIPTURE TO MEDITATE ON:

Listen to my testimony: I cried to God in my distress and he answered me. He freed me from all my fears! Gaze upon him, join your life with his, and joy will come. Your faces will glisten with glory. You'll never wear that shame-face again. When I had nothing, desperate and defeated, I cried out to the Lord and he heard me, bringing his miracle-deliverance when I needed it most. The angel of the Lord stooped down to listen as I prayed, encircling me, empowering me, and showing me how to escape. He will do this for everyone who fears God. (Psalm 34:4-7)

JULY 31

I love when you turn to me for what you need. You don't have to be afraid any longer. You will see that as you do grow through this and find that I am always here for you, your heart will learn that it is safe to trust me. Just as the enemy tried to destroy you over the years, how much more will I be here for you to bring you into the life I always intended for you to have. I want you to know a life of a peaceful quiet trust inside knowing that you are always safe with me, you are always accepted, and you are always celebrated. Just know that I want this to be your reality, a reality that is moving more and more away from trying to do life on your own. It is not always going to be a struggle, so get ready to go into new places with me. Get ready for the time of your life.

SCRIPTURE TO MEDITATE ON:

Never doubt God's mighty power to work in you and accomplish all this. He will achieve infinitely more than your greatest request, your most unbelievable dream, and exceed your wildest imagination! He will outdo them all, for his miraculous power constantly energizes you. (Ephesians 3:20)

AUGUST

AUGUST 1

So I have been talking to you about being the kind of father that loves to bless his kids with all kinds of good things, all kinds of surprises. Even if you think of the wildest, seemingly impossible dream, I am able to do so much bigger than that. What I want you to know is that I really have this for you. Sure life has its trials, but I also have days planned for you full of good things. I am just waiting for you to come to me to find this out for yourself, to taste and see that I am a good Father. Again, I want to remind you that I will never push my way into your life, but as soon as you open the door for me to come in, I will be right there eagerly waiting to be with you.

SCRIPTURE TO MEDITATE ON:

But whenever you pray, go into your innermost chamber and be alone with Father God, praying to him in secret. And your Father, who sees all you do, will reward you openly. (Matthew 6:6)

AUGUST 2

I have heard you say, "I don't know how He is going to do this, but we need a miracle," when you were facing some impossible looking situations. You stood there in shock as I came through in ways you never expected. Now you say this again about my love for you. You wonder about me, and you say once again, "How is He going love me from heaven?" I made heaven and earth and I know how I am going to help you feel deep inside the feelings that a child feels when they receive the love and nurturing that they need. I see you wondering if you are as special as the next guy. I am your God and your Father, and I ask you, my dear child, is there anything too hard for me? I will convince you, I will fill all those empty places where your needs were not met.

SCRIPTURES TO MEDITATE ON:

The Lord loves seeing justice on the earth. Anywhere and everywhere you can find his faithful, unfailing love! (Psalm 33:5)

I pray that the light of God will illuminate the eyes of your imagination, flooding you with light, until you experience the full revelation of the hope of his calling— that is, the wealth of God's glorious inheritances that he finds in us, his holy ones! (Ephesians 1:18)

I am the Lord, the God of all mankind. Is anything too hard for me? (Jeremiah 32:27 NIV)

AUGUST 3

I am so glad you came to see me today because there is something that I have been wanting you to do. I will help you if you let me. I ask you to be aware of the way you see yourself when you mess up and to learn to be kind to you and know that I don't look at you any differently. If you turn to me when you are feeling like a failure, you will always find my love there. You need to see for yourself that I am not a punishing God. I will never change my mind about you. The way you see yourself or treat yourself is how you will be with others. Ask me to show you how I see you, I am sure that you will be surprised when your eyes are opened, and you see how I feel. You have risked your heart with others, but I am the safest place for you to risk your heart.

SCRIPTURES TO MEDITATE ON:

The Lord alone is our radiant hope and we trust in him with all our hearts. His wrap-around presence will strengthen us. (Psalm 33:20)

You are to love the Lord Yahweh, your God, with every passion of your heart, with all the energy of your being, with every thought that is within you, and with all your strength. This is the great and supreme commandment. And the second is this: 'You must love your neighbor in the same way you love yourself.' You will never find a greater commandment than these. (Mark 12:30-31)

AUGUST 4

You really need your eyes opened to see how much I am in your world and in your life. My yoke is easy, and my burden is light, so I am saying to you that I don't want it to be hard for you when you are faced with life's challenges. I will give you the security you need as you realize I am right here, and that I am bigger than anything you are facing. Just know as soon as you turn to me I promise to be there and promise to take good care of you. I understand your struggle to trust and I reassure you that my love will calm that part of your heart. I am here to nurture you and I will patiently wait until you are able to come to me. Your adult mind knows this is true, but you cannot open your heart fully to me until the little child inside of you receives what it needs to feel safe again.

SCRIPTURES TO MEDITATE ON:

Lord! I'm bursting with joy over what you've done for me! My lips are full of perpetual praise. I'm boasting of you and all your works, so let all who are discouraged take heart. Join me, everyone! Let's praise the Lord together. Let's make him famous! Let's make his name glorious to all. Listen to my testimony: I cried to God in my distress and he answered me. He freed me from all my fears! Gaze upon him, join your life with his, and joy will come. Your faces will glisten with glory. You'll never wear that shame-face again. When I had nothing, desperate and defeated, I cried out to the Lord and he heard me, bringing his miracle-deliverance when I needed it most. (Psalm 34:1-6)

For all that I require of you will be pleasant and easy to bear. (Matthew 11:30)

AUGUST 5

My love is greater than anything you could possibly imagine, but my Holy Spirit can help you to know and experience it. The healing I have for you is at the cross and it is always available; it never ends, and it never runs out. That same power that raised my son from the dead lives in you and it is the same healing power that my son demonstrated that is healing you. I love being with my children, but I sit and wait for the day that their guarded hearts are healed enough and they know they can freely come to me anytime . As I heal your broken hearts and wash off the shame and unworthiness you feel, you will see for yourself the kind of father I am. You will find what you need from me as I reparent you. I will not disappoint you.

SCRIPTURES TO MEDITATE ON:

Yes, God raised Jesus to life! And since God's Spirit of Resurrection lives in you, he will also raise your dying body to life by the same Spirit that breathes life into you! (Romans 8:11)

I pray that you will continually experience the immeasurable greatness of God's power made available to you through faith. Then your lives will be an advertisement of this immense power as it works through you! This is the mighty power that was released when God raised Christ from the dead and exalted him to the place of highest honor and supreme authority in the heavenly realm! (Ephesians 1:19-20)

Blessed and prosperous is that nation who has God as their Lord! They will be the people he has chosen for his own. (Psalm 33:12)

AUGUST 6

I have been loving you all along, and there were many times you were not aware of it. I loved you in the past when you did not know me and when you were making many bad decisions. I loved you when you sinned against me and your brothers. I love you now in the midst of your struggling to figure all this out and wondering how you will ever fully trust me. I will never stop loving you, and never will I ever give up on trying to reach you, trying to convince you. Do not try and understand this on your own. Only with my Spirit can you know the height, width, and depth of my love for you. He will help you to grasp this love that is not common to man.

SCRIPTURES TO MEDITATE ON:

He offers a resting place for me in his luxurious love. (Psalm 23:2)

And I pray that you, being rooted and established in love, may have power, together with all the Lord's holy people, to grasp how wide and long and how high and deep is the love of Christ, to know this love that surpasses knowledge....that you may be filled to the measure of all the fullness of God. (Ephesians 3:17)

The Lord appeared to us in the past, saying: "I have loved you with an everlasting love; I have drawn you with unfailing kindness." (Jeremiah 31:3 NIV)

AUGUST 7

My children walk around so unaware of their need to be fathered. Fatherlessness has left a huge hole in the hearts of my children. The painful memories leave you with crip-pling emotions and an almost constant war on the inside. At times you may feel an emptiness, a restlessness that keeps you busy or in addictions; anything to not have to feel the pain of the past. But I am here to fill that hole and meet all those unmet needs, to give you a healthy attachment to me, something every child needs to have identity and security. So now you can live to your fullest expression of life that I put in you . I can and I will do this for you. When you turn to me you will find the Father you always wanted and I will be so happy to have you in my life.

SCRIPTURES TO MEDITATE ON:

The Lord is close to all whose hearts are crushed by pain. (Psalm 34:18)

You will seek me and find me when you seek me with all your heart. (Jeremiah 29:13)

AUGUST 8

I have given you an imagination to help you to relate to me. So now I ask you to sit there and close your eyes and try to imagine this place that we will go to. I take you to a warm, cozy home with shutters at the windows, happy flowers and ivy growing up the wall. A fireplace is burning while your mom is cooking your favorite meal and your dad is out in his workshop, excited about what he is making you. Dad comes in for supper and he is so happy to see you, that he picks you up and swings you around. You sit around the table and Dad listens to every word you say as if he couldn't get enough of you. At bedtime, Mom is there singing to you with her comforting arms wrapped around you to drive away all the bedtime fears. Just take this in and imagine the peace and love in this moment, not a care in the world, knowing you are completely loved and cared for. I will help you to know this kind of love and make it your reality.

SCRIPTURES TO MEDITATE ON:

Jesus replied, "Loving me empowers you to obey my word. And my Father will love you so deeply that we will come to you and make you our dwelling place." (John 14:23)

The Lord your God is with you, the mighty warrior who saves. He will take great delight in you; in His love he will no longer rebuke you, but will rejoice over you with singing. (Zephaniah 3:17)

AUGUST 9

Don't be afraid, my dear child. Ask my Holy Spirit for help to see me as the kind of Father who is big and strong, yet tender and compassionate when it comes to his children. I want you to know that I am always looking out for you. I am your father that you can run to when you are afraid, and I will scoop you up and hold you close. I am your Father that you can run to when you are hurting, or if you just need someone to listen and understand you. I enjoy being your Dad. I enjoy giving you my time and love our times together. I love watching your face light up when I give you gifts and things that you like . Whatever it is that you are going through at the moment, I want you to feel secure in knowing that I will give you all the reassurance you need.

SCRIPTURES TO MEDITATE ON:

So do not fear, for I am with you; do not be dismayed, for I am your God. I will strengthen you and help you; I will uphold you with my righteous right hand. (Isaiah 41:10 NIV)

So don't ever be afraid, dearest friends! Your loving Father joyously gives you his kingdom realm with all its promises! (Luke 12:32)

AUGUST 10

There was never a time when I didn't love you, for I have always loved you. There was never a time that I didn't want you, for I have always wanted you. Just as I opened the Red Sea and walked on water, it is not too hard for me to make this truth go to the innermost part of your being where you struggle with trusting a love that you are not use to. No matter how dark your sin was, no matter how much you didn't want me in your life, I never stopped loving you. Over the years since you turned to me, you started to believe you had to be good and work for me in order for me to be pleased with you. Ask me and I will show you because I want this settled in your heart that you don't have to do anything to get me to love you. I want to remove and heal the pain that has gotten in the way of how you see me.

SCRIPTURE TO MEDITATE ON:

But God still loved us with such great love. He is so rich in compassion and mercy. Even when we were dead and doomed in our many sins, he united us into the very life of Christ and saved us by his wonderful grace! He raised us up with Christ the exalted One, and we ascended with him into the glorious perfection and authority of the heavenly realm, for we are now co-seated as one with Christ! (Ephesians 2:4-6)

AUGUST 11

I think you are spending too much time looking at the mess in your life. I want you to just relax and accept the truth that you are okay with me no matter how bad you think you are. I love you, even when you don't get it, even when you don't quite love yourself. What is it that you are feeling bad about right now? That thing will never change my love for you. Man reacts, but I do not. I am not sur-prised about your shortcomings. I just want to get through to you that I am here to stay and that nothing about you will ever make me change my mind. You don't have to hide from me, nor be afraid that I will ever reject you. So just try and learn to be patient with yourself as you work through these things and find your way to me.

SCRIPTURES TO MEDITATE ON:

See if there is any path of pain I am walking on, and lead me back to your glorious, everlasting ways…the path that brings me back to you. (Psalm 139:24)

So now the case is closed. There remains no accusing voice of condemnation against those who are joined in life-union with Jesus, the Anointed One. (Romans 8:1)

August 12

Another thing I want to mention to you is that it is important for you to find me in your mess, so that you can experience my unconditional love there. It's in this place that you will be convinced. You hear it with your ears, you read it in the books, but you need to experience my love in the middle of your guilt, shame and condemnation. Nothing else settles it like the presence of my love. All these things you felt bad about for so long and the shame that you carried, I took care of on the cross. You are free, my dear child. I don't want you feeling bad another moment. Just enter into this moment with me and see me washing off all the junk, fussing over you, and know that I am so excited to see you blossom, to watch you walk into all the wonderful things I have planned for you.

SCRIPTURES TO MEDITATE ON:

But he was pierced for our transgressions, he was crushed for our iniquities; the punishment that brought us peace was on him, and by his wounds we are healed. (Isaiah 53:5 NIV)

The Father now judges no one, for he has given all the authority to judge to the Son. (John 5:22)

August 13

Was I not there for you in the past? Think of all the times I pulled you through, when I showed up to reassure you. I was there then, and I am still here with you now. I have never left you and I never will. I will always keep my word to you, and you can count on that. I long to be a haven for you in the midst of the battle. Remember that I am not only God who created heaven and earth, but I am also your Father that cares about every detail of your life. Come, talk to me about what weighs on your heart. Come, share your concerns, your thoughts with me. Remember also that my healing does not dribble from the cross; it is a steady flow that is always there for you. I am a generous Father and love to lavish my goodness on you.

SCRIPTURE TO MEDITATE ON:

Pour out all your worries and stress upon him and leave them there, for he always tenderly cares for you. (1 Peter 5:7)

AUGUST 14

Don't waste your time and energy trying to figure out how to make things happen or spend hours worrying about the problem, because I already know how I am going to work this out for you. When you can trust me with this, you will see that I always have your best interests in mind. I know what you need, and I know what you want. You are limiting me and slowing up the process when you try to make these things work on your own. You only see in part, but if you ask me, I will show you things that you don't know. There is always a very good reason behind my timing for all things. I am a good Father and only want good for my children. So, rest my child, and remember that I am working behind the scenes.

SCRIPTURE TO MEDITATE ON:

If you, imperfect as you are, know how to lovingly take care of your children and give them what's best, how much more ready is your heavenly Father to give wonderful gifts to those who ask him. (Matthew 7:11)

AUGUST 15

My children say they know I love them, but I know their hearts and see that they are not fully convinced. You can say you know I love you and not really know it. You hear about it from others but you need to find out for yourself what my love is all about for you. I know you catch glimpses of me but quickly lose touch when looking at all that is going on in your life. Think about your children and how much you love them, how much you want to be in their lives, this will help you understand that this is how I feel about you. I would love to be more involved in your life but you have to open the door to let me in. I am waiting for the day when you will realize just how much I love you and that I am the Father that you always longed for. I will always be with you on your journey as you struggle through at times learning the truth about me. You have listened to the lies for a very long time now, and I would like you to consider listening to the truth about what I am telling you.

SCRIPTURES TO MEDITATE ON:

Fix your heart on the promises of God and you will be secure, feasting on His faithfulness. (Psalm 37:4)

Jesus, the Anointed One, is always the same—yesterday, today, and forever. (Hebrews 13:8)

If you hear my words and refuse to follow them, I do not judge you. For I have not come to judge you but to save you. (John 12:47)

AUGUST 16

When you talk to me about being my child, it melts my heart. It moves me beyond anything else. It is true; I am really your Father, and you are my sons and daughters. I am so excited about being your Father and I really enjoy being around you. These are the things that I want you to know and I will make real for you. I tell you, my child, you can know this truth and you can experience my love that will change your world as you know it. The love that you thought you would never have, I have always felt for you. A big part of what I do here is healing and convincing my children that I so deeply love them. Just know there is so much more that you can know and experience with me.

SCRIPTURES TO MEDITATE ON:

See what great love the Father has lavished on us, that we should be called the children of God! And that is what we are! (1 John 3:1)

For if you embrace the truth, it will release more freedom into your lives. (John 8:32)

AUGUST 17

There are those who practice my presence, but there is something else that you should practice as well. There is a blessing when you practice focusing on my presence being there to Father you in this very moment. Dwell on that for a while, that your God is also your Father who is with you at all times. Think of everything you have ever wanted in your relationship with your mother and father and know that you can have that with me. All those years you walked around feeling so alone in your pain, unaware of how I longed to take you under my wings. There is so much I can do for you when you turn to me and realize that I am the parent who will give you what your heart needs and longs for. It may be hard for you to trust this, but ask me and see what I will do for you. Be at rest, my child, your Father is home for you.

SCRIPTURES TO MEDITATE ON:

Jesus cautioned her, "Mary, don't hold on to me now, for I haven't yet ascended to God, my Father. And he's not only my Father and God, but now he's your Father and your God! Now go to my brothers and tell them what I've told you, that I am ascending to my Father—and your Father, to my God—and your God!" (John 20:17)

His massive arms are wrapped around you, protecting you. You can run under his covering of majesty and hide. His arms of faithfulness are a shield keeping you from harm. (Psalm 91:4)

When Jacob awoke from his sleep, he thought, "Surely the Lord is in this place, and I was not aware of it." (Genesis 28:16 NIV)

AUGUST 18

I wash off the shame, I wash off the labels, and I wash off the burdens that you were never meant to carry. Please, just sit and enjoy being with me in this very moment. I will give you freedom and peace that you never knew. I call you by name and give you a new name, a new identity which is not new to me but new to you. It is the person I created you to be, but who got lost along the way by all that you went through. You will see that you can trust me and have all that you longed for and more. You will feel the affirming looks, the approving smile, the tender hugs, and the accepting arms that are there to pick you up when you fall. The constant presence of your Father is what you need from me to secure your world. Please don't ever think you are bothering me; I want you to come to me. I will never turn you away.

SCRIPTURES TO MEDITATE ON:

Instead of your shame you will receive a double portion, and instead of disgrace you will rejoice in your inheritance. And so you will inherit a double portion in your land, and everlasting joy will be yours. (Isaiah 61:7 NIV)

So now we come freely and boldly to where love is enthroned, to receive mercy's kiss and discover the grace we urgently need to strengthen us in our time of weakness. (Hebrews 4:16)

August 19

Don't be afraid to ask me anything. Don't feel that you have to be a certain way around me. I want you to come freely to me as a child would run to their Papa and jump in his lap. My desire is for you to feel comfortable enough around me that you could raid my refrigerator or even be an emotional mess. I do not have a set of rules for you to approach me. I am just so happy to see you and be with you. I encourage you to come, my child, I just want you to come. The parts of your heart that have unknowingly held you back from me I have healing for. You will see that I have always cared about all that you have been through, that I do understand your pain. I promise to be there and take good care of what you give to me. I will touch your heart with my loving kindness and you will never be the same. Watch and see what I will do for you.

SCRIPTURE TO MEDITATE ON:

He understands humanity, for as a Man, our magnificent King-Priest was tempted in every way just as we are, and conquered sin. So now we come freely and boldly to where love is enthroned, to receive mercy's kiss and discover the grace we urgently need to strengthen us in our time of weakness. (Hebrews 4:15-16)

AUGUST 20

What do you feel when you hear the name 'Father?' I know that for many people it does not stir up warm feelings. My desire is to bring life to those desolate places. I am looking forward to you getting to know me as your Father. It will be a whole new world compared to what you knew. I will be there when you are afraid, and when you need protection. I will be there when you need support and direction. I will be there taking care of all of your needs, and even your wants. I will be there to help you get back up when you fall. I will fill the emptiness inside that you feel from not having a father or mother present for you. I will not let you down as you look to me. This is what I want to give to you and this is what I want to make happen for you. Dwell on this truth for a while and let it sink in.

SCRIPTURES TO MEDITATE ON:

I have revealed to them who you are and I will continue to make you even more real to them, so that they may experience the same endless love that you have for me, for your love will now live in them, even as I live in them! (John 17:26)

For here is what the Lord has spoken to me: "Because you have delighted in me as my great lover, I will greatly protect you. I will set you in a high place, safe and secure before my face. I will answer your cry for help every time you pray, and you will find and feel my presence even in your time of pressure and trouble. I will be your glorious hero and give you a feast. You will be satisfied with a full life and with all that I do for you. For you will enjoy the fullness of my salvation!" (Psalm 91:14-16)

AUGUST 21

There are some things you just need to explore with me and find out for yourself as you experience what I am telling you. You can hear many stories from others that are encouraging, but you also need to have your own encounters with me, your very own stories . Many times, you think that you alone will make things happen, but I am the one that is looking for you and wanting to make these things happen to help you to learn to trust again. I will make the rough places smooth, and I will open the doors that are shut tight. I will heal those painful broken relationships, and I will restore what was lost. I want to birth this hope in your heart, so that you can walk in expectations of good things to come.

SCRIPTURES TO MEDITATE ON:

For I know the plans I have for you," declares the Lord, "plans to prosper you and not to harm you, plans to give you hope and a future. (Jeremiah 29:11 NIV)

When Jacob awoke from his sleep, he thought, "Surely the Lord is in this place, and I was not aware of it." (Genesis 28:16 NIV)

God, hear my cry. Show me your grace. Show me mercy, and send the help I need! Lord, when you said to me, "Seek my face," my inner being responded, "I'm seeking your face with all my heart." (Psalm 27:7-8)

AUGUST 22

As you look at my word, you can ask my Holy Spirit to help you find me in it. Jesus said that when you see him, you also see me, your Father. Look at Jesus to get a picture of me. Jesus was always hanging out with the disciples, he didn't care about hanging out with the rich and famous. They talked and ate together and he cared about people that nobody took notice of. He was not afraid to touch the man with leprosy. He could have been born in a castle, but instead he came to you in a manger. He washed the dirty feet of the disciples before he went to the cross and after he rose from the dead, he made them breakfast. So, you can see me when you look at Jesus and realize that I am the almighty God, but I am also your very own down to earth Father.

SCRIPTURES TO MEDITATE ON:

"And from now on you will realize that you have seen him and experienced him." Philip spoke up, "Lord, show us the Father, and that will be all that we need!" Jesus replied, "Philip, I've been with you all this time and you still don't know who I am? How could you ask me to show you the Father, for anyone who has looked at me has seen the Father." (John 14:7-9)

But when the Father sends the Spirit of Holiness, the One like me who sets you free, he will teach you all things in my name. And he will inspire you to remember every word that I've told you. (John 14:26)

August 23

My children can be distracted by so many things. Some of them go after the gifts, some go after ministry, some after education and the list goes on. There is nothing wrong with these endeavors, but when you pursue your relationship with me that will be the place of your greatest fulfillment. Many hide behind all of the other things because relationships have been too painful for them, and they are not aware of how much I want to bring them comfort. Many do not even know what I am talking about when I mention comfort and don't even realize how much they need it. As long as you keep turning to other things instead of facing your pain, you will not experience my comfort that is always there for you. Once you taste and see that I am good, you will know that a relationship with me is what your heart needed all along.

SCRIPTURE TO MEDITATE ON:

All praises belong to the God and Father of our Lord Jesus Christ. For he is the Father of tender mercy and the God of endless comfort. He always comes alongside us to comfort us in every suffering so that we can come alongside those who are in any painful trial. We can bring them this same comfort that God has poured out upon us. And just as we experience the abundance of Christ's own sufferings, even more of God's comfort will cascade upon us through our union with Christ. (1 Corinthians 1:3-5)

August 24

I am always so happy to see you. I hope that you will come sit with me and stay for a while. I know it's been a hard road for you, and I understand all that you have been through. I have been watching and waiting for the first sign of life as I rain down on the hard soil of your heart. As your Father, I couldn't be happier as I see new life spring forth from those guarded places that had your emotions and hopeful expectations shut down. As your Father, I couldn't be happier to see your heart responding to me as I make myself known to you. The enemy tried to hurt you but watch what I will do with this. Don't be discouraged. I know the timing of all things, and I have plans for you that just might surprise you.

SCRIPTURES TO MEDITATE ON:

This is why the Scriptures say: Things never discovered or heard of before, things beyond our ability to imagine—these are the many things God has in store for all his lovers. (1 Corinthians 2:9)

I will repay you for the years the locusts have eaten (Joel 2:25)

AUGUST 25

I do see the good, the bad and the ugly, and it does not change for one second how I see you. I also see that you are not convinced of this. You need to know that even though you don't like what you see, my love for you never changes. Sit with that for a while and just take it in. I hear you asking how could He love me after what I did, but this is the place where you need to be deeply convinced. I also hear my children say that they know that I love them, but they need to know me here in this place where they are feeling the shame of the past. Next time you are feeling bad about yourself, just come to me and ask me what I think. You just might be surprised to hear what your Papa thinks of you as I share my heart with you.

SCRIPTURE TO MEDITATE ON:

Love is large and incredibly patient. Love is gentle and consistently kind to all. (1 Corinthians 13:7)

AUGUST 26

I am not going to let fear hurt you anymore. You will know my parental care and you will walk in a new confidence knowing that your Papa is right here by your side. I know you are not used to this, but you will see me personally caring for you in ways that you were never cared for before. This is what will put your heart to rest. You don't want to miss this by focusing on your problems, nor running from them. Just as you learned to be self-sufficient and strong, now you must learn about my care and how to receive from me. You don't have to be strong anymore because I am here for you to lean on. You don't have to be afraid anymore, my love is greater than any fear you are facing. Someone can tell you to not be afraid, but it is experiencing my love that will really make you brave.

SCRIPTURES TO MEDITATE ON:

Simply join your life with mine. Learn my ways and you'll discover that I'm gentle, humble, easy to please. You will find refreshment and rest in me. For all that I require of you will be pleasant and easy to bear. (Matthew 11:29-30)

So do not fear, for I am with you; do not be dismayed, for I am your God. I will strengthen you and help you; I will uphold you with my righteous right hand. (Isaiah 41:10 NIV)

August 27

The day will come when you will walk with me realizing and believing that I am not looking at what is wrong in your life. I know your heart, and I know your struggles and it is how sincere you are about our relationship that couldn't make me happier. We will work those quirks out, but it is you coming to me that I look forward to. Most days I don't think many of my children realize how much I long to be with them. When they come to me they think that I want them to always be working for me. First, I want you to believe how important a relationship is to me, how important you are to me. Come, and let go of everything weighing on you at the moment and let's just enjoy our time together.

SCRIPTURE TO MEDITATE ON:

Look with wonder at the depth of the Father's marvelous love that he has lavished on us! He has called us and made us his very own beloved children. The reason the world doesn't recognize who we are is that they didn't recognize him. (1 John 3:1)

AUGUST 28

There are things that you are carrying that you don't need to, things that weigh on you. I will grace you to lay them down, let them go, and gently remind you of this when you pick them back up. Don't use your precious time and energy trying to figure out a solution when I am here to tell you that I have an answer and can work this out in ways that you have not thought of. You can try to make things happen, but I have a greater plan and reasons for any delayed answers. So, if you don't see me in a situation, don't get the wrong idea that I am not there working on your behalf. You can fall into a habit of worrying and fretting, or you can turn to me to heal your heart that struggles with trusting me. You have carried things for a long time, now it is time for you to be as a carefree child and let go of all that stuff that was put on you, things that you were never meant to carry.

SCRIPTURES TO MEDITATE ON:

Pour out all your worries and stress upon him and leave them there, for he always tenderly cares for you. (1 Peter 5:7)

I leave the gift of peace with you—my peace. Not the kind of fragile peace given by the world, but my per-fect peace. Don't yield to fear or be troubled in your hearts—instead, be courageous! (John 14:27)

AUGUST 29

You are so important to me, so it is hard for me to watch you struggling with yourself when feeling out of the loop with others. It will be harder to run the race if you are busy comparing yourself to them. You need to stay focused on me and what I am telling you, so you can accomplish the task at hand that I have for you. You can ask me as many times as you need to, and I will help you each time. Just look at my son and how he reached out to the seemingly insignificant ones, the ones nobody paid attention to. That is how I love. You don't need to impress me with anything. If you don't get invited to the ball, I will stay behind with you. I will do whatever it takes to convince you.

SCRIPTURE TO MEDITATE ON:

For God has proved his love by giving us his greatest treasure, the gift of his Son. And since God freely offered him up as the sacrifice for us all, he certainly won't withhold from us anything else he has to give. (Romans 8:32)

AUGUST 30

I speak to the deep fears in your heart about making mistakes. Not knowing that you were so okay with me being imperfect with the rest of the human race, a lot of energy went into striving to be good. You didn't want to take the chance of losing the love of your daddy, so you listened to the drill sergeant voice inside screaming at you to toe the line. I have allowed you to enter into a season where you made many mistakes; this was so that you could learn about my love for you there and how to accept yourself as an imperfect human being. I wanted you to learn to be tenderhearted and kind to that child inside that never knew she was okay. I speak to that child now, to that precious one and tell them it's okay to spill your milk.

SCRIPTURES TO MEDITATE ON:

So don't worry. For your Father cares deeply about even the smallest detail of your life. (Matthew 10:31)

So do not fear, for I am with you; do not be dismayed, for I am your God. I will strengthen you and help you; I will uphold you with my righteous right hand. (Isaiah 41:10 NIV)

AUGUST 31

You will see as time passes that you can trust in my care for you. I will not let things happen to you like you experienced in your past. I will be to you a refuge and fortress like you have never known. Just turn to me, so I can help you to trust what I have for you. As I take you to new places with me that you have not been to, you will be amazed at all that I have for you that you have not even begun to imagine. I tell you as your Father that you will be able to trust the blessing of things going well. I want to fill your heart with the hope, and joyful expectation you once had a very long time ago.

SCRIPTURE TO MEDITATE ON:

For here is what the Lord has spoken to me: "Because you have delighted in me as my great lover, I will greatly protect you. I will set you in a high place, safe and secure before my face. I will answer your cry for help every time you pray, and you will find and feel my presence even in your time of pressure and trouble. I will be your glorious hero and give you a feast. You will be satisfied with a full life and with all that I do for you. For you will enjoy the fullness of my salvation!" (Psalm 91:14-16)

SEPTEMBER

SEPTEMBER 1

I am the Father you have always longed for and I will give to you the love that you always needed, the love that was not there for you. I have always loved you, even when you didn't know me, even when you acted foolishly making bad choices. All those years you ignored me, I longed to be close to you and I remember the times I reached out to you grabbing your attention for a fleeting moment. I loved you then and I love you now in this very moment, and I would wait a lifetime for you. I gave my only son to reach you because I knew one day I would have your heart.

SCRIPTURES TO MEDITATE ON:

"I will be a true Father to you, and you will be my beloved sons and daughters," says the Lord Yahweh Almighty. (2 Corinthians 6:18)

And so that we would know for sure that we are his true children, God released the Spirit of Sonship into our hearts—moving us to cry out intimately, "My Father! You're our true Father!" (Galatians 4:6)

September 2

I just want to remind you how happy I am to see you. I want this to become the norm for you, to freely come and see me anytime of the day or night, whether you are happy or just falling apart. There is so much trouble in this life, but my world is not like that. I have security, peace, lots of fun, and big hugs for you. I have not been out of touch with what you have been through. I have been there when you were not aware of me. It was sad for me not to be able to connect with you as your heart was being broken. I longed to help you then but I had to wait for you and the day that I knew your heart would finally turn to me. My promise to you is that I will restore all that was taken from you. I will not push my way in, but wait for your heart to be open to receive all that I have for you. There is more, so much more to our relationship that we can have together that I look forward to.

SCRIPTURE TO MEDITATE ON:

I will repay you for the years the locusts have eaten—the great locust and the young locust, the other locusts and the locust swarm—my great army that I sent among you. (Joel 2:25 NIV)

SEPTEMBER 3

Don't feel bad when you need reassurance from me. I want you to feel confident in that you can come to your Papa anytime for whatever it is you need. I don't want you to let anything keep you away. I am always here for you. I see you struggling, feeling bad about yourself and I see you feeling alone in what you are facing. I have always been here waiting for you to invite me into your life, into your problems. Try and remember to turn to me and not to other places for comfort. Those other things cannot give you the comfort, or the answers you need. No one knows you or understands what you are all about like I do. I love the person you are and look forward to you connecting with this reality.

SCRIPTURE TO MEDITATE ON:

You formed my innermost being, shaping my delicate inside and my intricate outside, and wove them all together in my mother's womb. I thank you, God, for making me so mysteriously complex! Everything you do is marvelously breathtaking. It simply amazes me to think about it! How thoroughly you know me, Lord! (Psalm 139:13-14)

September 4

Your Father is having a big party to celebrate His children. I invited them all, but there are still some that do not realize how important they are to me. They are surprised their name is on the list because they are focused on what is wrong with them and they are still trying to be good so their Papa God will think well of them. They are surprised as they enter, and I proudly announce them as my sons and daughters and not by their titles. Some are uncomfortable because their lives and identities have been built on their titles. They do not understand what it is to be a beloved son, or a beloved daughter. They don't know who I created them to be and are still finding their identity in what they do. But I call them one by one by their names, waiting for the day that they will realize I am the one that accepts them just as they are. That I am their Father that calls them beautiful, that calls them my beloved children.

SCRIPTURES TO MEDITATE ON:

Lord, you know everything there is to know about me. You perceive every movement of my heart and soul, and you understand my every thought before it even enters my mind. You are so intimately aware of me, Lord. You read my heart like an open book and you know all the words I'm about to speak before I even start a sentence! You know every step I will take before my journey even begins. You've gone into my future to prepare the way, and in kindness you follow behind me to spare me from the harm of my past. With your hand of love upon my life, you impart a blessing to me. This is just too wonderful, deep, and incomprehensible! Your understanding of me brings me wonder and strength. (Psalm 139:1-6)

But the true Shepherd walks right up to the gate, and because the gatekeeper knows who he is, he opens the gate to let him in. And the sheep recognize the voice of the true shepherd, for he calls his own by name and leads them out, for they belong to him. (John 10:2-3)

SEPTEMBER 5

I have given to you pictures of what my love is and what it looks like in my Word. I told you that while you were in sin I loved you by giving my son to reach you and that was when you were not doing so well. I showed you how I washed the disciples' feet before I went to the cross. Listen for me calling you by your name and see me washing your feet. I made them breakfast on the beach while they were working. I loved sharing meals with them and I love being with you at the table. The 'Prodigal Father' happily ran to his son, and I want you to see that I am this happy to see you. Ask my Holy Spirit and He will help you to see this and give you the capacity to receive this incredible love that I have for you.

SCRIPTURES TO MEDITATE ON:

Jesus knew that the night before Passover would be his last night on earth before leaving this world to return to the Father's side. All throughout his time with his disciples, Jesus had demonstrated a deep and tender love for them. And now he longed to show them the full measure of his love. (John 13:1)

So the young son set off for home. From a long distance away, his father saw him coming, dressed as a beggar, and great compassion swelled up in his heart for his son who was returning home. So the father raced out to meet him. He swept him up in his arms, hugged him dearly, and kissed him over and over with tender love. (Luke 15:20)

SEPTEMBER 6

How thrilled I get the moment you are in touch with the reality that I am in this moment of your life with you. Be mindful of the things that try and pull you away from our time. I will help you with the struggles you have when you come to me, the restlessness and lack of confidence. I understand why you hold back from me, you just don't realize how much I want you in my life. It will help you tremendously when you know that I want to come to you just to be with you. You are so important to me and this is what you also need to know to help your self-worth. I am the one that can help you with all that is going on inside of you. I have carefully planned out your healing for all the broken places. You are the only one that can accept what I have for you. I will not force myself on you, but encourage you to be open so I can reparent you and nurture you back to life.

SCRIPTURES TO MEDITATE ON:

I look up to the mountains and hills, longing for God's help. But then I realize that our true help and protec-tion come only from the Lord, our Creator who made the heavens and the earth. (Psalm 121:1-2)

The Lord is close to all whose hearts are crushed by pain, and he is always ready to restore the repentant one. (Psalm 34:18)

SEPTEMBER 7

All of these things that you are concerned with or worry about I was already planning on taking care of for you. But there are hurtful things that have happened to you which interfere with your ability to see me as a Father who cares about your needs and even about the things that you want. So, you go to work independently of me trying to make things happen for yourself, you work hard and still worry. I am here to tell you that I have the healing for that part of your heart that just can't seem to connect with me. Ask me and I will show you the kind of Father I am, the kind of Father I want to be for you. I love to see your face light up when I give you the desires of your heart and you realize it is me making this happen for you.

SCRIPTURES TO MEDITATE ON:
I pray that the Father of glory, the God of our Lord Jesus Christ, would impart to you the riches of the Spirit of wisdom and the Spirit of revelation to know him through your deepening intimacy with him. (Ephesians 1:17)

So don't ever be afraid, dearest friends! Your loving Father joyously gives you his kingdom realm with all its promises! (Luke 12:32)

September 8

I would love to see you relax a little more when you come and see me. Please don't think you have to be a certain way or say something clever to impress me. I will try to convince you until you believe that I know you well, and I couldn't love you anymore than I do right now. Just know you are so okay with me even though you have imperfections and don't always seem to get it right. I am not expecting you to be more, you are just fine right now in this moment with all the things that you struggle with. What stands out to me are all the wonderful things I see in your life that I love about you. Ask me and I will tell you how I see you.

SCRIPTURES TO MEDITATE ON:

Lord, you know everything there is to know about me. You perceive every movement of my heart and soul, and you understand my every thought before it even enters my mind. You are intimately aware of me, Lord (Psalm 139:1-3)

Love is a safe place of shelter, for it never stops believing the best for others. (1 Corinthians 13:7)

September 9

Though your heart condemns you, I will never do that to you. I am not here to condemn you, but here to convince you of how special you are to me, even while I see you out there trying to get all your ducks in a row. I am not alarmed or surprised by your attitudes, or wrong thoughts of others. It will help you knowing you are fully accepted by me when you just come to me and talk to me about all these things. I will never hurt you, but I am here to be your Papa. My love and my healing will just keep coming to you, over and over, flowing like a river from my heart with acceptance and warm tender mercies. Just receive it, my dear child, just receive, it is yours.

SCRIPTURES TO MEDITATE ON:

Whenever our hearts make us feel guilty and remind us of our failures, we know that God is much greater and more merciful than our conscience, and he knows everything there is to know about us. (1 John 3:20)

"For I know the plans I have for you," declares the Lord, "plans to prosper you and not to harm you, plans to give you hope and a future." (Jeremiah 29:11 NIV)

September 10

When you look at yourself and become discouraged at what you see, your natural reaction is to ignore it and get busy. I see the original self that I made in you. I know this child, who is quite special to me. I am here to father that little one, the little one that is hiding. I want you to see what I see when I look at you. It is important for you to see this, for it will help you walk in the emotional wellness and the fullness of life that I have for you. I will not just barge my way into your life like others have done, out of respect for you, so I remind you to ask for my help and to let me in. I keep telling you these things over and over hoping that one of these times you will really hear me. So, I will just wait for you, my child, because you are so worth waiting for.

SCRIPTURE TO MEDITATE ON:
Not one promise from God is empty of power, for nothing is impossible with God! (Luke 1:37)

September 11

Be aware of the many things that vie for your attention. When you find me, that is when you find your real life. There is no security here on earth that compares to the security you will have when you realize that you are worth so much more than anything you turn to here. It is not in titles, positions, fame, wealth, or any of the distractions that keep you from me. All of these pretty bright lights are so enticing but there is no life in them; they don't hold a candle to knowing me. I am more, and I have so much more for you than this world has to offer. Even if you are going after all those other things, I will wait for you to return to me. I do love to watch your expression as you discover that I truly am your Father who is waiting at the door for you, who runs to you when I see you coming. This is the kind of Father I am.

SCRIPTURES TO MEDITATE ON:

We look away from the natural realm and we fasten our gaze onto Jesus who birthed faith within us and who leads us forward into faith's perfection. His example is this: Because his heart was focused on the joy of knowing that you would be his, he endured the agony of the cross and conquered its humiliation, and now sits exalted at the right hand of the throne of God! (Hebrews 12:2)

So the young son set off for home. From a long distance away, his father saw him coming, dressed as a beggar, and great compassion swelled up in his heart for his son who was returning home. So the father raced out to meet him. He swept him up in his arms, hugged him dearly, and kissed him over and over with tender love. (Luke 15:20)

SEPTEMBER 12

I want to heal that thing inside of you that struggles to believe that I will talk to everyone else but you. The outward signs of this are how much you look to prophets and teachers. It's not just about you getting a word from a prophet, but it's more important for you to know my heart. My heart is to talk to my children, and I want you to know this about me. You just don't know how important you are to me. You settle for crumbs when I have a royal dinner waiting for you. Many earthly fathers do not know how to talk to or be present with their children, so I know you don't have a frame of reference to draw from. I will show you that I so love being with you, and that I enjoy you. I am more present than the person you see right in front of you. This is the truth that I will make real to you. This is one of your unmet needs that I will take care of, that I will make up to you. My promise to you is that, over time, you will come to know that I keep all of my promises.

SCRIPTURES TO MEDITATE ON:

Pour out all your worries and stress upon him and leave them there, for he always tenderly cares for you. (1 Peter 5:7)

God is not human, that he should lie, not a human being, that he should change his mind. Does he speak and then not act? Does he promise and not fulfill? (Numbers 23:19 NIV)

SEPTEMBER 13

Today we will do something different from the usual. We will lay aside all worries and all pressures, and just do things that you always wanted to do as a child that you didn't get a chance to do. You can give yourself permission to have some fun because I am going to take care of your problems anyway. There is so much more to life than you know that I want to show you. I bless you from being free of all fear of stepping out and trying new things. I bless you with being free to enjoy life. I bless you with the grace and ability to release all things to me, so that you may go off and enjoy your day. It will be good for you to take the time to do this, so I encourage you to be intentional and make the decision to make it happen and not just think about it anymore.

SCRIPTURE TO MEDITATE ON:

A thief has only one thing in mind—he wants to steal, slaughter, and destroy. But I have come to give you everything in abundance, more than you expect—life in its fullness until you overflow! (John 10:10)

SEPTEMBER 14

I am your God and I am passionate about my children. There is nothing I wouldn't do for you, even giving up my son to reach you. I am always near you, wanting to father you, even in times that you are not aware of me being there. My voice is not hard to hear, but many times you are not hearing me because it is so hard for you to believe how much I want to talk to you. I don't just talk to certain people; any one of my children can learn to hear my voice. The truth is, I am here in this very moment with you talking to you right now. Ask my Holy Spirit to remove all these things that get in the way of you hearing me. My Holy Spirit is the best teacher, listen to him and he will tell you many things about me.

SCRIPTURES TO MEDITATE ON:

But when the Father sends the Spirit of Holiness, the One like me who sets you free, he will teach you all things in my name. And he will inspire you to remember every word that I've told you. (John 14:26)

My own sheep will hear my voice and I know each one, and they will follow me. (John 10:27)

SEPTEMBER 15

I see a reaction when I tell my children there is a need to be childlike. I understand the triggers from the memories of your childhood. What does it look like to be at total rest not worrying about your needs? What does it feel like to have someone there for you cooking your favorite meals, to walk in the door and have someone home who is so happy to see you?What is it like just to be able to be a child, to enjoy the wonders and simplicity of childhood and not be afraid that your world is a scary place? My child, I come to you to tenderly heal and restore. You can rest now, your Papa is here. My arms long to comfort you. When you find out the kind of Father I am, you will be able to have a confidence that your Papa will take good care of you and whatever you give to me. I will take care of the things you carried for a very long time. I look forward to you letting me father you.

SCRIPTURES TO MEDITATE ON:

O Jerusalem, Jerusalem—you are the city that murders your prophets! You are the city that stones the very messengers who were sent to deliver you! So many times I have longed to gather a wayward people, as a hen gathers her chicks under her wings—but you were too stubborn to let me. (Matthew 23:37)

May joyous grace and endless peace be yours continually from our Father God and from our Lord Jesus, the Anointed One! I am always thanking my God for you because he has given you such free and open access to his grace through your union with Jesus, the Messiah. In him you have been made extravagantly rich in every way. You have been endowed with a wealth of inspired utterance and the riches that come from your intimate knowledge of him. (1 Corinthians 1:3-5)

SEPTEMBER 16

I look forward to the day that you can feel completely at home with me, when you realize that I am sitting with you here and we can have a two-way conversation. I noticed when my children talk to me they are not realizing that I am right there listening. They talk but have no idea how much I am listening to them. This is not what I had in mind when you come in to see me and close the door. I wanted to see you and for us to have heart to heart talks together. I also know many do not know how to relate to me as Father and this is the biggest struggle of all. I want to show you who I am and open up your world to the relationship we can have. The truth is, I love talking to my kids, and as I show you who I am, you will be blessed to know that you have a Father who really cares, that I am present listening to every word you speak.

SCRIPTURES TO MEDITATE ON:

But whenever you pray, go into your innermost chamber and be alone with Father God, praying to him in secret. And your Father who sees all you do, will reward you openly. When you pray, there is no need to repeat empty phrases, praying like those who don't know God, for they expect God to hear them because of their many words. (Matthew 6:6)

You are so intimately aware of me, Lord. You read my heart like an open book and you know all the words I'm about to speak before I even start a sentence! (Psalm 139:3-4)

SEPTEMBER 17

I don't mind reminding you as many times as you need how much I want to father you. I love every minute that you are aware of me being with you. All that you feel you were robbed of growing up, I want to give you. Rejection and abandonment pain run deep and are very difficult to face, but not too hard for me to reach and heal. There is no pain too deep for me to heal. The greater the pain of rejec-tion, the greater my acceptance of you is. In every sense of the word, your home is with me and my home is with you, and I will help you to have a true sense of that deep within as I heal your orphan pain. For me, my child, it's not about riches, fame and intelligence. It is about my heart longing for you to grow in the reality of how much you mean to me, how much I love you.

SCRIPTURES TO MEDITATE ON:

Then, by constantly using your faith, the life of Christ will be released deep inside you, and the resting place of his love will become the very source and root of your life. Then you will be empowered to discover what every holy one experiences—the great magnitude of the aston-ishing love of Christ in all its dimensions. How deeply intimate and far-reaching is his love! How enduring and inclusive it is! Endless love beyond measurement that transcends our understanding—this extravagant love pours into you until you are filled to overflowing with the fullness of God! (Ephesians 3:17-19)

I will repay you for the years the locusts have eaten—the great locust and the young locust, the other locusts and the locust swarm—my great army that I sent among you. (Joel 2:25 NIV)

SEPTEMBER 18

Many of my children relate well to me when they come to me to receive their assignments to work. They believe I am pleased because of what they are doing, and it makes them feel good. They toil the fields, work the sweat of their brow, and receive recognition for a job well done, but they never asked me what I was thinking about. They could not believe that I simply just wanted to be in a loving relationship with them, unless they worked hard. They wanted me to think well of them, to make sure that I would be pleased and therefore would not leave them. Jesus only did what he saw me doing and that came out of a loving relationship with me. This would be good to think about before you run off to start your day.

SCRIPTURES TO MEDITATE ON:

So Jesus said, "I speak to you timeless truth. The Son is not able to do anything from himself or through my own initiative. I only do the works that I see the Father doing, for the Son does the same works as his Father." (John 5:19)

Who could ever separate us from the endless love of God's Anointed One? Absolutely no one! For nothing in the universe has the power to diminish his love toward us. Troubles, pressures, and problems are unable to come between us and heaven's love. What about persecutions, deprivations, dangers, and death threats? No, for they are all impotent to hinder omnipotent love. (Romans 8:35)

SEPTEMBER 19

If you could see into my world, you would never worry about another thing again. You only see with your natural eyes the problems in front of you. You hear with your ears the terrible things going on with others. The peace from my world can overflow into your life as you realize how much activity is going on behind the scenes here on your behalf. All your worries came from a time in your life when you didn't know me. The lies will hang around until you find out about me and my world. You will realize that you don't have to be afraid of the things you used to be afraid of once you know the depth of my love. Remember my plans are good, my child, and I will never hurt you.

SCRIPTURES TO MEDITATE ON:

"For I know the plans I have for you," declares the Lord, "plans to prosper you and not to harm you, plans to give you hope and a future." (Jeremiah 29:11 NIV)

For now we see but a faint reflection of riddles and mysteries as though reflected in a mirror, but one day we will see face-to-face. My understanding is incomplete now, but one day I will understand everything, just as everything about me has been fully understood. (1 Corinthians 13:12)

September 20

Do you know I would drop everything for you? Do you know if they came to get me if you were sick, I would stop what I was doing and go to you? Do you know that if you and the President called me at the same time, I would answer you first and put him on hold? Do you know that I know all the things you like and don't like? Do you know it makes me smile when I think of you and my heart happy when I know you are coming to see me? You may know many things, but these are the things that I want you to know more than anything else. I don't mind you asking, in fact I encourage it because I am the one who will help you.

SCRIPTURES TO MEDITATE ON:

I look up to the mountains and hills, longing for God's help. But then I realize that our true help and protection come only from the Lord, our Creator who made the heavens and the earth. (Psalm 121:1-2)

The believer who is poor still has reasons to boast, for he has been placed on high. (James 1:9)

For if you embrace the truth, it will release more freedom into your lives. (John 8:32)

SEPTEMBER 21

When you are struggling to talk to me, or wondering where I am, I encourage you to come and not be afraid of telling me just how you feel. We can work through this together. I know that you were used to facing life alone many times, but those were the times you didn't know I was there. I will always be here for you, and my promise to you is that I will never leave, you will never have to be alone again. I understand why you might have a hard time believing this, so just like a loving Papa I will give you all the reassurance you need. You can taste and see that I am a good Father, the Father that you didn't have, the Father that I said I would be to you.

SCRIPTURE TO MEDITATE ON:

Drink deeply of the pleasures of this God. Experience for yourself the joyous mercies he gives to all who turn to hide themselves in him. (Psalm 34:8)

September 22

I long to speak comfort to your heart, to tell you that you are not alone anymore. How different you will feel, how exciting life will be as your heart is convinced of my faithfulness to you. As this becomes more of a reality for you, this truth will secure you. And when life throws some difficult punches your way, and you don't understand what I am doing, it will not rattle you the same way. You will stay calm inside because you finally know you have a good Papa. You will rely less on your own understanding of the situation and your heart will rest securely in knowing that your Papa God is always right here in the present moment with you.

SCRIPTURES TO MEDITATE ON:

So, what does all this mean? If God has determined to stand with us, tell me, who then could ever stand against us? (Romans 8:31)

Trust in the Lord completely, and do not rely on your own opinions. With all your heart rely on him to guide you, and he will lead you in every decision you make. (Proverbs 3:5)

SEPTEMBER 23

I understand the restlessness I see when you come to me. I know you are not used to the love that I have for you. It is beyond anything you have known or experienced here. Some of my children have experienced little to no love at all, and it was not because you were unlovable. Your hurting parents could only give to you what they received from their hurting parents. As children we do not know this and take it personally. We come to our own conclusions that are colored by a very wounded life experience. I am here to remind you that I make all kinds of miracles happen, so it is not a hard thing for me to make my love known to you. I know how to get through to this heart of yours that has been trampled on and shut down. Just watch out for the lies of the enemy that tell you I don't care. That is a classic lie he uses over and over, to tempt you to believe when you are hurting. You don't have to jump through hoops to receive my love. Just come to me and share your honest thoughts and feelings with me so I can help you.

SCRIPTURES TO MEDITATE ON:

For the greatest love of all is a love that sacrifices all. And this great love is demonstrated when a person sacrifices his life for his friends. "You show that you are my intimate friends when you obey all that I command you. I have never called you 'servants,' because a master doesn't confide in his servants, and servants don't always understand what the master is doing. But I call you my most intimate friends, for I reveal to you everything that I've heard from my Father. You didn't choose me, but I've chosen and commissioned you to go into the world to bear fruit. And your fruit will last, because whatever you ask of my Father, for my sake, he will give it to you! (John 15:13-16)

So then, we must cling in faith to all we know to be true. For we have a magnificent King-Priest, Jesus Christ, the Son of God, who rose into the heavenly realm for us, and now sympathizes with us in our frailty. He understands humanity, for as a Man, our magnificent King-Priest was tempted in every way just as we are, and conquered sin. So now we come freely and boldly to where love is enthroned, to receive mercy's kiss and discover the grace we urgently need to strengthen us in our time of weakness. (Hebrews 4:14-16)

SEPTEMBER 24

I would like you to think on this for a while using the imagination I gave you. Close your eyes and remember all that I did to make this world and everything on it. The land, the bodies of water, the universe and you. I am God and have the ability to do this, yet I will never cross a person's will. I have given man free choice to decide and will never take that away from him. My son talks to me all the time about all of you and prays for you to choose life, for you to know that his Father is yours and that you would know that we can be close just as Jesus and I and Holy Spirit are. Even though you can't see me, you can know and experience this closeness with me. I hope this makes you feel cared for knowing my son is here praying for you. No matter who you are or what you have done, when you turn to me, I will greet you with open arms and a heart full of love.

SCRIPTURES TO MEDITATE ON:

Who then is left to condemn us? Certainly not Jesus, the Anointed One! For he gave his life for us, and even more than that, he has conquered death and is now risen, exalted, and enthroned by God at his right hand. So how could he possibly condemn us since he is continually praying for our triumph? (Romans 8:34)

He is able to save to the uttermost those who draw near to God through him, since he always lives to make intercession for them. (Hebrews 7:25)

SEPTEMBER 25

There is a place that I would like to take you to this morning. Continue to use your imagination and come and watch this with me. I see this child of mine all caught up in the hustle and bustle of worldly activities, trying to make things happen because she/he is on a mission. Their mission is to secure their world by making sure their needs are met. They know a degree of truth about me providing but work independently of me. What would their lives be like if they knew that I had everything taken care of, that they are the focus of my affection? I want to take them to this place, to show them and help know that I am a very generous Father. That is my mission!

SCRIPTURE TO MEDITATE ON:

I am convinced that my God will fully satisfy every need you have, for I have seen the abundant riches of glory revealed to me through the Anointed One, Jesus Christ! (Philippians 4:19)

SEPTEMBER 26

Because you are so used to carrying your own burdens and cares, I think it would be a good idea to get into a new habit of giving them to me daily. This is my way of caring for you. Remember that because you have done it for years, you don't always realize you are worrying about so many things. Use the imagination that I have given you and see yourself releasing all these things to me, one by one. I have given you the grace to do this, so you can start right now; I will show you how. Just see yourself giving me that burden, that problem, and putting it into the hands of a loving and committed Father who knows how to take care of everything. You will feel so much better as you let go, you don't need to carry this and you will see that you worried for nothing. As you do this, enjoy being carefree, something maybe that is not to familiar. This will be a new place for many, but I do have this carefree place for you and I know you will enjoy it. You will finally know what it feels like to be a carefree child without a care in the world. Remember, You don't have to beg me, for I will gladly receive all your cares because I love you.

SCRIPTURE TO MEDITATE ON:

Pour out all your worries and stress upon him and leave them there, for he always tenderly cares for you. (1 Peter 5:7)

SEPTEMBER 27

O child of mine, how I wait for the day for you to have an ever-increasing awareness of my presence and my love for you. I am everywhere and in everything. I keep waiting for you to realize I am here for you. My love is never ending, it will never stop, and you can never be separated from me and what I feel in my heart for you. I understand the pain of separation because of the day that I was separated from my children when they had to leave the garden. My son took care of that at the cross and we will never be separated again. That is my promise to you. As you let me heal your heart from all that you have been through, you will experience my love like you have never known it before. Jesus rested in my love because he knew and trusted, and you can too.

SCRIPTURE TO MEDITATE ON:

For I am convinced that neither death nor life, neither angels nor demons, neither the present nor the future, nor any powers, neither height nor depth, nor anything else in all creation, will be able to separate us from the love of God that is in Christ Jesus our Lord. (Romans 8:38-39)

SEPTEMBER 28

Many times, you hear the words and know in your head that you are my child, but it is not known to your heart. It is when you know in your heart that you are my child, that you will know security and freedom that your heart always longed for. Life as you have known it for many years will look different. Just as a child explores with wonder, you will have that childlike trust again, as your heart returns to me. Your heart will be at rest in knowing that all is well because your Father who created heaven and earth is at home with you. Your heart knows and can hear me, but your mind gets in the way when your heart is not healed. The very best part of what I am telling you is that I am here to stay. I want you to know, as your Father, that I will never let anything nor anyone separate us or come between us again.

SCRIPTURE TO MEDITATE ON:

Who could ever separate us from the endless love of God's Anointed One? Absolutely no one! For nothing in the universe has the power to diminish his love toward us. Troubles, pressures, and problems are unable to come between us and heaven's love. What about persecutions, deprivations, dangers, and death threats? No, for they are all impotent to hinder omnipotent love. (Romans 8:35)

September 29

As your heart heals and learns that it is truly safe to trust in your Father God, a new adventure will begin for you. Your eyes will see what they have never seen before. Your ears will hear the things that you needed to hear from me so you know that I am a Father that loves to talk to his children. You were used to the old, but I ask you to be open to the new and all the wonderful things I have planned for us together, plans that you have not even begun to realize. Sure, there are trials in life, but you need to know that you are not alone, I am always with you. Sit with this truth as my Holy Spirit helps you to take it in.

SCRIPTURE TO MEDITATE ON:

This is why the Scriptures say: Things never discovered or heard of before, things beyond our ability to imagine—these are the many things God has in store for all his lovers. (1 Corinthians 2:9)

September 30

Stay with me here for a little while more as I need to convince you of an important truth that will be a blessing to you. It would be good for you to stop watching what I am doing for everyone else and start to listen to what I have for you. I am so happy you are here and so glad I got your attention on this. When you are busy watching everyone else, you are not free to hear from me and what I want to show you about your life. Somewhere along the way you have accepted the lie that others are more important. This makes my heart sad for you because nothing could be farther from the truth. Keeping your eyes on me, as your doting Father who thinks of you all the time, will come easier for you as you find out for yourself how I feel about you. I will never give up trying to get through to you just how special you are to me.

SCRIPTURE TO MEDITATE ON:

You even formed every bone in my body when you created me in the secret place, carefully, skillfully shaping me from nothing to something. You saw who you created me to be before I became me! Before I'd ever seen the light of day, the number of days you planned for me were already recorded in your book. Every single moment you are thinking of me! How precious and wonderful to consider that you cherish me constantly in your every thought! O God, your desires toward me are more than the grains of sand on every shore! When I awake each morning, you're still with me. (Psalm 139:15-18)

OCTOBER

OCTOBER 1

All the change that is constant around you can feel a little unnerving. We change in our bodies, others can change in how they feel about us, and people come and go. These are just a few changes that occur in our lives. There is one thing you can be sure of and that is, I will never change. I will never change the way I feel about you no matter what you do or don't do. So, if you are having a bad day and you are struggling with yourself, you can count on me being right there for you. I am not like man that I should ever lie to you. You can count on my love remaining the same. If you are in a time when you don't feel connected to me, or you feel out of sorts, just come and tell me and you will discover your Father is home waiting for you and that I am very good listener.

SCRIPTURES TO MEDITATE ON:

Let everyone thank God, for he is good, and he is easy to please! His tender love for us continues on forever! (Psalm 136:1)

Jesus, the Anointed One, is always the same—yesterday, today, and forever. (Hebrews 13:8)

OCTOBER 2

My children see me in so many different ways. I am seen as a judge, a distant God, powerful and unfeeling, and the list goes on and on. Many walk around unaware of how they are relating to me. Ask and it shall be given according to my will. It is my will for you to know that I am your loving, understanding, and compassionate Father who you have always needed, and always longed for. I can open the eyes of your heart and give you revelation of who I truly am and not what others project me to be. Yes, I am almighty God, but I am also your Father who understands you and all that you have been through. There is healing as you experience this truth about me.

SCRIPTURE TO MEDITATE ON:

He understands humanity, for as a Man, our magnificent King-Priest was tempted in every way just as we are, and conquered sin. (Hebrews 4:15)

OCTOBER 3

You thought for a while that life was about being successful and making your mark financially. You thought it was about having a grand anointed ministry. This is good, but nothing compares to knowing me and the healing I have for your heart, the kind of healing that gives you peace, and the kind of healing that helps you to be present. If you did not have this healing and relationship with me, you would really be missing out on the most important things in life. There is a strong pull here which drives my children to work endlessly, being filled with the cares of this life, without trusting me to provide and care for them. If you will trust me enough to let me in here, you will see for yourself what I can do for you. I can go into your past and get rid of any fears that have driven you and hurt you when your many needs were not taken care of. Watch and see what I will do for you.

SCRIPTURE TO MEDITATE ON:

Pour out all your worries and stress upon him and leave them there, for he always tenderly cares for you. (1 Peter 5:7)

OCTOBER 4

When I tell you that I can do more than you could ever ask or think, I am saying this in order to break the limits you have set on me and bring your vision higher. I am your Father and would love to bless you, would love to do more for you. Think about what you would like me to do for you and what you want to see happen in your life. I know why you have a hard time trusting this and I can see that it comes mostly from all the disappointments you had to endure. I am so excited to do this for you and can't wait to finally set you free to be all you were created to be, to have a heart that can feely receive from me all the love you have longed for.

SCRIPTURES TO MEDITATE ON:

Never doubt God's mighty power to work in you and accomplish all this. He will achieve infinitely more than your greatest request, your most unbelievable dream, and exceed your wildest imagination! He will outdo them all, for his miraculous power constantly energizes you. Now we offer up to God all the glorious praise that rises from every church in every generation through Jesus Christ—and all that will yet be manifest through time and eternity. Amen! (Ephesians 3:20-21)

I pray that you will continually experience the immeasurable greatness of God's power made available to you through faith. Then your lives will be an advertisement of this immense power as it works through you! This is the mighty power that was released when God raised Christ from the dead and exalted him to the place of highest honor and supreme authority in the heavenly realm! (Ephesians 1:19-20)

OCTOBER 5

You don't have to beg me for help. Many come to me with an orphan mindset and think they have to plead with me for help, unsure of what kind of father I am. A loving father would not want his child to feel like they needed to plead for his help. Intercession is led by my Spirit, but begging in prayer is led by a heart with unmet needs, a heart that learned very early that they had to take care of themselves. My children say they know I love them, but really know very little and experience very little of my love because their hearts are guarded. I want you to know that you don't have to beg me. If you only knew the storehouse of blessings I have for you and how much I sincerely long to be close to my children.

SCRIPTURE TO MEDITATE ON:

Ask, and the gift is yours. Seek, and you'll discover. Knock, and the door will be opened for you. (Matthew 7:7)

October 6

Because you have no frame of reference for what a loving father is, you have nothing to draw on. I see you watching other fathers with their children, wondering what it would be like to have that. I am here to tell you that I will make this real for you. I will give you all of the things you never received so you to can feel that security that you longed for. I always wanted this for you. It may be hard for you to believe the lengths I will go through to convince you. It is going to be a whole new world from what you knew. You will discover things about me and yourself that will leave you standing in awe and wonder. It is time to receive now from me, your Father God, who has always longed to father you.

SCRIPTURES TO MEDITATE ON:

I will repay you for the years the locusts have eaten—the great locust and the young locust, the other locusts and the locust swarm—my great army that I sent among you. (Joel 2:25 NIV)

I hear the Lord saying, "I will stay close to you, instructing and guiding you along the pathway for your life. I will advise you along the way and lead you forth with my eyes as your guide." (Psalm 32:8)

OCTOBER 7

As your Father, I watch you daily and I come to you now to show you who I am, to let you know your Papa is home for you. Watch for me so you don't miss what I have for you. Even in this very moment I am here, and I come to you many times to be with you but you are preoccupied. Its hard for you to comprehend that you have a Father who loves hanging out with you. As your heart heals and you desire revelation about me, you will see me more clearly; it is then that you will be more receptive to me. You will learn to draw your life from me and not from what others think of you. I will cause the parts of your heart that were shut down to live again. What you have wondered about as you watched the little children full of life expressing freedom as their true selves, you will have. At one time you didn't believe you could ever have this, but with me you can, with me all things are possible.

SCRIPTURES TO MEDITATE ON:

A thief has only one thing in mind—he wants to steal, slaughter, and destroy. But I have come to give you everything in abundance, more than you expect—life in its fullness until you overflow! (John 10:10)

Jesus said to him, "What do you mean 'If?' If you are able to believe, all things are possible to the believer." (Mark 9:23)

OCTOBER 8

No matter where you are at in your life, I want you to know I just want to be with you. I do not want anything from you like many others have in your life. Just as parents love to be with their children, so I love to be with you. You don't have to be concerned with impressing me or proving anything to me. That is a waste of time because I already loved you completely when I created you and I knew then what your imperfections would be. I call you by your name to be open to my love as I come to you knowing all your weaknesses and flaws. I have always longed to be close to my children. Pray for open eyes and ears, that you may see and hear, but also pray for an open heart, a heart that has been touched, healed and restored by me.

SCRIPTURES TO MEDITATE ON:

I will give them an undivided heart and put a new spirit in them; I will remove from them their heart of stone and give them a heart of flesh. (Ezekiel 11:19 NIV)

Teach me more about you, how you work and how you move, so that I can walk onward in your truth until everything within me brings honor to your name. (Psalm 86:11)

But now, this is what the Lord says—he who created you, Jacob, he who formed you, Israel: "Do not fear, for I have redeemed you; I have summoned you by name; you are mine." (Isaiah 43:1 NIV)

OCTOBER 9

Don't worry, my child. I will make my love known to you and you will learn to trust me and rest in my love. My heart of love will never demand for you to be a certain way to be loved by me. Remember that my yoke is easy and my burden is light. I am your Father who will always be at home for you. You can keep checking and you will see that I will always be there, and you will know a security you have never known. This is part of the good plans I have for you. You think you are already receiving from me, but when I show you what I have, you will need my help to receive because it is bigger than what you are thinking. You will stand in amazement and ask, "Is this really for me?" And I say, "Yes, my dear child, start getting used to being surprised by your Papa who loves to lavish his love on you."

SCRIPTURES TO MEDITATE ON:

This is just too wonderful, deep, and incomprehensible! Your understanding of me brings me wonder and strength. (Psalm 139:6)

For all that I require of you will be pleasant and easy to bear. (Matthew 11:30)

OCTOBER 10

Many of my children do not see me as the kind of father who loves to talk to his kids. They think of me as a silent God, who is too busy for them. On a daily basis, they are not connecting to the reality of me being their Father that is watching and waiting for them. They think they know but have very little revelation of how much I want to interact with them throughout the day. My children cannot bring themselves to believe that the creator of all heaven and earth wants to come and talk to them, that I call them by their name. They, like Peter, feel unworthy of having their feet washed by God. You ask, "Why, God, would you want to wash my feet? Why, God, would you want to come and hang out and talk?" Just like any loving parent, I love being with my kids and there is nothing I wouldn't do to express my love to them.

SCRIPTURES TO MEDITATE ON:

If you, imperfect as you are, know how to lovingly take care of your children and give them what's best, how much more ready is your Heavenly Father to give wonderful gifts to those who ask. (Matthew 7:11)

And because the gatekeeper knows who he is, he opens the gate to let him in. And the sheep recognize the voice of the true Shepherd, for he calls his own by name and leads them out, for they belong to him. (John 10:3)

OCTOBER 11

There is much to learn, but more than anything, I want you to know how important you are to me. Each one of you are so special and so dear to my heart. There will be a day where you will be able to come to me and just be so free with who you are as you realize who I created you to be. My life is all about my children. I see the orphan that lingers in their hearts and I want to help them know in every sense what it means, what it feels like to be my sons and daughters. The more you see me working in your life as your Father, the more at rest you will feel inside, and the more at home you will feel with me. I look forward to the moment when you realize that I am in this very present moment just being so happy to be with you.

SCRIPTURES TO MEDITATE ON:

And you did not receive the "spirit of religious duty," leading you back into the fear of never being good enough. But you have received the "Spirit of full acceptance," enfolding you into the family of God. And you will never feel orphaned, for as he rises up within us, our spirits join him in saying the words of tender affection, "Beloved Father!" For the Holy Spirit makes God's fatherhood real to us as he whispers into our innermost being, "You are God's beloved child!" (Romans 8:15-16)

But when the truth-giving Spirit comes, he will unveil the reality of every truth within you. He won't speak his own message, but only what he hears from the Father, and he will reveal prophetically to you what is to come. (John 16:3)

OCTOBER 12

I hear my children crying out for many things, almost from a place of begging, not knowing how approachable I am. Without realizing it, you look at me through the lenses of your earthly father. My children are more in touch with what is in front of them and are not so much with me. They rely on their limited ways of looking at things and are not seeing the bigger picture of what I have in mind for them. This is why I tell you not to worry. So many do not know this place of childlike trust with me and worry fills their days for they are not used to being cared for and cannot relate to a father that they cannot see. They wonder if I will really take care of all of their needs? Their lives have been filled with disappointment and they are not quick to turn to me. They do not know that I am a Father who longs to take them under his wings, to comfort, and to nurture all those desolate places. Just ask me, and I will be very happy to show you many things you do not know about me, things that you need to know to be able to be at rest

SCRIPTURES TO MEDITATE ON:

Call to me and I will answer you and tell you great and unsearchable things you do not know. (Jeremiah 33:3 NIV)

This is why I tell you to never be worried about your life, for all that you need will be provided, such as food, water, clothing—everything your body needs. (Matthew 6:25)

OCTOBER 13

I know that I am repeating myself but I see you are not yet convinced of my care for you. All of these things that you are concerned about will seem like a speck of sand in comparison to me and the loving plans that I have for you. You don't have to work for my love, nor be the perfect model Christian. I will be waiting for you until you realize the kind of father I want to be for you. I understand that this is not a familiar love, so your heart and mind are not fully connecting to this reality. I see you thinking as you catch glimpses of my love, how can He love me like this? This is too good to be true! Then I watch your excitement as you take baby steps and sometimes big leaps toward me as I keep calling to you in many different ways to let you know I am here and always happy to be with you.

SCRIPTURES TO MEDITATE ON:

And never forget that I am with you every day, even to the completion of this age. (Matthew 28:20)

So do not fear, for I am with you; do not be dismayed, for I am your God. I will strengthen you and help you; I will uphold you with my righteous right hand. (Isaiah 41:10 NIV)

OCTOBER 14

I want you to hear these words that I speak so tenderly to you. You are so worth waiting for as I wait for your heart to fully connect to mine. I look forward to the day that you no longer hold back anymore and freely give your heart to me. Lay down all these ideas you have about the way you think it should be when you come to me. You don't have to pray a certain way or act a certain way so as to please me, this will just keep you from connecting to me as your Father that is already pleased without you doing a thing. I see this as a concern of yours, but I am more concerned with all the ideas that people have of me that keeps them at a distance. I want you to feel my smile, and know that you have my full attention when you walk in.

SCRIPTURES TO MEDITATE ON:

Jesus answered him, 'Love the Lord your God with every passion of your heart, with all the energy of your being, and with every thought that is within you.' (Matthew 22:37)

So we proclaim to you what we have seen and heard about this life-giver so that we may share and enjoy this life together. For truly our fellowship is with the Father and with his Son, Jesus, the Anointed One. (1 John 1:3)

OCTOBER 15

I have so much for you to experience. I encourage you to come to me so we can do life together. As your Father, there are places I want to take you and so many doors of revelation that I want to open. Don't rely on what you have created to secure your world but turn to me and I will heal the broken trust that has keeps you from me. The security that you need will come from me once you know me better. I sent my son to go through all the pain and suffering, so that you could know that I fully understand your pain, your fears, and your struggles. As you turn to me, I will show you that I am the Father that your heart always longed for since your early days. I so look forward to being closer to you as you realize your heart is safe with me.

SCRIPTURE TO MEDITATE ON:

For this is how much God loved the world—he gave his one and only, unique Son as a gift. So now everyone who believes in him will never perish but experience everlasting life. (John 3:16)

OCTOBER 16

I am the extreme opposite of all you know here when it comes to a father. Your father might not have been there for you, but I am always here, all the time, even though you are not aware of my presence. The more you get to know that about me, the more you will notice me throughout your day. Maybe you had a father that was silent, never talked to you and in that case, there is something you need to know about me. I love when you come to talk to me, day or night. I love our times together. I love hearing your voice and listening to you share your thoughts and ask me what I think. Even if you don't have much to say, that's okay too, because it is all about being together.

SCRIPTURE TO MEDITATE ON:

But whenever you pray, go into your innermost chamber and be alone with Father God, praying to him in secret. And your Father, who sees all you do, will reward you openly. (Matthew 6:6)

OCTOBER 17

I encourage you to ask me about this restlessness that you feel at times when you come to me. I know you better than you know yourself and I can show you what is happening for you. There are times when you get in touch with my love and you feel unworthy, but I call you by your name to come to me. Then there are times when you just can't imagine anyone loving you like I do. I am your Father who truly wants to reveal myself to you and clear up the distorted way you see me. The same power that raised my son from the dead lives in you and that same power can break through the lies of your guarded heart to let you know that you are safe with me. You will rest when you know that I am a safe place for you in the midst of all the pain. Just as I heal the sick, I can heal the pain that hurts your heart. I know, my dear child, that it has been quite a healing journey for you but wait until you see what is up ahead.

SCRIPTURE TO MEDITATE ON:

He heals the wounds of every shattered heart. (Psalm 147:3)

OCTOBER 18

Ask my Holy Spirit to help you hear my heart for you when I tell you how I often longed to gather you as a hen gathers her chicks, but you were not willing. This is my heart to comfort and give you security, and to protect you. Sometimes my children don't feel as if they can trust me to protect them, because of the things that have happened to them. You may not even have thought much about being comforted if you didn't have this. This is a real human need and we all need to be comforted; every painful place buried inside needs to be comforted. My Holy Spirit, who I sent to you, is called the Comforter, and he will help you to know what this is and help you to trust and receive it. Just ask him to help you hear my heart in Matthew 23:37 and to open the eyes of your heart.

SCRIPTURES TO MEDITATE ON:

I pray that the light of God will illuminate the eyes of your imagination, flooding you with light, until you experience the full revelation of the hope of his calling— that is, the wealth of God's glorious inheritances that he finds in us, his holy ones! (Ephesians 1:18)

Open my eyes to see the miracle-wonders hidden in your word. (Psalm 119:18)

OCTOBER 19

There is so much to look forward to with me. Before you knew me, I saw you wishing and hoping for things, hoping that your luck would change. With me in your life, it is not a matter of wishing or luck; it is a sure thing the blessing I have for you. You have my word that I will work all things out for your good, things you find difficult and do not understand. There have been many times that others have disappointed you, but as you turn to me you will find me faithful. You will see in time that I was there all the time for you but your troubled heart was not able to see me or trust in a Father that you could not see.

SCRIPTURES TO MEDITATE ON:

So we are convinced that every detail of our lives is continually woven together to fit into God's perfect plan of bringing good into our lives, for we are his lovers who have been called to fulfill his designed purpose. (Romans 8:28)

The one who calls you by name is trustworthy and will thoroughly complete his work in you. (1 Thessalonians 5:24)

OCTOBER 20

Ask me, and I will speak to your restless heart. I understand you like no one else. You can come just as you are, in whatever condition, and you will find a safe haven. I see the times in your life where you were hurting and there was no one there to talk to about it, no one that seemed to care about what was going on inside of you. I know how hard that was for you. Now, it is time for you to realize that I am always present, and you can talk to me at any time. I don't just want to talk to you about praying for others, but I want to talk to you about you and our life together. We will be together for a very long time, so I would suggest to you, my dear child, to start getting used to being loved, and start getting used to having your Papa around.

SCRIPTURE TO MEDITATE ON:

Love is large and incredibly patient. Love is gentle and consistently kind to all. It refuses to be jealous when blessing comes to someone else. Love does not brag about one's achievements nor inflate its own importance. (1 Corinthians 13:4)

OCTOBER 21

I know what happened in your past and how painful it was when you felt used by others. I have something I want you to listen very carefully to. I don't ever want you to feel that I just want to use you to build my kingdom. Our relationship means more to me than any work you could possibly do for me. This is another reality that I want you to have settled in your heart. When Adam and Eve were on the earth, I loved our times together and I was not trying to get them to work for me. We were a family and that's what I wanted. Yes, you will want to tell others about me, but it should come from what you have experienced with me, and never out of duty or trying to earn my love.

SCRIPTURES TO MEDITATE ON:

For you bring me a continual revelation of resurrection life, the path to the bliss that brings me face to face with you. (Psalm 16:11)

On the day of judgment many will say to me, 'Lord, Lord, don't you remember us? Didn't we prophesy in your name? Didn't we cast out demons and do many miracles for the sake of your name?' (Matthew 7:22)

OCTOBER 22

When I talk to you my child I share with you from my heart. My words to you are not empty but full of life. When you are guarding your heart it is harder to embrace what I am telling you. There will always be the question of, does he really feel this way about me. As you open up and let me heal those places, my Word will come alive again and you will feel that excitement once again that you felt the day you met me. You will once again feel excited as you read my Word and it comes to life. Ask my Holy Spirit; he will help you know the truth about what I am saying. He will give you understanding and insight into all the scriptures that speak of my care for you. As my son and Holy Spirit intercede for you, I want you to know that it is from a heart of love that we want to reach you and help you experience life with us.

SCRIPTURES TO MEDITATE ON:

So he is able to save fully from now throughout eternity, everyone who comes to God through him, because he lives to pray continually for them. (Hebrews 7:25)

And in a similar way, the Holy Spirit takes hold of us in our human frailty to empower us in our weakness. For example, at times we don't even know how to pray, or know the best things to ask for. But the Holy Spirit rises up within us to super-intercede on our behalf, pleading to God with emotional sighs too deep for words. (Romans 8:26)

God is not human, that he should lie, not a human being, that he should change his mind. Does he speak and then not act? Does he promise and not fulfill? (Numbers 23:19 NIV)

OCTOBER 23

When you are looking at life, situations and people from a limited human perspective, you will naturally not see the whole picture. It would be good to talk to me about what you have concluded and not rely on this as a final word. When you come to me, I can open up a whole new world of thoughts and ideas for you to look at. I love when you come to me and we share our hearts and I love to see the excitement on your face as you come into new understanding. This happens as you learn to trust that everything I do for you is out of a heart of love. As your heart heals and learns to trust what I am revealing to you, you will know that my fatherly love and guidance is safe, that I am not a Father who would use you or hurt you in any way.

SCRIPTURES TO MEDITATE ON:

"For I know the plans I have for you," declares the Lord, "plans to prosper you and not to harm you, plans to give you hope and a future." (Jeremiah 29:11 NIV)

Become intimate with him in whatever you do, and he will lead you wherever you go. Don't think for a moment that you know it all. (Proverbs 3:6)

"For my thoughts are not your thoughts, neither are your ways my ways," declares the Lord. (Isaiah 55:8 NIV)

OCTOBER 24

My dear child, if you only knew how much I know and understand you. You put demands on yourself that I am not asking of you. I am not demanding that your broken heart must trust me when you never learned to trust as a child. I am not upset with you the way you get upset with yourself. I can see that you are not aware of what it is you really need. My child, I speak tenderly to your heart and ask you to be kind to yourself in this very moment as I speak the truth of my loving thoughts that I have toward you. It is my plan to show you how much I love you, so you will feel safe coming close to me in whatever condition you are in. I have healing for your troubled heart and you will see my faithfulness.

SCRIPTURES TO MEDITATE ON:

Your love is so extravagant, it reaches higher than the heavens! Your faithfulness is so astonishing, it stretches to the skies! (Psalm 108:4)

The Lord is close to all whose hearts are crushed by pain, and he is always ready to restore the repentant one. (Psalm 34:18)

Every single moment you are thinking of me! How precious and wonderful to consider that you cherish me constantly in your every thought! O God, your desires toward me are more than the grains of sand on every shore! When I awake each morning, you're still with me. (Psalm 139:17-18)

OCTOBER 25

I know about all the times you felt alone and uncared for. I know about all the times you were scared and didn't have comfort. I have longed to take you under my wings, but you did not know me, you did not know I was there. Man has hurt you by violating your will, so I will never force myself on you. I gently keep trying to reach you and I wait patiently for you to respond to me. I am here waiting with everything you need. I do understand your struggling to trust what I am telling you, but once you let me help you, you'll be able to freely receive from me. I am here to father you in every way that you need a father and to give to you what you missed out on. You wonder how I am going to father you and I tell you to watch and see.

SCRIPTURES TO MEDITATE ON:

Look with wonder at the depth of the Father's marvelous love that he has lavished on us! He has called us and made us his very own beloved children. (1 John 3:1)

I will repay you for the years the locusts have eaten—the great locust and the young locust, the other locusts and the locust swarm—my great army that I sent among you. (Joel 2:25 NIV)

OCTOBER 26

I know I repeat myself to you, but some things you need to hear over and over. I would like for you to get in the habit of bringing things to me. It is so easy to walk around carrying all this stuff without realizing it. I would like for you to see me as the kind of father that is excited about his kids, that celebrates them. For way to long, you have not seen me as I truly am, but you can know me, and it is my heart's desire that you know the truth about me. I have so much to tell you and so much to show you. You won't be afraid anymore as you realize that your God is your Papa and I am the safest place in the world for you to come to.

SCRIPTURE TO MEDITATE ON:

Love never brings fear, for fear is always related to punishment. But love's perfection drives the fear of punishment far from our hearts. Whoever walks constantly afraid of punishment has not reached love's perfection. (1 John 4:18)

OCTOBER 27

I knew that you would eventually turn and give your life to me and I also knew there would be a battle to win your heart. All that you have gone through has caused your heart to hold back from me. You know in your head, but your heart doesn't know yet the depth of my love, and the security it brings. I will never give up on trying to get through to you. I see at times you struggle with believing I love you the way I do. It is not always going to be hard. As your heart heals you will experience what I am telling you. If you ask me to show you your heart, I will be happy to show you know-ing that as your heart heals we will become closer. I will be gentle with you as you receive from me the nurturing you need.I have all the plans and provisions for this important part of your life.

SCRIPTURES TO MEDITATE ON:

The same way a loving father feels toward his children.... that's but a sample of your tender feelings toward us, your beloved children, who live in awe of you. (Psalm 103:13)

Our love for others is our grateful response to the love God first demonstrated to us. (1 John 4:19)

OCTOBER 28

I am right here always ready to connect, always ready and anticipating our times together. Right now, I want to help you with your fears about me. I want my children to realize what is going on inside for them, but they are very busy working for me. Even as you wait before me, you are not aware how guarded your heart is with me. You know something is not happening but you are not sure what it is. I see you struggling. I see the restlessness at times, with the idea of just being quiet before me so that you may receive my love. You don't have to do anything, you don't have to be interceding, praising, or saying amazing sounding prayers, for me to love you. I just want you to come and receive my love, to be close to you. For some it might sound to good to be true, but this is truth you can know. The lies have kept you from me long enough.

SCRIPTURE TO MEDITATE ON:

Let everyone everywhere shine with praise to Yahweh! Let it all out! Go ahead and praise him! For he has conquered us with his great love and his kindness has melted our hearts. His faithfulness lasts forever and he will never fail you. So go ahead, let it all out! Praise Yah! O Yah! (Psalm 117:1-2)

OCTOBER 29

I was just wondering if you thought about how much time you spend worrying. Think about how much time you have taken to entertain orphan ways of thinking. I just want to bring this to your attention. I don't believe you realize how much you need my help with accepting the way I feel about you. My Spirit will help you discover how much you are in my heart. He will help you to know in the midst of your biggest failures and mistakes how much I am there to love and encourage you, not to scold you nor shame you in any way. Quiet yourself with me and just receive my love. If you are feeling any blocks, trust me, I will help you with them. I want you to know that I don't want anything between us, and remind you that I have listened to every word you have spoken to me

SCRIPTURES TO MEDITATE ON:

So don't worry. For your Father cares deeply about even the smallest detail of your life. (Matthew 10:30-31)

If you hear my words and refuse to follow them, I do not judge you. For I have not come to judge you but to save you. (John 12:47)

Look with wonder at the depth of the Father's marvelous love that he has lavished on us! He has called us and made us his very own beloved children. The reason the world doesn't recognize who we are is that they didn't recognize him. (1 John 3:1)

October 30

I am here to remind you that I am not upset with you. The things that upset you about yourself, I am not bothered by. You don't need anyone to scold you or set you straight. I know what you need, and it is the exact opposite of what you are allowing yourself to have. It is my nurturing love that calms your fears and lets you know that you are okay. It is kindness that you need when you are discouraged about the things in your life that you don't like. I believe in you, my dear child. Ask me, and I can open up your eyes, your ears and your heart to my nurturing love. I don't want you to miss what I long to show you. It is the longing of my heart to give this to you.

SCRIPTURES TO MEDITATE ON:

Do the riches of his extraordinary kindness make you take him for granted and despise him? Haven't you experienced how kind and understanding he has been to you? Don't mistake his tolerance for acceptance. Do you realize that all the wealth of his extravagant kindness is meant to melt your heart and lead you into repentance? (Romans 2:4)

We know that the truth lives within us because we demonstrate love in action, which will reassure our hearts in his presence. Whenever our hearts make us feel guilty and remind us of our failures, we know that God is much greater and more merciful than our conscience, and he knows everything there is to know about us. (1 John 3:19-20)

OCTOBER 31

My desire is for you to know how much I really want you come to me with your concerns. These are not empty words that I speak to you. Because you were alone so much in your past carrying things by yourself, this has become almost a daily way of life for you. Believe me when I tell you that you don't have to carry these problems any longer. Ask my Holy Spirit to show when you are carrying burdens that I have not given you. I am here to heal and convince your heart that I am a good Papa. The more you know this, it will become easier for you to release your cares to me and be confident that I will take care of you and anything that concerns you. Think how wonderful it will feel to walk into your day free of all worries. I want you to know me as a good Papa that takes care of his kids. I want to give you warm feelings inside when you think of me, and your heart can know the rest I have for you.

SCRIPTURES TO MEDITATE ON:

Pour out all your worries and stress upon him and leave them there, for he always tenderly cares for you. (1 Peter 5:7)

But when the truth-giving Spirit comes, he will unveil the reality of every truth within you. He won't speak his own message, but only what he hears from the Father, and he will reveal prophetically to you what is to come. (John 16:13)

NOVEMBER

NOVEMBER 1

Yes, I believe in you in spite of all your mistakes because I know your heart and I know it is a heart that is for me. Even when no one else seemed to believe you were worth the time to listen to, I was right there wanting you to know how I felt about you, wanting to listen to every word and every thought you had. I know you better than anyone and so I know that you are going to make it even though you might not always feel that way. You can safely rely on the fact that I will finish the work I started in you. Watch for me, I will keep speaking these words that your heart needs to hear of how much I believe in you. This is very important for you to hear this from your earthy father, who was not able to do this for you, but I promise I can, and I do not speak empty words. So, don't be concerned with what you didn't receive from your parents because I am here now and know just how to make things better for you.

SCRIPTURES TO MEDITATE ON:

I pray with great faith for you, because I'm fully convinced that the One who began this glorious work in you will faithfully continue the process of maturing you and will put his finishing touches to it until the unveiling of our Lord Jesus Christ! (Philippians 1:6)

My own sheep will hear my voice and I know each one, and they will follow me. (John 10:27)

November 2

I want to father you in your struggles, and you will see that I am a present Father. Come and see all that I have for you and come find out for yourself. There will never be lack for you, just come and see for yourself. My eyes are always aware of you throughout the day and night, and my ears are sensitive to your cries. I do hear you when you are talking to me and you are not aware of how much I am listening. You may be wondering about everything you are going through and wondering where I am, but I am right here. I am right here, in this very moment wanting you to know the truth about me. This is the kind of Father I am. I will wipe away your tears, sing over you and hold you close, and love you over and over again.

SCRIPTURES TO MEDITATE ON:

When I had nothing, desperate and defeated, I cried out to the Lord and he heard me, bringing his miracle-deliverance when I needed it most. (Psalm 34:6)

The eyes of the Lord are everywhere and he takes note of everything that happens. He watches over his lovers, and he also sees the wickedness of the wicked. (Proverbs 15:3)

November 3

So many of my children are unaware of the kind of father I want to be to them. They are not in touch with how involved I want to be in their daily lives. I have been involved all along in times of celebrating, crying, laughing or just sitting with or doing nothing at all, just because I wanted to be with them. I know it is hard to comprehend this if you did not have a father present in your life that cared for you, but I know how to make myself known to you. I don't mind waiting for you to be convinced, waiting for you to be able to trust again. You will see that I will not break your heart, I will not hurt you as you take even baby steps toward me experiencing that my love is the safest place for you to give your heart to.

SCRIPTURE TO MEDITATE ON:

"For I know the plans I have for you," declares the Lord, "plans to prosper you and not to harm you, plans to give you hope and a future." (Jeremiah 29:11 NIV)

November 4

Sometimes you see me as so small in the midst of all your daily happenings. You forget in the moment, just how big a God I am, and just how much I am able and wanting to help you. The problem is not what is happening; the real issue is that your heart is not able to trust me. You don't realize that it is I who will heal your broken heart, so that you can trust again. When you know this about me, it will make you feel much better. Your heart won't be using your energy to guard it, but will finally be able to enter the rest. You will know that you have a compassionate Papa who is in touch with all you are feeling. This is a reality I long for my children to experience with me.

SCRIPTURES TO MEDITATE ON:

See, I am doing a new thing! Now it springs up; do you not perceive it? I am making a way in the wilderness and streams in the wasteland. (Isaiah 43:19 NIV)

He understands humanity, for as a Man, our magnificent King-Priest was tempted in every way just as we are, and conquered sin. (Hebrews 4:15)

November 5

Every unmet need you ever had, all those moments that there was no one there for you, I will make up to you. I have always wanted to care for you in this way, but until your healing came, you were not able to see me nor trust that I would actually do this for you. And even as you are reading this in this very moment, I am longing to father you and hold you close to me, to comfort all those desolate places. With time and with my consistent reaching out to you, your heart will learn to rest as it realizes I am a Father that you can finally trust. Think about how you feel about your children to help you get in touch with my love I have for you, a love that will never stop, never end, never change, and never leave you.

SCRIPTURES TO MEDITATE ON:

I the Lord do not change. So you, the descendants of Jacob, are not destroyed. (Malachi 3:6 NIV)

I will repay you for the years the locusts have eaten—the great locust and the young locust, the other locusts and the locust swarm—my great army that I sent among you. (Joel 2:25 NIV)

NOVEMBER 6

Out of anything you could possibly know or learn I would want you to know I am compassionate about my children. Lay down all your preconceived ideas you have of me and let me show you what I am truly like. Maybe you never thought about the possibility of knowing me as your Father, but Jesus talked about me all the time referring to me as his Father and yours. I know when my Son , Jesus, told you to come and see me in private and close the door, you didn't know what to expect. You had no idea what was about to unfold for you. You can be reading this and maybe still not understand the way I feel about you, but I will make it happen for you. You will need my help because it is a love that you are not familiar with, a love that feels so good and that leaves you wondering if it is too good to be true.

SCRIPTURES TO MEDITATE ON:

The Lord appeared to us in the past, saying: I have loved you with an everlasting love; I have drawn you with unfailing kindness. (Jeremiah 31:3 NIV)

Not one promise from God is empty of power, for nothing is impossible with God! (Luke 1:37)

NOVEMBER 7

Please come to me in whatever condition you are in even if you are angry at me. If you are troubled, restless, scared, I still want you to come. I don't judge you or think less of you. My heart goes out to you because you are not aware yet of how much you are accepted by me in whatever state you are in. You don't have that sense deep inside of how important you are, that you are so okay with me. You needed this acceptance from your parents who were not able to give, they were broken and you live in a broken world, so I am here to give this to you. I am here to work with you and make every orphan mindset go away. Only I can heal the kind of pain that is buried deep inside your heart that has left you feeling so uncared for. I will keep at it until you feel like that much-loved child that you always longed to be.

SCRIPTURE TO MEDITATE ON:

I myself said, "How gladly would I treat you like my children and give you a pleasant land, the most beautiful inheritance of any nation.' I thought you would call me 'Father' and not turn away from following me. (Jeremiah 3:19 NIV)

November 8

Listen to me, my child, and be intentional about putting effort into what I am telling you. You have been listening to lies far too long that have really hurt you. I have things to say to you that you need to hear and this is the truth that I ask you to listen to. I tell you that your value is not based on your looks or achievements, and I want to address who you really are. You need to believe how important you are to me, as I have made you a very special person. It has nothing to do with your looks. You had no one value you as the person you are, or call forth the gifts and abilities I put in you. The world puts far too much emphasis on outward appearance, and one's talents, but I do not. When beauty fades, what will you have? I look at the heart, and man looks at outward appearance. I can open your eyes, if you ask, and let you see what I am seeing when I look at you.

SCRIPTURES TO MEDITATE ON:

But the Lord said to Samuel, "Do not consider his appearance or his height, for I have rejected him. The Lord does not look at the things people look at. People look at the outward appearance, but the Lord looks at the heart." (1 Samuel 16:7 NIV)

You formed my innermost being, shaping my delicate inside and my intricate outside, and wove them all together in my mother's womb. I thank you, God, for making me so mysteriously complex! Everything you do is marvelously breathtaking. It simply amazes me to think about it! How thoroughly you know me, Lord! You even formed every bone in my body when you created me in the secret place, carefully, skillfully shaping me from nothing to something. You saw who you created me to be before I became me! Before I'd ever seen the light of day, the number of days you planned for me were already recorded in your book. (Psalm 139:13-16)

NOVEMBER 9

Many of my children do not know that they are okay. They are busy at work for me or thinking they will be okay once they change in a certain area that they struggle with. When do you think you will be okay? Will it be once you get your degree, once you look a certain way, or once you get the ministry you always wanted? You never heard what your ears needed to hear; to know how lovable you are even though you may have had selfish motives or a bad attitude. Some people you look at seem to have it together, but there are a lot of normal looking people out there that are very uncertain about themselves and don't know how much I love them. This needs to be your reality, this is what you need to know more than anything else, that your Papa God loves you. I will keep telling you this until your heart can hear it, and this becomes your very own experience with me.

SCRIPTURE TO MEDITATE ON:

But Christ proved God's passionate love for us by dying in our place while we were still lost and ungodly! (Romans 5:8)

November 10

There are moments when you look at the natural circumstances, and you wonder what is going on. It might not look like what you thought or what you had planned but let me reassure you that I am right here at work in your life. As you come to a place of trusting me, but not fully understanding what I am doing, just know that this is a very good place to be. Just remember all the times I have come through for you. I am glad that you are starting to believe that your Papa knows what He is doing. It is good for you to come and see me to talk these things over with me, so you can get the perspective you need and some reassurance. Once you get my perspective it will help you tremendously on a situation that has made no sense to you and has caused you to wonder about me. The great thing for me is that I get to be with you because I look forward to our times together.

SCRIPTURES TO MEDITATE ON:

Call to me and I will answer you and tell you great and unsearchable things you do not know. (Jeremiah 33:3 NIV)

"For my thoughts are not your thoughts, neither are your ways my ways," declares the Lord. (Isaiah 55:8 NIV)

NOVEMBER 11

Imagination time.....using your imagination that I gave you. Someone calls you and tells you that the King of England heard about you and thought you were a very interesting person and wanted you to come and see Him. He would consider it an honor for you to come and meet with him. Think about how that would make you feel. How much more exciting it will be for you when you realize this is true about how your Father, creator of the universe, feels about you. Your Papa thinks you are amazing. I love when you come and talk to Me. I love doing things with you and love hearing your thoughts about life.. Now here our my thoughts that you need to know about me.... My children are the ones that make my heart happy. If you are uncomfortable with love, you will need to come to me for the help to embrace this truth, and keep coming to receive it deep into your heart.

SCRIPTURES TO MEDITATE ON:

And realize what this really means....we have the privilege of worshiping the Lord our God. For he is our Creator and we belong to him. We are the people of his pleasure. (Psalm 100:3)

For the Lord is always good and ready to receive you. He is so loving that it will amaze you.....so kind that it will astound you! And he is famous for his faithfulness toward all. Everyone knows our God can be trusted, for he keeps his promises to every generation! (Psalm 100:5)

NOVEMBER 12

Just as a mother speaks tenderly to her child, so I long for you to hear my tender-hearted words spoken over you. Just as a child needs to hear reassuring words from mommy in the night when they are frightened, so I want you to be comforted in the truth that I am here for you also. Just as a mother hugs her baby close to her chest, so I long for you to feel this embrace from me. I want my children to enjoy and know this security that I freely offer them. I long for you to be at home with me as my sons and daughters. My Holy Spirit is here to give you all the comfort and reassurance you need, this is my Father's heart reaching out to you, calling you by your name to welcome you home.

SCRIPTURE TO MEDITATE ON:

And I will ask the Father and he will give you another Savior, the Holy Spirit of Truth, who will be to you a friend just like me—and he will never leave you. The world won't receive him because they can't see him or know him. But you will know him intimately, because he will make his home in you and will live inside you. (John 14:16-17)

November 13

Be aware of the business on the inside and try to relax, there is nothing you have to do to get my love. Just relax and receive. I understand all that goes on inside of your heart, and inside your thoughts. I know it hasn't been easy and understand why your heart is guarded and struggles to believe the things I tell you. I have plans for healing and restoration so that you can know how much you are wanted by me, that you have always been a part of my family. I have never forgotten you. You will no longer be living from an identity that your past gave you, but from your true authentic self, the person I have created you to be, the person that I know and love.

SCRIPTURES TO MEDITATE ON:

God, I invite your searching gaze into my heart. Examine me through and through; find out everything that may be hidden within me. Put me to the test and sift through all my anxious cares. See if there is any path of pain I'm walking on, and lead me back to your glorious, everlasting ways—the path that brings me back to you. (Psalm 139:23-24)

So then we must give our all and be eager to experience this faith-rest life, so that no one falls short by following the same pattern of doubt and unbelief. (Hebrews 4:11)

NOVEMBER 14

As you experience my love, it will make it easier for you to turn to me in the midst of your battles. You are not alone, my child, in what you are going through. Many have the same struggles, the same kind of pain, but hide it well. Letting others freely see you can be so healing as you experience acceptance and not judgement. I am the one that truly knows who you are, and I am the one that can help you. You might think others are more put together, so therefore you might think they are more special. All my children are special to me, and all have their own struggles. I am with you in the good times and the difficult times, and you can rely on that. I don't leave you nor upset when you are not acting right or not responding well to a situation, or to me. You are not alone in your battles for there is no temptation that is not common to man.

SCRIPTURES TO MEDITATE ON:

We all experience times of testing, which is normal for every human being. But God will be faithful to you. He will screen and filter the severity, nature, and timing of every test or trial you face so that you can bear it. And each test is an opportunity to trust him more, for along with every trial God has provided for you a way of escape that will bring you out of it victoriously. (1 Corinthians 10:13)

Then Jesus came close to them and said, "All the authority of the universe has been given to me. Now go in my authority and make disciples of all nations, baptizing them in the name of the Father, the Son, and the Holy Spirit. And teach them to faithfully follow all that I have commanded you. And never forget that I am with you every day, even to the completion of this age." (Matthew 28:18-20)

NOVEMBER 15

No one influences you like your father and mother, so how much more will I have an impact on you when you realize my love. When they speak, their words shape the lives of those in their care, for the negative or positive. I want to remind you not to listen to thoughts that make you feel bad, don't just accept them and don't be quick to agree with them. Any thoughts that come from me will encourage, nurture and build you up. I don't want you listening to anything that makes you feel bad. When I look at you, I see all the flaws, all the imperfections and I do not judge you. Others may, and you might judge yourself unfairly, but I do not judge you. You know enough about being judged, it is time for you to bask in my unconditional love. Get your focus off what is wrong with you and on the love that I have for you. Stay with my loving thoughts and stay away from the opinions of others. Remember, just as parents have so much influence on their children, how much more will my love touch your life when you let me in.

SCRIPTURES TO MEDITATE ON:

If you, imperfect as you are, know how to lovingly take care of your children and give them what's best, how much more ready is your heavenly Father to give wonderful gifts to those who ask him? (Matthew 7:11)

The Father now judges no one, for he has given all the authority to judge to the Son. (John 5:22)

November 16

My dear child, I see you wondering about many things. I want to take you somewhere today to show you something. It is good to get some healthy perspective on how I see things. I want you to see all this worrying does not one thing to change any situation. Just relax and let it all go. Shift gears here and look at the butterfly, so light and peaceful. I created this beautiful, graceful insect. Why would I take the time to create so much beauty? Yes, I love beauty, but I did this for you to enjoy, and for you to get a picture of what I am like. So, rest from all your troubles and watch the butterfly, and remember that there is so much more that I want to show you about who I am that will help you to let go and rest. Just realized I am not at all worried about your outcome, because I already know what I am going to do for you.

SCRIPTURE TO MEDITATE ON:

I have revealed to them who you are and I will continue to make you even more real to them, so that they may experience the same endless love that you have for me, for your love will now live in them, even as I live in them! (John 17:26)

NOVEMBER 17

I have loved you the whole time that you have hated yourself, hated your past choices, and hated the mistakes you made. It saddens me to see you struggle and I have been waiting for the day that you would come and talk to me about it. You have been used to the voice that condemns you but listen closer and you will hear me calling your name to come to me just as you are. I want you to get used to my voice, the voice that tells you just how special you are to me. I know you are not used to this kind of love, a love that never changes based on your behavior. My Holy Spirit is here to make this your reality. Learn to enter into this moment with me and just receive from your Father who adores you.

SCRIPTURES TO MEDITATE ON:

Call to me and I will answer you. (Jeremiah 33:3 NIV)

God is not human, that he should lie, not a human being, that he should change his mind. Does he speak and then not act? Does he promise and not fulfill? (Numbers 23:19 NIV)

NOVEMBER 18

I see you having a hard time with the idea of how much I want to spend time with you. There is so much about me that you haven't yet experienced, so much about me that you need to know. I want you to feel the security of knowing that I will never let you down. I want you to feel safe knowing I will never let you go. I am guiding you when you are not even aware of my presence being there. I know at times you feel left out of what I am doing, but I assure you that I am right here caring for you, working to bring about my purposes in your life. It won't always be hard to trust me as I heal your heart and you see my continual faithfulness.

SCRIPTURE TO MEDITATE ON:

When you sit enthroned under the shadow of Shaddai, you are hidden in the strength of God Most High. He's the hope that holds me and the Stronghold to shelter me. (Psalm 91:1-2)

NOVEMBER 19

It is time to imagine...using the imagination that I have given you. Imagine your Papa calling you to spend the day with you. He took time off from work because he misses you and when you walk into his office he tells the others to wait instead of making you wait for him. He smiles from ear to ear as soon as he sees you. Your Papa takes you to lunch and shopping and asks you what you would like. He loves walking in the park with you, where you have special bonding times and when he talks to you, he gives you his full attention. As you talk, he smiles, admiring you and what you have to say. He wants to hear all about what is on your heart. This is a story, but it is also true about your Papa God and the way He is with each one of us. How often do we think of Him this way?

SCRIPTURES TO MEDITATE ON:

For the Father tenderly loves you, because you love me and believe that I've come from God. (John 16:27)

Jesus replied, "Loving me empowers you to obey my word. And my Father will love you so deeply that we will come to you and make you our dwelling place." (John 14:23)

NOVEMBER 20

Come in, my dear child, and close the door. I am so glad you came because there are a few important things I want to talk to you about that will affect your whole life. There are things you have been believing that have really hurt you, the way you see me, and the way you see yourself. Closely listen to what I am about to tell you. There comes a moment when you have to decide who you will believe. You are not what others have told you that you are, you are who I created you to be. You have believed for a long time the lies spoken over you, but now it is time for you to listen to me and take me seriously when I tell you that I created you in love, smiling and enjoying every moment as I thought about you and what you would be like. Stay with this for a while and let my Holy Spirit reveal this truth to you until it becomes your reality.

SCRIPTURES TO MEDITATE ON:

For if you embrace the truth, it will release more freedom into your lives. (John 8:32)

But whenever you pray, go into your innermost chamber and be alone with Father God, praying to him in secret. And your Father, who sees all you do, will reward you openly. (Matthew 6:6)

You formed my innermost being, shaping my delicate inside and my intricate outside, and wove them all together in my mother's womb. (Psalm 139:13)

November 21

Everything you ever longed for from your father, I long to give you. I understand your struggle to believe this, but I know just how to help you. It is not too hard for me to reach you with my love. I come to you to take care of all the rejection, all the trauma, and all the self-hatred that has hurt you and kept you from me. Where you have known rejection, my love can come and break down any guarded walls you have. Where you have buried trauma, the power of the cross can heal the deepest pain. Where you lived with self-hatred and anger, my constant love will always be there to believe in you. My love will win your trust and help you see what I see when I look at you. Just relax and let my Holy Spirit minister truth and comfort to all the places inside your heart that need to be fathered.

SCRIPTURES TO MEDITATE ON:

His tender love for us continues on forever! (Psalm 136:1)

To the fatherless he is a father. To the widow he is a champion friend. To the lonely he gives a family. To the prisoners he leads into prosperity until they sing for joy. This is our Holy God in his Holy Place! But for the rebels there is heartache and despair. (Psalm 68:5-6)

November 22

I am a Father that enjoys being with his children. I long to show you what I am like, to let you see that I am different in many ways than what you are familiar with here. I do want to remind you not to rely on your own understanding of events, but to ask my Holy Spirit to help you hear what I am saying to you. He is always here and always ready to help, always ready and available to bring you the comfort you need. You have been used to a certain kind of care, so you do not know what to expect from me. I have so much more for you than what you are expecting, than what you know about. There is so much more you can know about me and there is so much more that I want to tell you.

SCRIPTURES TO MEDITATE ON:

Trust in the Lord completely, and do not rely on your own opinions. With all your heart rely on him to guide you, and he will lead you in every decision you make. Become intimate with him in whatever you do, and he will lead you wherever you go. Don't think for a moment that you know it all. (Proverbs 3:5-6)

God, you're such a safe and powerful place to find refuge! You're a proven help in time of trouble—more than enough and always available whenever I need you. (Psalm 46:1)

His massive arms are wrapped around you, protecting you. You can run under his covering of majesty and hide. His arms of faithfulness are a shield keeping you from harm. (Psalm 91:4)

November 23

My people see me in many different ways with many names, and many titles. The name father can trigger very painful memories for some. There are many distorted images of me because of this and how I have been misrepresented. I am here to tell you I am not like your father. He was broken and could only father you the way he was fathered. It's important for you to know not to take it personally, it had nothing to do with you the way he could or could not love you. The enemy is out to destroy the father image because he wants to give my children a distorted picture of me. I want my children to know what kind of father I want to be to them. The only thing you have to do is ask my Holy Spirit to show you and get ready to go on an adventure of being blessed in ways you didn't know possible. I know it's hard to trust this since many have experienced fatherlessness, or abuse from someone that was suppose to give nurturing and stability. I took care of all the healing you will ever need at the cross. There is no pain that is bigger than the healing that I have for you. I have provided the healing you need for your heart to live and trust again. You can and will know just how special you are to me.

SCRIPTURE TO MEDITATE ON:

Surely he took up our pain and bore our suffering, yet we considered him punished by God, stricken by him, and afflicted. But he was pierced for our transgressions, he was crushed for our iniquities; the punishment that brought us peace was on him, and by his wounds we are healed. (Isaiah 53:4-5 NIV)

November 24

While I am trying to get your attention, you have been distracted by many things. Once I can get you to look my way, you will see me again and you will know that everything is going to be alright. When you see my love, it will calm you down. As your Father I know your needs, and I know how to help you calm down and get perspective. No one knows you like I do, so do not be afraid, but be secure in knowing that I am right here. I am bigger than any of your problems that you are facing, and even bigger than the impossible looking ones.

SCRIPTURES TO MEDITATE ON:

We look away from the natural realm and we fasten our gaze upon Jesus who birthed faith within us and who leads us forward into faith's perfection. His example is this: Because his heart was focused on the joy of knowing that you would be his, he endured the cross and conquered its humiliation, and now sits exalted at the right hand of the throne of God! (Hebrews 12:2)

Don't worry or surrender to your fear. (John 14:1)

NOVEMBER 25

I want you to learn to just receive from me and learn this well. Just relax and enjoy being my child and all the blessings that come with that. You don't have to do a song or dance, or anything to try and impress me to get my attention. You lived with the belief that you had to be good, follow the rules, do everything that a good Christian does in order to be okay with me, to get my favor and attention. The truth is that you do not have to do a thing. I loved you when you didn't know me, and I love you now. I will tell you this as many times as I need to, until it starts sinking in from your head to your heart. Many of my kids are working for me, but we have very little time together and many times when we are together they don't believe how much I want to be with them. It seems to be all about what they are doing for me, but that is not what I want. This is what they settle for, but I long for them to know the blessings that come with being my sons and daughters.

SCRIPTURE TO MEDITATE ON:

So answer me this: Did the Holy Spirit come to you as a reward for keeping all the Jewish laws? No, you received him as a gift because you believed in the Messiah. Your new life in the Anointed One began with the Holy Spirit giving you a new birth. Why then would you so foolishly turn from living in the Spirit by trying to finish by your own works? Have you endured all these trials and persecutions for nothing? Let me ask you again: What does the lavish supply of the Holy Spirit in your life, and the miracles of God's tremendous power, have to do with you keeping religious laws? The Holy Spirit is poured out upon us through the revelation and power of faith, not by keeping the law! Abraham, our father of faith, led the way as our pioneering example. He believed God and the substance of his faith released God's righteousness to him. (Galatians 3:2-6)

NOVEMBER 26

If I told you I am here to reparent you and give to you all the things you didn't receive, not knowing what that means nor what that would look like, you might question this and hope at the same time. You have learned to look at life and handle it in such a way that brings you the security you need. Ask me, and I will show you what it looks like to be fathered by me, for again I will not push my way into your life because I know your father pain has caused your heart to distance itself from me. I promise not to hurt you, but to nurture all those places that have been deprived of love, a love that is necessary to thrive and live fully with a trusting heart. Finally,I want you to be at rest knowing that you have a Papa who will take good care of you. Start looking to me to make this happen for you.

SCRIPTURE TO MEDITATE ON:

"For I know the plans I have for you," declares the Lord, "plans to prosper you and not to harm you, plans to give you hope and a future." (Jeremiah 29:11 NIV)

NOVEMBER 27

It's okay for you to feel restless when you come see me because you might just need to be held by your father. Whatever frame of mind you are in, it is okay with me. I also want you to know that it's okay if you don't have anything to say, or if you just feel like an emotional mess. You might not even know what you need. I love to just sit with you and hold you close. There are times that this is all you need, just to be held by your Papa. I know that this might not be a familiar love, so my Spirit is right here to help you receive it and take it in. I want you to know that your needs are important to me and it might even surprise you that I care about the things you want. Think about what it means to have a Father who cares about everything that concerns you, even the little things that you might think I am too busy to notice Be aware of the things that try to distract you from coming to me, things that I can take care of for you. My Father's heart longs to care for my children!

SCRIPTURE TO MEDITATE ON:

"I will be a true Father to you, and you will be my beloved sons and daughters," says the Lord Yahweh Almighty. (2 Corinthians 6:18)

NOVEMBER 28

Just as I am moving on this earth, so I am personally moving in your heart to convince you that you are my child. You are my first priority. You have watched me for years doing all kinds of miraculous things and still did not connect the miracles to my love. It was exciting to watch, and it encouraged your faith, but you still did not connect it to the love I feel toward you as your Father. The greatest thing for you to see is the look on my face when I look at you. Just as some need glasses for their eyes to see better, so you need my Holy Spirit to help you see me. Life will get pretty exciting as you realize how involved my Holy Spirit is in your life. And we get pretty excited here when we see you responding as we come to you. You are usually more in touch with what is happening there but just be aware that there is a lot going on here on our end. I am always loving you, my child.

SCRIPTURES TO MEDITATE ON:

See this great thing the Lord is about to do before your eyes. (1 Samuel 12:16)

It is through him that we live and function and have our identity; just as your own poets have said, 'Our lineage comes from him.' (Acts 17:28)

For the Holy Spirit makes God's fatherhood real to us as he whispers into our innermost being, "You are God's beloved child!" (Romans 8:16)

NOVEMBER 29

If there is one thing I could convince you of today, it would be how much I cared about what you went through as a child. I have been here all along watching over you, and that is how you are here today. In your pain it is hard for you to see me accurately, but Jesus said he will make me known to you and will continue to make me known. It will no longer be a wish of something you want to grab a hold of but can never seem to reach it. I am so happy that you relate so well with my son, but I would love for you to see me as your father who runs to you, who thinks about you constantly. Many see me as the complete opposite of this, if they only knew. But I tell you now, you can know me. This was my son's prayer for you, and he prays for you still, that you would continue to know me and would know that I love you as much as I love my son Jesus. And I talked to him, and I will talk to you.

SCRIPTURES TO MEDITATE ON:

I have revealed to them who you are and I will continue to make you even more real to them, so that they may experience the same endless love that you have for me, for your love will now live in them, even as I live in them! (John 17:26)

Then they asked, "Just who is this 'Father' of yours? Where is he?" Jesus answered, "You wouldn't ask that question if you knew who I am, or my Father. For if you knew me, you would recognize my Father too." (John 8:19)

Jesus replied, "Loving me empowers you to obey my word. And my Father will love you so deeply that we will come to you and make you our dwelling place." (John 14:23)

NOVEMBER 30

It makes me sad to see how guarded my children's hearts are with me. I do understand why and the enemy thinks he's won. It might be hard to believe in the moment but I will turn this whole thing around for good. Many say they know I am their Father, but their guarded hearts are keeping them from getting to close. Not seeing the whole picture, they are relying on their own understanding and believing the lies that I am upset, or love others more than them. Ask me to bring the people in your life that you need to help you with the healing I have for you. You have taken many risks in your life, and I encourage you to take this one with me. I promise that I will not disappoint you, your heart is safe with me.

SCRIPTURE TO MEDITATE ON:

Listen carefully, my dear child, to everything that I teach you, and pay attention to all that I have to say. Fill your thoughts with my words until they penetrate deep into your spirit. Then, as you unwrap my words, they will impart true life and radiant health into the very core of your being. So above all, guard the affections of your heart, for they affect all that you are. Pay attention to the welfare of your innermost being, for from there flows the wellspring of life. (Proverbs 4:20-26)

DECEMBER

DECEMBER 1

You have a need to be heard and to have loving significant others that are able to be present for you. I am all around my children and present with them at all times and they have not realized this. The same happened for the disciples when they did not realize I was with them when my son was here. I try to get your attention through miracles but then I lose you again by many distractions that bombard your days. I can only be as personally involved as you allow me. There is so much pain and fear from abuse and unmet needs, that your trust level is not close to being able to trust a Father you cannot see. My heart goes out to my children as I see them struggle so much, not being able to grasp just how I feel about them. They say, "Yes, I know he loves me," but it comes from head knowledge and not from a healed heart. It's in the heart that we relate to each other with trust and compassion.

SCRIPTURES TO MEDITATE ON:

As a father has compassion on his children, so the Lord has compassion on those who fear him. (Psalm 103:13)

If you really know me, you will know my Father as well. From now on, you do know him and have seen him. (John 14:7)

DECEMBER 2

I am looking forward to you getting to know me as a kind Father. For you to know that I want to take care of the unmet needs you had as a child, have someone there to go to your school events, to have your dental needs cared for, spend time with you doing all kinds of fun things together, to take you shopping for what you not only need but for what you would love to have, and to talk to you with honor and respect, asking you what your thoughts are. I am here to reparent you, to give you this kind of security. You will see as you watch me come through, that I will restore and give back to you what the enemy has stolen from you. And in time you will know that I am your father who keeps his promises as you watch me do this. No more struggling alone. Ask me to show you what is really going on in your heart. I want to do this not because I want something from you, but just because my heart is full of love and I am your Father.

SCRIPTURES TO MEDITATE ON:

The Lord is close to all whose hearts are crushed by pain, and he is always ready to restore the repentant one. (Psalm 34:18)

Trust in the Lord completely, and do not rely on your own opinions. With all your heart rely on him to guide you, and he will lead you in every decision you make. (Proverbs 3:5)

December 3

When others are upset with you because you didn't act right, or live up to their expectations, this is not the way I love you. I do not deal with you according to your actions. I am not shocked, and my love does not change. I don't look at you any differently. In spite of all that you see that you don't like, or others may see that bother them about you, you are perfectly okay with me. I know that you are used to living with all this conditional love, but my desire is for you to get used to the way I love you. Get used to me being so happy to see you right after you mess up. Get used to the fact that I see all that is not right with you and I still long to be with you. Get used to the truth that others may leave, but I am always here for you even though you don't always see me. I know that when there is no bonding or healthy attachments in childhood, that it is harder to trust, so I will let you know in many different ways that I am here when you need reassurance from me.

SCRIPTURES TO MEDITATE ON:

For he knew all about us before we were born and he destined us from the beginning to share the likeness of his Son. (Romans 8:29)

Don't be obsessed with money but live content with what you have, for you always have God's presence. For hasn't he promised you, "I will never leave you alone, never! And I will not loosen my grip on your life!" (Hebrews 13:5)

DECEMBER 4

I am just trying to get through to you that I just want to be with you. I am especially happy when your heart is open, and you fall into my arms and rest there. Just as you long to hold your children, I long to hold you, but I am also here whenever you need to talk. There are ideas floating around that I don't talk to my children very much. This couldn't be farther from the truth. Think about how much you like to talk to your own children. My children don't know, they don't realize how much I want to talk to them, so they are not listening or expecting this kind of relationship with me. Ask me for ears to hear and I will remove the blocks for you and I will heal that little child inside who was never heard and who didn't have a voice. I want you to know that I hear your cries and I hear every word you ever spoke . I am listening even as you are wondering could this be true, can I really have a Father in my life that is this present for me?

SCRIPTURES TO MEDITATE ON:

But Jesus called for the parents, the children, and his disciples to come and listen to him. Then he told them, "Never hinder a child from coming to me. Let them all come, for God's kingdom realm belongs to them as much as it does to anyone else. They demonstrate to you what faith is all about." (Luke 18:16)

Lovers of God have been given eyes to see with spiritual discernment and ears to hear from God. (Proverbs 20:12)

DECEMBER 5

It would be a good idea to remember to come to me for direction, advice or whatever guidance you need. It would be a good habit to get into to and realize that there would be a very different outcome if you took things into your own hands. Try me and ask; I assure you that life will get pretty interesting when you include me in the picture. Maybe you just don't realize how much I want to be involved in your life in the little things as well. Also, I want to remind you that I am available at all times. You don't have to wait for me to show up or wonder where I am. Asking me for what you need is like opening the door and inviting me into your life, this is what makes my Father's heart happy.

SCRIPTURES TO MEDITATE ON:

And if anyone longs to be wise, ask God for wisdom and he will give it! He won't see your lack of wisdom as an opportunity to scold you over your failures but he will overwhelm your failures with his generous grace. (James 1:5)

So here's what I've learned through it all: Leave all your cares and anxieties at the feet of the Lord, and measure-less grace will strengthen you. (Psalm 55:22)

DECEMBER 6

It is good to desire my presence and it is good to desire revival, praying for the fire of heaven to come down. I heard the cries of my people for more. I am telling you here and now that there is more. The more is in the relationship that you can have with me. I can give you a heart to know me and there is nothing in this life that compares to this. While all these other things are good, it is my desire that you know me, it is my desire for us to be close, and it is my desire to be your friend, your savior, your God and your Father.

SCRIPTURES TO MEDITATE ON:

I will give them a heart to know me, that I am the Lord. They will be my people, and I will be their God, for they will return to me with all their heart. (Jeremiah 24:7 NIV)

For your tender mercies mean more to me than life itself. How I love and praise you, God! (Psalm 63:3)

DECEMBER 7

I want to heal that child inside of you who believes that no one is there when facing difficult situations. I want you to get used to me being there. Ask me to show that I am a good Papa who can fix anything. This truth needs to replace the lie that you are all alone. Just remember not to always try to figure out what is going on, but to turn to me, your Papa, and watch for my guidance. I want you to experience being carefree and secure knowing you have a Father who adores you and there is nothing I wouldn't do for you to convince you of my love.

SCRIPTURES TO MEDITATE ON:

Trust in the Lord completely, and do not rely on your own opinions. With all your heart rely on him to guide you, and he will lead you in every decision you make. Become intimate with him in whatever you do, and he will lead you wherever you go. Don't think for a moment that you know it all. (Proverbs 3:5-6)

I promise that I will never leave you helpless or abandon you as orphans—I will come back to you! Soon I will leave this world and they will see me no longer, but you will see me, because I will live again, and you will come alive too. So when that day comes, you will know that I am living in the Father and that you are one with me, for I will be living in you. (John 14:18-20)

DECEMBER 8

Here is something I would like you to think about. I created the heavens and earth with excellence and everything is securely in place. It's hard to fathom all the beauty and breathtaking places to see. Who can fathom the galaxies and the countless stars? Look at the human body, so well made in how it works in spite of much abuse and still survives for a long time and longer if well taken care of. This is just to give you a picture of what I am like, and what I can do. In all that I have created, you still could not see me as your loving Father until my son came to tell you about me and my Spirit revealed Him to you. He loved the outcasts, healed the sick, reached out to sinners, and told you that when you see him, you see me. This is what I am like. So everything that I did from the beginning of time was with you in mind.

SCRIPTURES TO MEDITATE ON:

You keep all your promises. You are the Creator of heaven's glory, earth's grandeur, and ocean's greatness. (Psalm 146:6)

Your word is truth! So make them holy by the truth. I have commissioned them to represent me just as you commissioned me to represent you. And now I dedicate myself to them as a holy sacrifice so that they will live as fully dedicated to God and be made holy by your truth. And I ask not only for these disciples, but also for all those who will one day believe in me through their message. I pray for them all to be joined together as one. I pray for them to become one with us so that the world will recognize that you sent me. For the very glory you have given to me I have given them so that they will be joined together as one and experience the same unity that we enjoy. You live fully in me and now I live fully in them so that they will experience perfect unity, and the world will be convinced that you have sent me, for they will see that you love each one of them with the same passionate love that you have for me. Father, I ask that you allow everyone that you have given to me to be with me where I am! Then they will see my full glory— the very splendor you have placed upon me because you have loved me even before the beginning of time. You are my righteous Father, but the unbelieving world has never known you in the way that I know you! And all those who believe in me also know that you have sent me! I revealed to them who you are and I will continue to make you even more real to them, so that they may experience the same endless love that you have for me, for your love will now live in them, even as I live in them! (John 17:17-26)

Compared to all this cosmic glory, why would you bother with puny, mortal man or be infatuated with Adam's sons? (Psalm 8:4)

DECEMBER 9

If you didn't have a loving emotional connection with your earthly parents, which is common for many, you will not know what you can expect and experience with me. You have no idea what you are missing, until I show you. Many have shut down their hearts not knowing what else to do with the pain. People are not heartless, they are just numbed to the point of not feeling. This is why I tell you that I am close to the broken-hearted, whether they are aware or not. I am there for when they are ready to turn to me. I have the healing that you need, and I speak life and hope over those desolate places. I want you to be able to rest knowing your Papa is here and I have no plans of ever leaving. I will help you to know and enjoy my goodness. It is time for you to become as a trusting child again and just receive, without hesitation, without questioning.

SCRIPTURES TO MEDITATE ON:

So now we come freely and boldly to where love is enthroned, to receive mercy's kiss and discover the grace we urgently need to strengthen us in our time of weakness. (Hebrews 4:16)

For this is what the Lord says: "I will extend peace to her like a river, and the wealth of nations like a flooding stream; you will nurse and be carried on her arm and dandled on her knees. As a mother comforts her child, so will I comfort you; and you will be comforted over Jerusalem." (Isaiah 66:12-13 NIV)

DECEMBER 10

The imprint left on your heart from an early age was one of feeling very alone and not knowing what to do about it. You have learned to live this way and even when someone is around, you feel isolated with your emotions. You may not be aware that you are doing this, but you naturally pull away from others and from me. When you come to me in tears, your heart is not totally open to me to comfort you. You still see yourself crying all alone. When I say I am close to the broken-heart, it is my heart longing to comfort you. I am right there for you to comfort you and let you know your feelings matter and what you are going through are very important to me. Your coping mechanism has been to shut down all emotions, telling yourself to get over it and stay busy by pouring yourself into whatever project is in front of you. It is time for new beginnings, fresh revelation of me being there to comfort, heal, and restore you. You don't have to do this alone anymore. Try me, taste and see that I am good, and you will see that I will be who I said I would be for you!

SCRIPTURES TO MEDITATE ON:

The Lord is close to all whose hearts are crushed by pain, and he is always ready to restore the repentant one. (Psalm 34:18)

Taste and see that the Lord is good; blessed is the one who takes refuge in him. (Psalm 34:8)

DECEMBER 11

As my love sinks deeper into your heart you will trust that depending on me is a good thing, and not an unhealthy dependency that many of you know here. I will show you that I am someone that you can safely trust. When I ask you to rely on me it is not for me to take over your life. It will not take away from you and the person I made you to be, I will only enhance and enrich your life. You have learned early on to be independent because no one was there for you and this is what you needed to do to survive. You also have been conditioned to believe lies that have hurt you and kept you from me. So turn to me and I can open your ears to hear the truth, which is greater and more powerful than any lie.

SCRIPTURES TO MEDITATE ON:

For if you embrace the truth, it will release more freedom into your lives. (John 8:32)

But when the truth-giving Spirit comes, he will unveil the reality of every truth within you. He won't speak his own message, but only what he hears from the Father, and he will reveal prophetically to you what is to come. (John 16:13)

December 12

You have taken on burdens and responsibilities that I have not given you. I see that you are having a hard time feeling bad about what you think you should be doing for others, and I know this is a very difficult place. I tell you, my child, I can see that you feel this out of a sense of duty and getting lost there. I have not called you to take care of everyone and want to free you from that false sense of responsibility. I want to lift all of the burdens that you are carrying that are not from me. You only have to do what I ask of you and I remind you that my yoke is easy, and my burden is light. I know these things have been put on you at an impressionable age and I am going to free you now because this is not from me. I am a Father who would never put burdensome things on my children. I know you will be surprised at what I have for you as I lift this weight of guilt and you move forward in freedom to enjoy the life that I have for you.

SCRIPTURES TO MEDITATE ON:

Come to me, all you who are weary and burdened, and I will give you rest. (Matthew 11:28)

For all that I require of you will be pleasant and easy to bear. (Matthew 11:30)

DECEMBER 13

I know when something is going on in your life, just the way a parent senses something is going on with their child. Just as you know your children, so I know you and every-thing that concerns you. Think about your child and how natural it feels to love them, how when they turn to you for help, you do whatever you can for them. Think about how you like to get them the things they like, how you like to surprise them. Think about how much you like to hang out with them, laugh with them, and cry with them. You would want them to know that they can freely and safely come to you if they needed to talk to someone that would not judge them. This is what you will find with me and even more than anything you will ever experience here.

SCRIPTURES TO MEDITATE ON:

You've gone into my future to prepare the way, and in kindness you follow behind me to spare me from the harm of my past. With your hand of love upon my life, you impart a blessing to me. This is just too won-derful, deep, and incomprehensible! Your understanding of me brings me wonder and strength. (Psalm 139:5-6)

Follow the example of all that we have imparted to you and the God of peace will be with you in all things. (Philippians 4:9)

DECEMBER 14

It is hard for me to watch you needing comfort, and not being able to receive it because of the things that hold you back. My heart aches to bring you comfort. So many of you don't know what comfort is or could even trust it if it was available to you. You might know what comfort is as to understand it in your head, but you have not yet experienced the comfort that your heart needs, the comfort that soothes and calm the aches and the fears. This is what you needed from your mother to make you feel that your world is safe. Fear, guilt, and distrust have taken up too much room in your heart over the years. There are many ways that you have learned to comfort yourself that are harmful without you even realizing it. You have not been able to trust that comfort will ever be there for you. But I reassure you that I have this for you.

SCRIPTURES TO MEDITATE ON:

For this is what the Lord says:For I will extend peace to her like a river, and the of nations like a flooding stream you will nurse and be carried on her arm and dandled on her knees. As a mother comforts her child, so will I comfort you. (Isaiah 66:12-13)

I will give them an undivided heart and put a new spirit in them; I will remove from them their heart of stone and give them a heart of flesh. (Ezekiel 11:19 NIV)

DECEMBER 15

I will help you with the anger that you harbored over what others have done to you. I will heal the shame that causes you to believe you were bad. I will wash it off, and even where it is hiding. You will feel brand new, you will feel something you hadn't felt for a long time. I will help you with the guilt that made you feel like it was all your fault. I will free you from the fears that came from all the abuse, neglect, and trauma. This is what my son went to the cross for. I am your Father, who promises to restore, and I will! Come to me and watch what I will do for you. Come to me and experience the comfort that I long to give you. Pray to have an open heart. I want you to feel the compassion in my heart for you concerning all those years of not understanding the things that you were going through. I am always here for you and that will never change. I do not come and go, I am here to stay. There is no other place I would rather be than with my children.

SCRIPTURES TO MEDITATE ON:

Why do you complain, Jacob? Why do you say, Israel, "My way is hidden from the Lord; my cause is disregarded by my God?" Do you not know? Have you not heard? The Lord is the everlasting God, the Creator of the ends of the earth. He will not grow tired or weary, and his understanding no one can fathom. He gives strength to the weary and increases the power of the weak. Even youths grow tired and weary, and young men stumble and fall; but those who hope in the Lord will renew their strength. They will soar on wings like eagles; they will run and not grow weary, they will walk and not be faint. (Isaiah 40:27-31 NIV)

So do not fear, for I am with you; do not be dismayed, for I am your God. I will strengthen you and help you; I will uphold you with my righteous right hand. (Isaiah 41:10 NIV)

And teach them to faithfully follow all that I have commanded you. And never forget that I am with you every day, even to the completion of this age. (Matthew 28:20)

DECEMBER 16

As a mother sings over her child, so I sing over you. Try and rise above all of the noise and listen closely so that you can hear me. As I sing comforting words over you, just enjoy and enter into this moment with me. Listen closely, and just receive. Try and let go of all of the things others and sometimes even yourself have put on you of unrealistic expectations of how you should be. I want you to know how much I miss you when all of these distractions come and take you away from our times together. The other thing I want you to know is that I will never leave you. I will say it again. I will never leave you. Just stay with this truth, sit there and drink it in as long as you need to. Receive my comfort my dear, dear child. If you will let me, my Spirit will take this truth deep within your heart and heal all of that abandonment pain that you have been trying to avoid. My love will never give up on you.

SCRIPTURES TO MEDITATE ON:

As a mother comforts her child, so will I comfort you; and you will be comforted over Jerusalem. (Isaiah 66:13 NIV)

Can a mother forget the baby at her breast and have no compassion on the child she has borne? Though she may forget, I will not forget you! (Isaiah 49:15 NIV)

He's the God who chose us when we were nothing! His tender love for us continues on forever! (Psalm 136:23)

December 17

I see you feeling discouraged about your circumstances, wondering if I am still around. Try to be aware of your thoughts about me. Feeling alone may be the familiar feelings you had as a child, but we are going to make new memories for you, so that when you think of me, you will automatically know that your Papa is home and he will make everything okay. There is so much going on in this world and very few are aware of just how present I am for them. When you sincerely look for me with all your heart, with just as much earnestness that you put into working for me, I promise you will find me in ways you haven't imagined possible. This is something I don't want you to miss. Nothing in this life compares to the good plans I have for you and our journey we can have together.

SCRIPTURE TO MEDITATE ON:

For I know the plans I have for you,"declares the Lord," plans to prosper you and not to harm you, plans to give you a hope and a future. (Jeremiah 29:11)

DECEMBER 18

My Holy Spirit will open up a whole new world for you to know and experience the truth about my love. As you get to know me better you will learn to rely less on your limited natural thinking, and more on what I have told you. Your heart will feel, and your heart will rest as it opens up to me. You will hear me with your heart, not just in your mind. No longer will it be using your energy to stay guarded. There are times when you feel like you lived in a certain place for a long time, you just can't imagine moving on to new places, but I promise that I will take you by your hand and guide you. I can see your heart and in spite of all, I know it's a heart that loves me. This makes my heart happy!

SCRIPTURES TO MEDITATE ON:

But when the Father sends the Spirit of Holiness, the One like me who sets you free, he will teach you all things in my name. And he will inspire you to remember every word that I've told you. (John 14:26)

So above all, guard the affections of your heart, for they affect all that you are. Pay attention to the welfare of your innermost being, for from there flows the wellspring of life. (Proverbs 4:23)

For I am the Lord your God who takes hold of your right hand and says to you, Do not fear; I will help you. (Isaiah 41:13 NIV)

DECEMBER 19

I love to see movement in your life, even if your heart is only taking baby steps toward trusting me. I know how hard it can be to trust me when you didn't have your needs met. That is why I said you could have mustard seed size faith to make things happen. I love to watch your face as you catch glimpses of me wanting to father you. I also feel sad for you when you reject yourself for the things you don't like. It's in those moments of feeling bad, that you forget how much I love you. As my love continues to become a greater reality for you, those feelings will become less, and you will find yourself moving more quickly from that lonely place. Always remember how much I believe in you, especially when you are struggling with yourself.

SCRIPTURES TO MEDITATE ON:

Love is a safe place of shelter, for it never stops believing the best for others. Love never takes failure as defeat, for it never gives up. (1 Corinthians 13:7)

I promise you, if you have faith inside of you no bigger than the size of a small mustard seed, you can say to this mountain, 'Move away from here and go over there,' and you will see it move! There is nothing you couldn't do! (Matthew 17:20)

DECEMBER 20

I am happy that my children believe in me, but they still don't believe how much I love them. So many things block this truth from getting into their hearts, the biggest block being unaware of how guarded their hearts are with me. You are to guard your hearts, but not from me. I want you to know that I am the safest place you could ever be. I see the struggle that my children face as they try to shake the orphan way of thinking and feeling, and it saddens me. When you know how much I want to come to the places in your life where there is deep pain, my love will finally convince you that I have always cared about you. Just like the day you met me and your life was changed forever, so I will once again make myself known to you as your Father and will continue until every last trace of orphan thinking is gone.

SCRIPTURES TO MEDITATE ON:

Jesus replied, "You are favored and privileged Simeon, son of Jonah! For you didn't discover this on your own, but my Father in heaven has supernaturally revealed it to you." (Matthew 16:17)

So above all, guard the affections of your heart, for they affect all that you are. Pay attention to the welfare of your innermost being, for from there flows the well-spring of life. (Proverbs 4:23)

DECEMBER 21

I want you to know that I am always happy to see you when you come to me and it is so good to be with you again. Even though I am always with you, it's those moments when I have your full attention that bring me the most joy. I am so excited about some of my thoughts that I want to share with you. There have been many things stolen from you in your life, and the most unmet need you had and still do have, is your need for a father that is present. It may be an area that you don't realize yet, but it can be recognized by what you are turning to for comfort. I long to care for you as your Father, whether you had one or not. I will father you in ways that may not be familiar, in ways you are not used to. I care about everything that concerns you, even down to the color of paint you were looking for. I will convince you of what kind of Father I will be for you in your daily lives. While you are looking at your flaws, I am busy admiring this lovable, interesting child of mine.

SCRIPTURES TO MEDITATE ON:

What is the value of your soul to God? Could your worth be defined by an amount of money? God doesn't abandon or forget even the small sparrow he has made. How then could he forget or abandon you? What about the seemingly minor issues of your life? Do they matter to God? Of course they do! So you never need to worry, for you are more valuable to God than anything else in this world. (Luke 12:6-7)

You will be guarded by God himself. You will be safe when you leave your home and safely you will return. He will protect you now, and he'll protect you forever-more! (Psalm 121:8)

DECEMBER 22

It is time to let go of those things that you picked back up. I want you to know that I am going to take care of you, so do not be worried. There is grace that I have for you to help you let go of all concerns and you will see how much better you will feel. This is why I tell you to become like a child; they do not worry. Now you can enter into this place where we can enjoy being together. Our relationship is very important to me and it needs to be the foundation of your life. It makes me sad when my children do not know this. They think working for me makes me happy and pleased with them, but I am not here to use you. I am here to father you and I long for you to know this. I know you want to do things for me, but whatever you do will flow out of that place.

SCRIPTURES TO MEDITATE ON:

Pour out all your worries and stress upon him and leave them there, for he always tenderly cares for you. (1 Peter 5:7)

I repeat it: Don't let worry enter your life. Live above the anxious cares about your personal needs. People everywhere seem to worry about making a living, but your heavenly Father knows your every need and will take care of you. Each and every day he will supply your needs as you seek his kingdom passionately, above all else. So don't ever be afraid, dearest friends! Your loving Father joyously gives you his kingdom realm with all its promises! (Luke 12:29-32)

December 23

We are here celebrating your healing because it means we are entering into new places. I am taking you to a new place where you are so comfortable with my love. A place where you can rest feeling so loved, loved even more than you ever felt. The unrest and the accusing voice that kept trying to tell you that you are orphaned will be silenced. Hear my Father's heart, my child, and know my favor that rests on your life. Things are going to change for you as you heal, so just know that it is a new day. It will no longer be hard for you like it was in the past. Just to have the ability to trust me and the things that I am telling you is a new and wonderful place to be in. Your heart can know that I will keep my word to you and you will see my goodness in the land of the living.

SCRIPTURES TO MEDITATE ON:

With your hand of love upon my life, you impart a blessing to me. This is just too wonderful, deep, and incomprehensible! (Psalm 139:5)

My heart will not be afraid even if an army rises to attack. I know that you are there for me, so I will not be shaken. (Psalm 27:3)

And God-Enthroned spoke to me and said, "Consider this! I am making everything to be new and fresh. Write down at once all that I have told you, because each word is trustworthy and dependable." (Revelation 21:5)

December 24

Just in case you were wondering, I am right here and I am going to take care of those things that are heavy on your heart. Take my hand, my child, and I will guide you, so you know exactly what it is you need from me. Listen closely as I speak tenderly to your heart not to worry. Think of all the times I have taken care of you and remember that I am faithful, and I will be there every time you need me. I know at times it seems too good to be true to have a father who is always there, but I will show you as you look for me that I am consistent and the security that you never had. Now just put out your hands and receive the grace to release these things to me, receive my help to be able to trust the love I want to shower on you. I am glad you are getting your eyes back on me, so you can rest now and enjoy being taken care of by your Father who adores you.

SCRIPTURES TO MEDITATE ON:

You lead me with your secret wisdom. And following you brings me into your brightness and glory! (Psalm 73:24)

For I am the Lord your God who takes hold of your right hand and says to you, Do not fear; I will help you. (Isaiah 41:13 NIV)

DECEMBER 25

When Jesus told you to come and see me, he said to go see your Father. In saying that, he is acknowledging that I am your Father. Just stay with that and drink in that truth that I am your Father. He just didn't say go see someone that cares about you, but instead he emphasized that you should go see your Father. It makes me sad that so many of my children do not have a sense of being my child. They have no idea how much I want to heal their father wound, so that they can relate to me as my sons and daughters and finally feel at home with me. It will no longer be about Christian zeal, programs, or working for me. There will no longer be a focus on being good or doing all the right things to make me happy or make me love you. You don't have to be concerned with your prayer time or saying the right prayers for me to be pleased. You already have all of my love and once you realize that, you will naturally respond to me.

SCRIPTURES TO MEDITATE ON:

"I will be a true Father to you, and you will be my beloved sons and daughters," says the Lord Yahweh Almighty. (2 Corinthians 6:18)

But whenever you pray, go into your innermost chamber and be alone with Father God, praying to him in secret. And your Father, who sees all you do, will reward you openly. (Matthew 6:6)

DECEMBER 26

I look forward to you coming around more. I assure you that I am not this serious, angry God that others portray me to be. Your happiest thought, the most loving person you have encountered, is a speck of dust next to me. I am full of life, love and happy thoughts about my world and my children. My son and I long to make our home with you and want you to feel at home with us. I want you to feel comfortable around me, to kick off your shoes, grab a bite to eat and sit around and chat. I showed you in my son what kind of Father I am. I love having dinner with my children, and even cooking for them. I want to show you that I am a Father who would get on my knees to wash your feet. Think on this for a while and take it in, that your Father is God and would bow down to wash your feet. It is my heart for you to see me as I truly am.

SCRIPTURES TO MEDITATE ON:

Jesus knew that the night before Passover would be his last night on earth before leaving this world to return to the Father's side. All throughout his time with his disciples, Jesus had demonstrated a deep and tender love for them. And now he longed to show them the full measure of his love. Before their evening meal had begun, the accuser had already planted betrayal into the heart of Judas Iscariot, the son of Simon. Now Jesus was fully aware that the Father had placed all things under his control, for he had come from God and was about to go back to be with him. So he got up from the meal and took off his outer robe, and took a towel and wrapped it around his waist. Then he poured water into a basin and began to wash the disciples' dirty feet and dry them with his towel. (John 13:1-5)

Jesus replied, "Loving me empowers you to obey my word. And my Father will love you so deeply that we will come to you and make you our dwelling place." (John 14:23)

DECEMBER 27

I know about the painful things you have been through and I want you to know that I am the one that brought you through those times even though you were unaware of me being there. I understand why you thought I didn't care, you just didn't know me well enough. I want to bring my comfort to the memories from when you felt so uncared for, the times of feeling so rejected and alone. Just as a mother nurses her sick child, so I am here to care for you. I want you to have this experience with me. I wait patiently for you until you are able to trust and receive from me. O how I long to gather you under my wings and give you the security you have always longed for.

SCRIPTURES TO MEDITATE ON:

Can a mother forget the baby at her breast and have no compassion on the child she has borne? Though she may forget, I will not forget you! (Isaiah 49:15 NIV)

When Jacob awoke from his sleep, he thought, "Surely the Lord is in this place, and I was not aware of it." (Genesis 28:16)

December 28

I have so much to give to my children that they have not realized yet, nor experienced. You don't have to beg me to bless or help you because it is in my heart to do this for you. Don't let the enemy lie to you about who I am when you are walking through difficult times. For it is in the difficult times that you learn of my faithfulness to you. He tried to lie to my son, so you can count on him trying to lie to you about me. Maybe you are not used to being blessed and are afraid to trust it out of fear of disappointment. Maybe feelings of unworthiness keep you from receiving from me. Either way, you need to find out for yourself the answers that will settle your heart and convince you that I am a generous Father who blesses his children. And then, you need to learn how to be good receivers.

SCRIPTURE TO MEDITATE ON:

For God has proved his love by giving us his greatest treasure, the gift of his Son. And since God freely offered him up as the sacrifice for us all, he certainly won't withhold from us anything else he has to give. (Romans 8:32)

DECEMBER 29

At times you might not feel so special when you think about how many children I have. But each one of my children are very special to me and I have no favorites. Maybe you had caregivers who gave you something, but they were not able to communicate to you just how special you are, that you were wanted and loved. I speak to your spirit with all sincerity that I want you to be my child. I come to you personally to speak this truth to your heart. I want you in my life, and you are not just a number added to my family. You are unique, and special to me in every way. Each one of you are dear to my heart, and I would leave the ninety-nine who are precious to me to go after you.

SCRIPTURES TO MEDITATE ON:

If a man owns a hundred sheep and one lamb wanders away and is lost, won't he leave the ninety-nine grazing on the hillside and go out and thoroughly search for the one lost lamb? And if he finds his lost lamb he rejoices over it, more than over the ninety-nine who are safe. Now you should understand that it is never the desire of your heavenly Father that a single one of these humble believers should be lost. (Matthew 18:11-14)

For God so loved the world that he gave his only son. (John 3:16)

For the Holy Spirit makes God's fatherhood real to us as he whispers into our innermost being, "You are God's beloved child!" (Romans 8:16)

DECEMBER 30

This has been fun for me watching you get excited as you discovered how much I want to talk to you, and it wasn't as hard as you thought it would be. You can make it hard in your mind when you believe the lies that I am too busy to talk to you, so you are not expecting to hear from me.. The other lie was you thought something was wrong because of the difficulty you had hearing me. That lie came from not having a father here that was able to talk to you because he didn't know how. I will continue to open up revelation to you that I am a very relational Father. I look forward to you being in my life where we can communi-cate daily now that you are being convinced of how much I want to talk to my kids.

SCRIPTURES TO MEDITATE ON:

For I know the plans I have for you, declares the Lord, plans to prosper you and not to harm you, plans to give hope and a future. (Jeremiah 29:11)

My own sheep will hear my voice, and I know each one and they will follow me. (John 10:27)

DECEMBER 31

Well, we made it through another year together. I commend you and acknowledge how well you have done in holding on in some difficult situations. You did the right thing by looking to Me for what you needed. I always believed in you even when you and others did not. I loved watching your trust in Me grow as you watched Me come through for you in small things as well as big. The one thing that I'm going to restore—that the enemy worked at stealing from my children—is the childlike trust and wonder that I put in them. I remind you he tries to make My children believe that I don't care and tries to get them focused on their problems. Just keep remembering to turn to Me and I will gently remind you that I am bigger than all of this. I am your Papa who will not let you down. I know how to open your Red Sea and make a way where there is none. Just remember, I am all about My children.

SCRIPTURES TO MEDITATE ON:

I will repay you for the years the locusts have eaten—the great locust and the young locust, the other locusts and the locust swarm—my great army that I sent among you. (Joel 2:25 NIV)

Then Moses stretched out his hand over the sea, and all that night the Lord drove the sea back with a strong east wind and turned it into dry land. The waters were divided. (Exodus 14:21 NIV)

A Word from the Author

A very strong emphasis in this book is the message that the Father wants to talk to us. I remember for years always want-ing to hear from a prophet because I didn't think I could hear Him. When you think of Him as being your Father, what kind of loving father doesn't want to talk to his kids? He does speak to us in many different ways, but I had no idea that the Father himself wanted to talk to me. It is actu-ally still sinking in.

This is what I longed for growing up with my Dad and all this time I didn't know I could have this with Father God. Psalm 139:6 says, "Such knowledge is too wonderful for me." In Matthew 6:6, Jesus tells us to go see the Father and close the door. Jesus knew that the Father wanted to see us, and not just to talk to us about ministry.

So many are not used to a loving relationship with their earthly dads. Is it possible that Father God just wants to be with you in the same way you want to be with your chil-dren? I hear Him say, "I don't want to be with my children to tell them where they need to change or how much I want them to work for me. I love being with them, love talking to them, they are very interesting people!"

Made in the USA
Middletown, DE
19 February 2021